Achieving Systems Safety

Related Titles

Aspects of Safety Management
Proceedings of the Ninth Safety-critical Systems Symposium, Bristol, UK, 2001
Redmill and Anderson (Eds)
1-85233-411-8

Components of System Safety
Proceedings of the Tenth Safety-critical Systems Symposium, Southampton, UK, 2002
Redmill and Anderson (Eds)
1-85233-561-0

Current Issues in Safety-critical Systems
Proceedings of the Eleventh Safety-critical Systems Symposium, Bristol, UK, 2003
Redmill and Anderson (Eds)
1-85233-696-X

Practical Elements of Safety
Proceedings of the Twelfth Safety-critical Systems Symposium, Birmingham, UK, 2004
Redmill and Anderson (Eds)
1-85233-800-8

Constituents of Modern System-safety Thinking
Proceedings of the Thirteenth Safety-critical Systems Symposium, Southampton, UK, 2005
Redmill and Anderson (Eds)
1-85233-952-7

Developments in Risk-based Approaches to Safety
Proceedings of the Fourteenth Safety-critical Systems Symposium, Bristol, UK, 2006
Redmill and Anderson (Eds)
1-84628-333-7

The Safety of Systems
Proceedings of the Fifteenth Safety-critical Systems Symposium, Bristol, UK, 2007
Redmill and Anderson (Eds)
978-1-84628-805-0

Improvements in System Safety
Proceedings of the Sixteenth Safety-critical Systems Symposium, Bristol, UK, 2008
Redmill and Anderson (Eds)
978-1-84800-099-5

Safety-Critical Systems: Problems, Process and Practice
Proceedings of the Seventeenth Safety-Critical Systems Symposium, Brighton, UK, 2009
Dale and Anderson (Eds)
978-1-84882-348-8

Making Systems Safer
Proceedings of the Eighteenth Safety-Critical Systems Symposium, Bristol, UK, 2010
Dale and Anderson (Eds)
978-1-84996-085-4

Advances in Systems Safety
Proceedings of the Nineteenth Safety-Critical Systems Symposium, Southampton, UK, 2011
Dale and Anderson (Eds)
978-0-85729-132-5

Chris Dale • Tom Anderson
Editors

Achieving Systems Safety

Proceedings of the Twentieth Safety-Critical
Systems Symposium, Bristol, UK,
7-9th February 2012

**Safety-Critical
Systems Club**

The publication of these proceedings is
sponsored by BAE Systems plc

BAE SYSTEMS

 Springer

Editors
Chris Dale
Dale Research Ltd
33 North Street
Martock TA12 6DH
United Kingdom

Prof. Tom Anderson
Centre for Software Reliability
Newcastle University
Newcastle upon Tyne NE1 7RU
United Kingdom

ISBN 978-1-4471-2493-1   e-ISBN 978-1-4471-2494-8
DOI 10.1007/978-1-4471-2494-8
Springer London Dordrecht Heidelberg New York

British Library Cataloguing in Publication Data
A catalogue record for this book is available from the British Library

Library of Congress Control Number: 2011944278

Printed on acid-free paper

Springer is part of Springer Science+Business Media (www.springer.com)

Preface

This proceedings volume contains papers presented at the twentieth Safety-critical Systems Symposium (SSS 2012). This year's authors have, as usual, delivered informative material touching on many topics that are of current concern to the safety-critical systems community; we are grateful to them for their contributions.

In his opening keynote address, Martyn Thomas highlights vulnerabilities in GPS and other global navigation satellite systems, thus illustrating that many general purpose systems can have an impact on safety. The two following papers address the importance of culture and community to the achievement of safety.

Roger Rivett's keynote paper looks at the challenge of technological change in the automotive industry. This is followed by three other papers on transport safety: one focuses on unmanned aerial systems, and the other two on railways.

Cyber-attacks on safety-critical systems form the subject of Chris Johnson's keynote talk. Four papers then look at improving our approach to systems safety: taking account of electromagnetic interference; treating safety as a viewpoint on systems engineering; safety architectural patterns; and Bayesian belief networks.

Next, two papers look at accidents: how should we investigate them and what can we learn thereby. The second of these is Peter Ladkin's keynote on the accident to the nuclear reactors at Fukushima.

Jens Braband's keynote paper presents a risk-based approach to assessing potential safety deficiencies. This is followed by two papers on validating safety-critical software, and on software testing.

The final keynote, by John McDermid and Andrew Rae, focuses on goal-based safety standards, and is followed by two papers that look in detail at safety levels.

We are grateful to our sponsors for their valuable support and to the exhibitors at the Symposium's tools and services fair for their participation. And we thank Joan Atkinson and her team for laying the event's foundation through their exemplary planning and organisation.

CD & TA
October 2011

A message from the sponsors

BAE Systems is pleased to support the publication of these proceedings. We recognise the benefit of the Safety-Critical Systems Club in promoting safety engineering in the UK and value the opportunities provided for continued professional development and the recognition and sharing of good practice. The safety of our employees, those using our products and the general public is critical to our business and is recognised as an important social responsibility.

The Safety-Critical Systems Club

organiser of the

Safety-critical Systems Symposium

What is the Safety-Critical Systems Club?

This 'Community' Club exists to support developers and operators of systems that may have an impact on safety, across all industry sectors. It is an independent, non-profit organisation that co-operates with all bodies involved with safety-critical systems.

Objectives

The Club's two principal objectives are to raise awareness of safety issues in the field of safety-critical systems and to facilitate the transfer of safety technology from wherever it exists.

History

The Club was inaugurated in 1991 under the sponsorship of the UK's Department of Trade and Industry (DTI) and the Engineering and Physical Sciences Research Council (EPSRC). Its secretariat is in the Centre for Software Reliability (CSR) at Newcastle University, and its Meetings Coordinator is Chris Dale of Dale Research Ltd. Felix Redmill of Redmill Consultancy is the Newsletter Editor.

Since 1994 the Club has been self-sufficient, but it retains the active support of the Health and Safety Executive, the Institution of Engineering and Technology, and BCS, the Chartered Institute for IT. All of these bodies are represented on the Club's Steering Group.

The Club's activities

The Club achieves its goals of awareness-raising and technology transfer by focusing on current and emerging practices in safety engineering, software engineering, and standards that relate to safety in processes and products. Its activities include:

- running the annual Safety-critical Systems Symposium each February (the first was in 1993), with Proceedings published by Springer-Verlag.
- organising a number of full day seminars each year.
- providing tutorials on relevant subjects.
- publishing a newsletter, *Safety Systems*, three times annually (since 1991), in January, May and September.
- a web-site http://www.scsc.org.uk providing member services, including a safety tools, products and services directory.

Education and communication

The Club brings together technical and managerial personnel within all sectors of the safety-critical-systems community. Its events provide education and training in principles and techniques, and it facilitates the dissemination of lessons within and between industry sectors. It promotes an inter-disciplinary approach to the engineering and management of safety, and it provides a forum for experienced practitioners to meet each other and for the exposure of newcomers to the safety-critical systems industry.

Influence on research

The Club facilitates communication among researchers, the transfer of technology from researchers to users, feedback from users, and the communication of experience between users. It provides a meeting point for industry and academia, a forum for the presentation of the results of relevant projects, and a means of learning and keeping up-to-date in the field.

The Club thus helps to achieve more effective research, a more rapid and effective transfer and use of technology, the identification of best practice, the definition of requirements for education and training, and the dissemination of information. Importantly, it does this within a 'club' atmosphere rather than a commercial environment.

Membership

Members pay a reduced fee (well below the commercial level) for events and receive the newsletter and other mailed information. Not being sponsored, the Club depends on members' subscriptions: these can be paid at the first meeting attended, and are almost always paid by the individual's employer.

To join, please contact Mrs Joan Atkinson at: The Centre for Software Reliability, Newcastle University, Newcastle upon Tyne, NE1 7RU, UK; Telephone: +44 191 221 2222; Fax: +44 191 222 7995; Email: csr@newcastle.ac.uk.

Contents

Keynote Address
Accidental Systems, Hidden Assumptions and Safety Assurance
Martyn Thomas 1

Do we truly understand Safety Culture?
Allan Bain 11

The Need for a Community for System and Functional Safety Professionals
Audrey Canning 25

Keynote Address
The Challenge of Technological Change in the Automotive Industry
Roger Rivett 35

Safety Process Implementation for Unmanned Aerial Systems
Sirma Celik 43

Risk Analysis and Development of an IP-Network-based Railway Signal Control System
Reiji Ishima and Minoru Mori 55

Taking Safe Decisions in the GB Railway Industry
George Bearfield 75

Keynote Address
CyberSafety: CyberSecurity and Safety-Critical Software Engineering
Chris Johnson 85

Including Electromagnetic Interference (EMI) in Functional Safety Risk Assessments
Keith Armstrong 97

Safety Engineering – a Perspective on Systems Engineering
Derek Fowler and Ronald Pierce 115

Survey of Safety Architectural Patterns
Paul Hampton 137

The Application of Bayesian Belief Networks to Assurance Case Preparation
Chris Hobbs and Martin Lloyd 159

Accident Investigation – are we reaching the Systemic Causes of Accidents?
Graham Braithwaite..177

Keynote Address
The Fukushima Accident
Peter Ladkin..189

Keynote Address
A Risk-based Approach towards Assessment of Potential Safety Deficiencies
Jens Braband...209

At the Sharp End: developing and validating Safety Critical Software
Fergus Duncan..225

The New Software Testing Standard
Stuart Reid..237

Keynote Address
Goal-Based Safety Standards: Promises and Pitfalls
John McDermid and Andrew Rae 257

Safety Levels in a Commercial Context
Mike Parsons..271

A Devil's Advocate on SIL 4
Odd Nordland..285

Author Index 293

Accidental Systems, Hidden Assumptions and Safety Assurance

Martyn Thomas

Martyn Thomas Associates Limited

London, UK

Abstract   In April, the Royal Academy of Engineering published the final report of a study into the world's increasing dependence on GPS and other global navigation satellite systems and the consequent vulnerabilities. The report, *Global Navigation Space Systems,* describes how GPS has been so useful and so reliable that a remarkable wide range of applications, ranging from financial trading to deep sea drilling, now depend on these extremely weak signals from space. As a consequence, if the GPS signals are disrupted or spoofed, many services that might be thought to be independent may fail simultaneously. Primary and backup systems may both be affected. In this paper, we explain some of the vulnerabilities in GPS and other GNSS and draw some conclusions about accidental systems, hidden assumptions and safety assurance.

1 Introduction

In May 2009, the US Government Accountability Office (GAO) published a report (GAO 2009) that concluded that the United States Air Force would have difficulty in maintaining its investment in the Global Positioning System (GPS) and in launching new satellites to schedule and cost[1]. At that time, the UK's National Academy for Engineering, the Royal Academy of Engineering (RAEng), already had concerns about the growing and largely unrecognised dependence of many services on GPS. They therefore asked me to convene a meeting to discuss the threats. This was a closed meeting, to permit the free exchange of views between government, public sector and private sector representatives, and the meeting concluded that it would be valuable for the RAEng to conduct a formal study into the

---

[1] The US GAO published a follow-up report in 2010 called *GPS: challenges in sustaining and upgrading capabilities persist.* The first IIF satellite was finally launched on 27 May 2010, almost 3.5 years late. They conclude: 'The IIIA schedule remains ambitious and could be affected by risks such as the program's dependence on ground systems that will not be completed until after the first IIIA launch...a delay in the launch of the GPS IIIA satellites could still reduce the size of the constellation to below its 24-satellite baseline, where it might not meet the needs of some GPS users.'

breadth of services that are dependent on GPS and other Global Navigation Satellite Systems (GNSS) and the vulnerabilities of such systems. The study reported in March 2011 and the report is freely available for download from the RAEng website (RAEng 2011). The report acknowledges the many experts who gave freely of their time to assist the study.

The study discovered that almost all industrial sectors and many important services had become dependent to some degree on GNSS signals. At present, the dependence is almost exclusively on GPS but our conclusions apply equally to other GNSS (Compass, Galileo, GLONASS, etc.) that are deployed or under development. In many cases, the degree to which a service is dependent on GNSS is not understood by organisations; this was illustrated dramatically by two jamming trials that were carried out by the UK General Lighthouse Authorities; one of these is described in detail in an appendix to the RAEng report.

When services that are otherwise independent share a common source of failure or interact in some unforeseen way, they become coupled into what John Rushby of SRI has felicitously called an *accidental system* (Jackson et al. 2007). The date-related Y2K errors had this effect at the turn of the millennium and I argue below that we have not properly learnt from the experience of that sentinel event.

2 GNSS basics

GNSS systems are satellite systems that transmit signals that can be used to provide three services: Position, Navigation, and Timing – known collectively as PNT.

GNSS can be considered as three related segments: ground, space and user.

- The ground, or control, segment is used to upload data to the satellites, to synchronize time across the constellation and to track the satellites to enable orbit and clock determination.
- The space segment of GPS consists of four satellites in each of six orbital planes. 24 satellites make a full constellation, although in January 2011 there were 32 in service, 2 of which had been declared unusable until further notice. For GPS, the satellite's code is used to identify it in orbit (GLONASS currently differentiates satellites by frequency channel although this is planned to change so that GLONASS becomes compatible with GPS and Galileo).
- The user segment consists of the receivers and associated antennas, used to receive and decode the signal to provide PNT information.

GNSS is a ranging system with three available carrier frequencies, all multiples of a fundamental frequency. The distance is derived primarily through measuring the time difference between the transmission from the satellite and reception at the receiver of a coded signal. This range is affected by a number of perturbations such as clock biases and propagation delays that must be solved for or estimated. Ranges to at least four satellites are required to determine position. Timing applications only need reception from a single satellite, although two are preferred for verification. The navigation message is transmitted from the satellite to the user and gives the satellite identifier together with information on satellite health, predicted range accuracy, ionospheric and clock correction coefficients as well as orbital ephemeris to allow the receiver to calculate the satellite position. The message also contains an almanac which gives status, location and identifier information for all satellites in the constellation.

With this information, it is possible for the receiver to determine the time to an accuracy of around one microsecond and, using the delays from satellites in what are now known positions, to calculate its 3D position to an accuracy of five to ten metres and its speed to an accuracy of about 20 centimetres per second. The accuracy can be improved using broadcasts from transmitters that know their own position to great accuracy and that can therefore calculate ionospheric delays and other sources of error. These transmissions allow accuracies between one metre and one centimetre.

GNSS signals are very weak: typically less than 100 watts transmitted from a distance of 20,000 km to 25,000 km. When received at the surface of the earth, the signal strength may be as low as -160 dBW (1×10^{-16}) watts, below the noise floor in the receivers. Deliberate or unintentional interference with this signal can easily defeat the signal recovery or overload the receiver circuitry. There are many potential sources of error described in the RAEng report and these can lead to partial or complete loss of the PNT, poorer accuracy, very large jumps in position, velocity or time, and incorrect but plausible data that may be hazardously misleading in safety critical applications.

3 The range of applications

The RAEng report lists applications in the following sectors:

- aviation (e.g. departure, en-route navigation, non-precision approach, precision approach, formation flying, mid-air refuelling, ground movement, ADS-B)
- road transport (e.g. in-car navigation, fleet management, urban traffic control, road user charging, lane control, intelligent speed assistance, information services, stolen vehicle recovery)
- marine applications (e.g. ocean, coastal and inland waterway navigation; port approach and docking; icebreakers; dredging; automatic docking; hydrography; beacon light synchronisation)
- rail (e.g. train location, movement authority, level crossing approach, door control at short platforms, supervision to buffers, speed warning, trackside personnel protection, power supply control, passenger information systems, management information systems)
- autonomous vehicles (land, sea and air)

- time synchronisation (e.g. synchronous telecommunications, power distribution, network control)
- precision agriculture (e.g. yield mapping, plot mapping, fertilizer application control, guidance of farm machinery)
- fisheries applications (e.g. navigation, monitoring, yield analysis, emergency location)
- oil and gas applications (e.g. drilling, exploration)
- emergency applications (e.g. emergency vehicle location and scheduling, dynamic route guidance, selective vehicle priority, search and rescue, aid and monitoring of disabled people, VIP protection)
- scientific applications (e.g. meteorology, surveying, bridge and dam monitoring)
- financial applications (e.g. time-stamping for high-velocity automatic trading).

Disruption to GNSS services could cause multiple simultaneous problems so that, for example, the likelihood of vehicle collisions would increase at the same time as the ability of emergency services to respond would be seriously degraded.

4 Vulnerabilities

4.1 Space weather

The speed of propagation of GNSS signals is reduced in proportion to the total electron count (TEC) in the ionosphere and this can cause significant PNT errors if uncorrected. Slow variations in the TEC happen constantly, for example as a consequence of the rotation of the earth, the 27 day rotation of the sun, and the 11 year sunspot cycle. These effects are relatively easy to mitigate but fast changes – typically caused directly or indirectly by solar flares and coronal mass ejections (CME) – can lead to large gradients in the TEC that are harder to mitigate (though easy to detect so that warnings can be promulgated to GNSS users).

In 1859, a very large CME occurred aligned with the earth and was detected at about 11:15 am UTC on 1 September.

At 11:18 AM on the cloudless morning of Thursday, September 1, 1859, 33-year-old Richard Carrington – widely acknowledged to be one of England's foremost solar astronomers – was in his well-appointed private observatory. Just as usual on every sunny day, his telescope was projecting an 11-inch-wide image of the sun on a screen, and Carrington skillfully drew the sunspots he saw.

On that morning, he was capturing the likeness of an enormous group of sunspots. Suddenly, before his eyes, two brilliant beads of blinding white light appeared over the sunspots, intensified rapidly, and became kidney-shaped. Realizing that he was witnessing something unprecedented and 'being somewhat flurried by the surprise, Carrington later wrote, 'I hastily ran to call someone to witness the exhibition with me. On returning within 60 seconds, I was mortified to find that it was already much changed and enfeebled.' He and his witness watched the white spots contract to mere pinpoints and disappear.

It was 11:23 AM. Only five minutes had passed.

Just before dawn the next day, skies all over planet Earth erupted in red, green, and purple auroras so brilliant that newspapers could be read as easily as in daylight. Indeed, stunning auroras pulsated even at near tropical latitudes over Cuba, the Bahamas, Jamaica, El Salvador, and Hawaii.

Even more disconcerting, telegraph systems worldwide went haywire. Spark discharges shocked telegraph operators and set the telegraph paper on fire. Even when telegraphers disconnected the batteries powering the lines, aurora-induced electric currents in the wires still allowed messages to be transmitted.[2]

There has never been such a large CME in the era of artificial satellites and digital communications, though the probability is estimated at about 0.005 per year (easily high enough to require inclusion in the hazard analysis for any safety-critical application).

4.2 Jamming, meaconing and spoofing

GNSS signals may be disrupted by being *jammed* (where the receiver cannot detect the very weak satellite signals because of stronger signals on the same frequency), by *meaconing* (where the satellite signals are rebroadcast and the receiver locks on to the rebroadcast signals instead of the original signals) and by *spoofing* (where signals that have the structure and content of genuine GNSS signals are broadcast on GNSS frequencies to cause the receiver to calculate an incorrect position chosen by the spoofer).

Jamming may be unintentional – for example where a badly designed transmitter generates harmonics on GNSS frequencies or where a powerful transmission on a neighbouring frequency band spreads into the GNSS band. Jamming may also be deliberate: circuit diagrams and commercial jamming equipment are widely available on the internet and jammers are routinely used by police and security services to defeat trackers, by criminals stealing valuable cars or cargoes, and by company car and lorry drivers who do not want their employers to know all their movements. These jammers are almost always extremely low power with deliberately limited range, but it would only require a few watts of transmitted power, in a well-chosen location, to disrupt all GNSS signals over hundreds of square miles. It was reported at a GNSS conference at the National Physical Laboratory in 2010 that the GPS Jammer Detection and Location System (JLOC) detects thousands of jamming incidents each day across the USA. In the UK, the GAARDIAN and SENTINEL (Chronos 2011) projects are building a detection capability with funding from the UK Technology Strategy Board.

---

[2] This description is copied from http://science.nasa.gov/science-news/science-at-nasa/2008/06may_carringtonflare.

Meaconing may also be unintentional (a typical example is where a poorly designed and mounted GPS antenna re-radiates the received signal) or deliberate (for example, where a GPS repeater is used to get GPS coverage in a location that does not have a clear view of enough of the sky. The most common effect is that receivers report their position as that of the meaconing antenna.

Spoofing is far less common currently because it requires a GNSS simulator to generate the signals and these simulators (which are designed and used legitimately for test and development of GPS receivers) have been very expensive. Prices are falling, however, and spoofing is a growing threat.

4.3 Other vulnerabilities and resilience measures

The RAEng report describes several other vulnerabilities, and some of the methods that may be adopted to increase the resilience of services and systems that rely on GNSS. Readers are encouraged to obtain the RAEng report if they wish to explore these issues in greater depth.

5 GNSS conclusions

It is clear that the UK is already highly dependent on GNSS and that this dependence is growing. No-one has a good oversight of the degree of dependence and the harm that would flow from significant GNSS disruption. The situation is no better in the USA; I have been told by a representative of the US Department of Homeland Security (DHS) that DHS carried out a survey of organisations with responsibilities for parts of the US critical national infrastructure, to discover their backup plans and readiness in the event of GPS disruption. Many organisations declared that they had no dependence on GPS (and hence no need for backup). They were almost all wrong.

Taking account of the difficulty that service operators have in discovering the extent to which they are vulnerable to GNSS disruption, the RAEng study recommended that:

- Critical services should ensure that GNSS vulnerabilities are included in their risk registers and that the risks are reviewed regularly and mitigated effectively.
- National and regional emergency management and response teams should review the dependencies (direct and indirect) on GNSS and mitigate the risks appropriately.
- Services that depend on GNSS for PNT, directly or indirectly, should document this as part of their service descriptions, and explain their contingency plans for GNSS outages (say, of duration 10 minutes, 2 hours, 5 days, 1 month).

It is illegal to place GNSS jamming equipment on the market in the EU, as it cannot be made compliant with the EMC Directive, which is transposed into UK and other European national legislation. The use of jammers is also a serious offence under the UK Wireless Telegraphy Act 2006. The UK telecommunications regulator, Ofcom, has the power to close remaining loopholes by putting in place a banning order under the 2006 Act which would prohibit import, advertisement and mere possession of jammers. The RAEng study recommended that Ofcom should introduce such a banning order, ideally in co-operation with other European legislators.

The RAEng study recognised that the provision of a widely available PNT service as an alternative to GNSS is already an essential part of the national infrastructure. Such an alternative should be cost effective to incorporate in civil GNSS receivers and free to use. Ideally it should provide additional benefits, such as availability inside buildings and in GNSS blindspots. The leading candidate for such a service is eLORAN, the enhanced LOng RAnge Navigation system that has been under development and trial by the UK General Lighthouse Authorities and others for several years and has proved to be effective and resilient. eLORAN is technically diverse from GNSS: it is terrestrial rather than space-based, long wave rather than extremely short wave, and the signals are powerful rather than weak.

If these recommendations are implemented, the risks from GNSS failures will be significantly reduced, but the danger of unforeseen accidental systems will always remain unless the general lessons of GNSS and Y2K lead to a change in engineering practice or oversight.

6 Lessons from Y2K

In the last decade of the 20th century, it became widely understood that the date change to a new century had the potential to cause a very wide range of computer-based systems to fail. The problem arose because very many software designers had chosen date formats that allowed only two digits for the year. As a consequence, when it became necessary to represent dates in 2000 and beyond, the dates would sort lower than earlier dates and would become ambiguous, leading to erroneous calculation of time durations and many other failures. Most major companies and large organisations found that they had to embark on a very expensive programme of work to detect and correct these errors. The difficulty was often compounded by poor software development practices: major companies discovered that they did not have the engineering disciplines in place to enable them to re-create the binaries that were currently running their business, as changes had been made that had not been properly documented or reflected in managed source libraries.

I led the international Y2K service line for Deloitte Consulting in the mid 1990s and, after I left Deloittes in 1998, I acted as the final Y2K assurance for the UK National Air Traffic Services systems, reviewing the considerable work undertaken by NATS in-house teams. (Despite heroic efforts, we missed one: the Runway Visual Range systems on every NATS airfield failed at 4am on 1 January 2000 when the runway equipment performed a routine health-check with the master system and discovered a discrepancy. There was no danger, of course, as no-one was flying over that night and the fault was quickly corrected).

Because there were no cascade failures of major systems or supply chains, the myth has arisen that Y2K was never a problem and that a small issue had been built up to something major by dishonest consultants and equipment manufacturers. Those who hold this point of view are dangerously ill-informed and complacent, for two reasons:

- Firstly, I know that my Deloitte and Praxis teams found and corrected many errors, some of which would have caused very great damage to major companies; on more than one occasion, individual errors that we found justified the entire cost of the organisation's Y2K remediation programme.
- Secondly, despite all the millions of person hours worked, serious failures did occur: one I know of threatened the continued existence of a major utility and led after some months to the replacement of the entire board of directors.

In my opinion, Y2K was a sentinel event – a near miss where serious consequences were averted by a combination of hard work and good fortune. The lessons that should have been learnt (and that appear not to have been) include:

- The development of all software for important applications should follow rigorous engineering disciplines, so that it is easy to analyse the software for key properties and to create a changed version that is based on the latest baseline and that incorporates all the latest maintenance changes.
- Important services should value resilience as highly as efficiency, and should incorporate checks, diverse sources of data and alternative paths so that systems are not tightly coupled and the failure of one system does not lead to a cascade of failures that halt a business process or a supply chain.
- For this reason, the preservation of adequate redundancy should be a high priority and appear in the risk registers and analyses for every important service or application.

7 Closing observations

The system safety community is inconsistent in the way that risk is addressed. It seems inconsistent to be critical of the environmental assumptions that were made by the designers and assessors of Fukushima Daiichi whilst ignoring the risk of a Carrington event that has roughly the same probability as the recent earthquake and tsunami in Japan.

A Carrington event is estimated at $p > 10^{-7}$/hr. Does it appear in your hazard analyses? If not, why not? If it does, what mitigations have you introduced to reduce and manage the risk? Is this a topic that should be debated widely, to develop an agreed professional best practice?

System safety engineers are very poor at winning arguments with finance directors and economists to preserve redundancy for resilience, perhaps because customers are very reluctant to spend money on resilience and dependability if they can avoid it. As a consequence, our profession is complicit in designing a technologically brittle society, with ever increasing coupling and the concomitant risk.

We must learn from sentinel events if we are to avoid major disasters. Please do what you can to increase awareness of the growing dependence on GNSS and try to ensure that eLORAN is properly funded as a long-term alternative source of PNT.

References

BGS (2011) The largest magnetic storm on record. British Geological Survey Archives. http://www.geomag.bgs.ac.uk/education/carrington.html. Accessed 31 August 2011

Chronos (2011) SENTINEL: Real-time detection of GNSS interference for critical infrastructure. http://www.chronos.co.uk/sentinel.php. Accessed 31 August 2011

GAO (2009) Global positioning system: significant challenges in sustaining and upgrading widely used capabilities. US Government Accountability Office. http://www.gao.gov/products/GAO-09-670T. Accessed 31 August 2011

Jackson D, Thomas M, Millett LI (eds) (2007) Software for dependable systems: sufficient evidence? Committee on Certifiably Dependable Software Systems, National Research Council. http://www.nap.edu/catalog/11923.html. Accessed 1 September 2011

RAEng (2011) Global navigation space systems: reliance and vulnerabilities. Royal Academy of Engineering. http://www.raeng.org.uk/gnss. Accessed 31 August 2011

Do we truly understand Safety Culture?

Allan Bain

Sea Systems Group, Ministry of Defence

Bristol, UK

Abstract Behavioural safety programmes seek to turn 'unsafe cultures' into 'safe cultures'. Although safety culture improvement campaigns often successfully reduce accident rates, their effectiveness fades over time, with a persistent rump of accidents and incidents remaining. It will be suggested that this is because the steps taken to improve occupational health and safety culture differ from those necessary to improve systems safety culture.

Behavioural safety programmes are unsuccessful due to an over-simplistic application of social science theories by we engineers. A more sophisticated cultural model will be offered to help improve future campaigns and help understand why systems safety needs contributions from multiple disciplines. Finally risk-free cultures will be contrasted with strategies to adapt an existing project culture.

1 One safety culture to rule them all

A contributing factor behind many accidents is poor safety culture. Every country, society and indeed, individual firms possess their own cultures. Many professions and teams are known to have unique cultures, often with certain values that are held with almost tribal intensity.

Why do so many safety professionals apparently seek common treatments to improve safety culture, when each of these cultures is different? It is more logical to suppose different treatments will be successful in changing different cultures.

It is often the case that behavioural safety programmes encourage safety managers to pick-up on small infractions in their workforce, reinforce 'positive behaviour' and let the big issues look after themselves. It is suggested however, that this concept misinterprets why cultural change is desirable in the first place. Schein's seminal work proposed a model of culture made of layers (Schein 1985), where the surface behaviour was driven by implicit assumptions, which were influenced by beliefs, that were formed by symbols, stories and artefacts (see Figure 1).

He defined group culture as 'a pattern of shared basic assumptions that the group learned as it solved its problems of external adaptation and internal integration, which has worked well enough to be considered valid and, therefore, to be taught to new members as the correct way you perceive, think, and feel in relation to those problems'(Schein 1985).

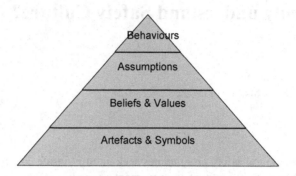

Fig. 1. A model of culture

This remains a good model for understanding cultures and offers insight into why it is so hard to change them, because what forms culture is buried deep. The model is based upon psychological studies of team behaviours. Any modern human factors text will differentiate between conscious and unconscious behaviour. Typical categories (Reason 1997) for specifying human error are:

- slips, lapses, mistakes, wrong/non-detections
- violations, unsafe acts.

To define any culture, the human behaviour that drives it must be understood (Schein 1990). The 'strength' of a particular culture can be measured by the 'amount' of artefacts and rituals performed in terms of:

1. the homogeneity and stability of group membership
2. the length and intensity of that group's shared experiences.

Schein found that to change culture, a leader must influence the layers. The more embedded and deeper the layer, the harder it is to change that cultural facet but the longer running the change will be. Behavioural programmes seek to identify 'free lessons' and challenge the behaviours that caused them. Too simplistic or formulaic a behavioural safety campaign can gloss over the true cause of the behaviour or human error that sit deeper, such as:

Skill-based. (Manage expectation, opportunity, power, planning)/(quality, reward, improvisation, mal-appliance)

Rule-based. Behavioural safety movement and the inspection culture

Knowledge based. Strive for excellence by removing error;

Behavioural safety tends to focus on workplace cleanliness and using peer pressure to enforce rules like wearing personal protective equipment. The changing of behaviour by tightening up 'rules' will not control a skill or knowledge-based error. Deeply-held cultures require consistent pressure to alter the undesired beliefs and values, informed by an understanding of the reasons why that surface behaviour occurred in the first place (cause-effect). The earliest accident theories stem from cause-effect models (Heinrich 1931) where a social environment:

1. sets preconditions for a personal fault to occur
2. when an unsafe condition
3. pre-empts an unsafe act until
4. an accident occurs
5. causing injury.

This domino theory's linear cause-effect has been discredited in recent times, replaced by networks and layers of causation and more than one underpinning 'cause'. The domino layers themselves have some parallels in the sequencing of more recent accident models such as the Swiss-cheese model of Figure 2 (Reason 1997). Just as there are several models of how systemic and random errors contribute to accidents, it is postulated that latent conditions can be explained and isolated within more than one cultural model.

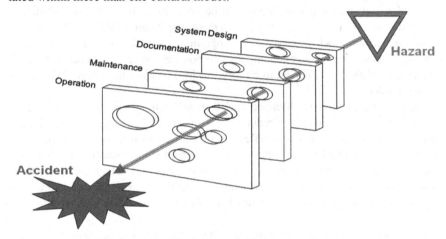

Fig. 2. Reason's cheese

Cultures are reinforced by what makes teams successful (skills, rules and violations that 'get the job done'). Therefore an attempt to change culture will work best when the cultural artefacts that bring success are understood. Team cultures become different when the teams are successful at different things.

2 A bad culture?

Successful change requires a compelling reason to move away from the habitual 'status quo' and begin that change (the burning bridge) and evidence (O'Neil 2006) that shows the change improved things. Entire societies are changed during social conflict and when new technologies are introduced and alter social dynamics. Such social shifts may accompany ideological shifts or complement other types of cultural change, e.g. the feminist movement (O'Neil 2006) or working patterns following a technological revolution. Therefore the best culture for one industrial sector working with one technology will be different than for others. The elements of a culture requiring change in response to one accident, within one industry, may not be the best solution within a different context, or the accident sequences for other industries and risks.

The idea that by addressing small accidents, serious (but rarer) accidents can be prevented from occurring was suggested by the accident triangle model (Heinrich 1931). This original research on accident statistics suggested a ratio where, for every major injury, there would typically be 29 minor injuries and 300 non-injuries (incidents); it was validated (Bird and Germain 1986) in their accident iceberg[1]. More recent versions of these models have added an additional layer for culture.

It has been widely held that by 'controlling' safety culture and removing all risky behaviour, that major accidents can be prevented. However the unthinking application of any technique without understanding it can undermine the noblest of intentions. Some behavioural safety programmes have become so doctrinarian that they encourage risk aversion and seek to pounce upon all small accidents and incidents, as they are perceived to be forewarnings of large ones according to the iceberg model.

More recent assessment (Bennett and Wilson 2010) of accident ratios shows reducing minor events does not reduce major events (Schouwenaars 2008), it just narrows the pyramid. It is worth reflecting why a universal reduction of small incidents or an improved safety culture will not reduce major incidents and only reduce the ratio. This may be because the 'wrong type' of safety culture is promoted. The Texas City, Piper Alpha and Nimrod disasters all had successful occupational health and safety regimes but poor systems safety engineering cultures.

It has been speculated (Schouwenaars 2008) that because accident sequences differ, the removal of minor events that do not contribute to major incidents within safety improvement programmes could result in the triangles in Figure 3. One set of accident sequences (occupational safety) are derived from the bottom right of Figure 4 and one set of sequences (process safety) from the top right. So accident statistics capture multiple accident sequences and are have multiple accident pyramids superimposed upon them.

An illustration of the 'wrong' safety culture from my own industry is the 1891 loss of HMS Victoria commanded by Admiral Tyron (Figure 5). The pervading culture cherished the preservation of the bright-work over physical gun drills that spoiled it (Massie 1991). When individual officers objected to instructing their men to shout bang instead of firing guns, they had been sent ashore.

---

[1] This work showed 1 serious injury (lost time or fatal) had a ratio of 10 minor injuries to 30 property damages and around 600 near misses.

The Hope
If smaller events are addressed, big ones improve

The Idea
Accident severities have a fixed ratio

In Reality
Addressing smaller events improves smaller events

Fig. 3. Narrowing of accident pyramids

Fig. 4. Risk matrices and accident types

Admiral Tyron was reputed to be a bit of a tyrant, insisting on spit and polish as he believed that attention to detail, immaculate appearance, regular drills and surprise exercises under pressure would help his men show initiative in battle. Whilst conducting a complex anchoring manoeuvre, at high speed, at half the safe separation distance, the warships HMS Victoria and HMS Cambertown collided.

Although his ideas encouraged innovation, the culture that had evolved reduced procedures and 'safety margins'. Despite a late order to 'close all watertight doors', some 358 of the 715 crew on board were drowned. It is alleged that the watertight doors had been so highly polished that they could no longer form a watertight seal (Massie 1991).

Fig. 5. Loss of HMS Victoria

Although many lessons can be taken from this accident, it is worth concluding teaching the 'wrong kind' of excellence can deliver unexpected consequences. Just as safe design begins with 'what is it for and how will it be used', those intending to change culture should ask the same questions. It is speculated that different types of safety culture can help avert different accidents. It would appear more useful if different accident sequences could be linked with specific types of hazardous event and specific behaviours. So what are the characteristics of a good systems safety culture, and is there another approach?

3 A different cultural model

What kind of safety culture is best for systems safety and what attributes would differ between an appropriate occupational work-based safety culture and one for process safety? Complex socio-technical systems can be understood by considering their failure modes and accident sequences from the major functions of these systems, sometimes called 'mission threads'. The largest and most complex systems have several threads to them and often multiple functions. Accident statistics can only be usefully collated together into pyramids of similar accident sequences. In other words, near misses and minor accidents only become helpful indicators of weaknesses in specific lines of defence that protect against serious accidents but are less helpful forewarning against dissimilar accident sequences. It is speculated that rather than promoting a blanket 'risk averse' safety culture, that an effective safety culture is one that is attuned to the core outputs, functions and mission threads of the system it is part of.

If we consider the 31 deaths from the Kings Cross fire (1987), a 'poor safety culture' was cited as a latent factor. The 'accident sequence' was a discarded cigarette which set light to an accumulation of rubbish under an escalator. In truth a poor cleaning regime (from Figures 4 and 5) permitted the accumulation of rubbish that may have been unsightly but was not thought to be important to safety. This culture was coupled with an ancient escalator design, which used unsuitable materials (wood) and an assumption that there was no credible fire source. These latent factors removed a line of defence and can be linked with other failed safety features such as the failure of fire fighting equipment and the lack of emergency training within underground staffs into a truthful cause-effect model. Rather than a blanket 'zero-risk' safety culture, the cultural changes necessary from this disaster appertain to fire prevention and accident sequences that lead to it.

Similarly the 'disease of sloppiness' and internal friction within Townsend-Thoresen caused a culture that underpinned a latent cause of the Herald of Free Enterprise disaster (1987). This safety culture did not require fire prevention awareness, but can be linked to ship seaworthiness. The overburdening commercial pressures and focus on the timetable within this company culture had overridden the seamanship culture where crews check and report key activities to the ship's master. The overloaded crew failed to close the bow doors in a flawed ship design and ultimately the collective behaviours of many killed 189.

A safety campaign that pushes hard for behavioural changes to a set timetable will be as counterproductive as a culture that seeks commercial savings irrespective of other priorities. Hypocritical leadership will not deliver the desired cultural changes. Conversely, leaders who insist safety is paramount and ignore other organisational pressures are unlikely to deliver sustained improvement by going bust. Before a risky behaviour can be understood and treated it is worth understanding the reasons why the risk is taken in the first place (see Figure 6).

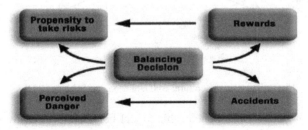

Fig. 6. Why we take risks (the Adams risk thermostat (MoD 2005))

One may wish to dismiss any 'hypocritical' leader who gives off mixed messages by encouraging staff to 'be safer', whilst driving team members to 'save money' and 'meet the programmes at all costs'. However, successful safety cultures are balanced and do not cast blame. Rather than a world of absolutes, safety regimes with widest support promote proportionate and balanced safety management that helps deliver business objectiveness (Bain 2008).

Large organisations are made up of people who form into teams of like-minded individuals. Different cultures evolve from groups of people from different backgrounds with different values, rewarded by specialisation. Safety should not become a barrier that is used to stop activities. The best cultures understand how core 'business' activities benefit from being done safely, e.g. military safety regimes recognise that 'who dares wins'. Allies can be gained outside of the immediate circle of safety practitioners when systems safety helps deliver other systems engineering disciplines. Zero risk can be taken as zero activity and no benefit.

To understand what elements of a corporate culture deliver core activities and what ensure safety, it is necessary to understand them in detail. Rather than a simple 3-layer model (Schein 1985) a culture can be understood in more detail using the model in Figure 7.

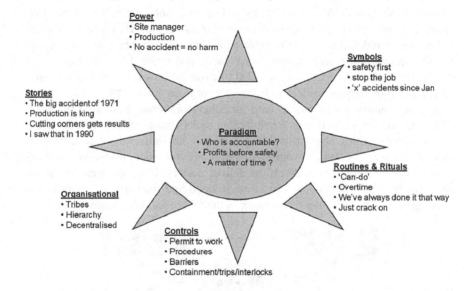

Fig. 7. Safety in the cultural web (Johnson and Scholes 1992)

Whilst still compatible with Schein, this model helps users to easily understand the specific features that make one culture different from another (Bain 2008). By shining light upon the prevailing strengths of one team's culture over another, the desirable traits of that culture can be understood, and the 'best' isolated. As this study progressed, it was shown that:

- Specific cultural types and preferences could be categorised into tables, aligned to professions, job types and skill areas.
- There is clear evidence that different cultural types are more successful at specific functions within different systems.

- Different cultures are dominated by certain personalities and attract others with compatible personalities.
- Each personality type was stimulated by different incentives.

Large organisations are actually formed from groups of tribes[2] (see Figure 8) and to change a large organisation's corporate culture, a change manager must influence multiple tribal cultures. No one culture is 'the best', this model just shows large organisations are made from 'teams of teams'. Indeed multi-disciplinary teams and multi-cultural groups of varied team disciplines are most effective.

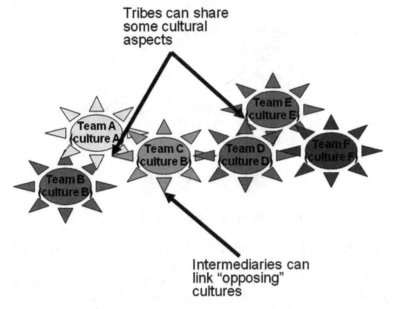

Fig. 8. Organisations are made from tribes (Bain 2008)

There is considerable evidence that multi-cultural organisations are more desirable than mono-cultures. Indeed, permitting different views allows counter-cultures which are a useful counter to 'group think' and should be encouraged by leaders. Leaders seeking to monitor the effectiveness of any team's culture are best advised to use a range of performance monitoring devices (Figure 7) appropriate to the element being assessed.

---

[2] A strong culture becomes 'tribal' when there are high-performing teams with strong, unifying cultures, containing individuals who share common values with familial intensity.

4 Improving cultures

A range of safety culture measurement techniques exist generically (HSL 2003, see Figure 9), as do tools for specific industries, e.g. rail and defence (Bain and De Fossard 2005). Such tools can be abused like any other, e.g. well meaning managers can set 100% targets in all areas. Intelligent target-setting can strengthen useful tribal strengths and tone down ineffective elements surgically.

Fig. 9. Safety climate measurement (HSL 2003)

It has been shown that setting team targets that encourage high performance in the key areas of each tribe's responsibility and which build on core skills are more successful 'carrots' than metrics that use 'sticks' (Bain 2008). Thus attention to quality paperwork is important to quality assurance whilst attention to material quality and physical performance is important to production. Both tribes may have common cause.

When a culture becomes too successful within highly complex industries, there have been occasions when barriers against high consequence low frequency events have been eroded over time and the reason for vigilance forgotten. Successful programmes can also make teams prone to violations as safety improvements deliver their fruit and time passes. The recurrent themes of accidents have been categorised (Reason 1998) as:

- universal hazards unique to an operating environment (like storms at sea)
- local traps of a task or workplace
- drivers, seen by psychologists as the motive forces that drive people to erroneous behaviour.

Many traps become larger when the short-term benefits of violations are reinforced (Figure 5) and outweigh the perceived 'theoretical' dangers as teams balance between ALARP and pressures to stay in business. Despite the comprehensive spread of safety cultural characteristics within cultural surveys, another dimension must be considered. This extra dimension is maturity and is shown well by DuPont's best practice model shown in the Bradley curve (Hewitt 2011).

The safety cultural characteristics of cultural maturity surveys can help assess cultural facets of both occupational and systems safety behaviour (Figure 10) but control is a mirage (Reason 1998) that can be nothing more than a lull in the occurrence of random accidents, rather than an effective barrier improved. Entirely risk-free activity (or the perception of this) can erode the collective understanding of the need for a defensive barrier and eternal vigilance. This is why the concept of 'perpetual unease' is so important as it continually searches for holes in barriers and drives a cultural characteristic of being a learning organisation.

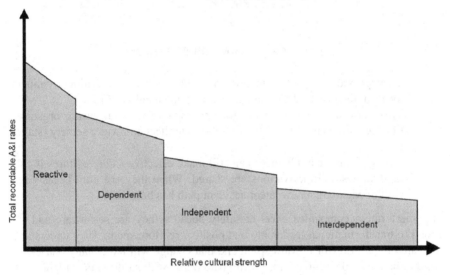

Fig. 10. Bradley curve (Hewitt 2011)

A sustainable corporate culture is a blend of individual tribe's cultures (Bain 2008). These strong tribes are made of people of similar background and personality (sociological grouping theory). The higher frequency events require high-workforce involvement whilst the low frequency events are more of a management system and strategic focus. The most effective type of intervention (Figure 11) varies:

- A single monolithic culture is counterproductive but positive elements of multiple cultures suitably aligned can be effective.
- Successful change creates alliances between willing tribes guided collectively to best influence the overall desired organisation culture.
- Tribes with 'counter-cultures' which may directly oppose some of an organisation's core assumptions, whilst creating the potential for conflict, serve three important functions:

  - They uphold standards of performance and ethical behaviour.

HIERARCHY OF SAFETY AUDITS AND OBSERVATIONS

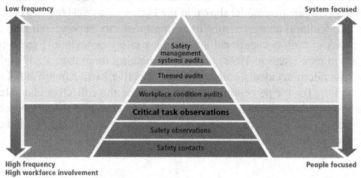

Fig. 11. Safety performance (BHP Billiton 2006)

– They provide corporate memory and intelligence that critiques/tempers over-dominance by the dominant organisational culture/fashion.
– They form a breeding ground for emerging values that ensure organisations remain connected with customers, suppliers and wider society (stakeholders).
– Strong commercial alliances can still make effective safety cultures if cultural values and motivations are shared. When they are not (Texas City, Gulf of Mexico), a new latent accident path has been laid.

High-performing companies excel at safety because they are self-aware and respond to transformational leadership and positive reinforcement. They understand they are on a journey or upward spiral and that change will have many phases toward a shared vision or goal and can slip backwards without drive (see Figure 12). Poor safety cultures look inward, are not self-aware, respond to negative reinforcement from transactional leadership and tend to be on a downward spiral, without a direction.

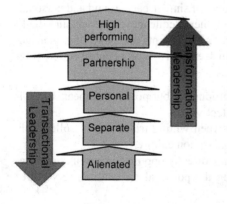

Culture exhibited	Language used
Multi-node, altruistic networks, innocent wonderment	Life's great, wow, miracle, lucky, vision, values, we
Triadic, collaborative relationships of champion tribes	Our team's great, do, we, them, have, did it, commit, value, team pride
Dyadic, competitive relationships between lone-warriors	I, me, my, job, did, do, have, went
Apathetic relationships of victims	My life sucks, boss, life, try, can't, give up, useless, quit
Despairingly hostile alienated gang relationships	All life sucks, *##@, break, can't, cut, whatever, don't care

Fig. 12. Layers of cultural maturity (Bain 2008)

5 Conclusions

Behavioural safety will not always succeed as a universal doctrine, in part due to an over-simplistic application of social science theories. By becoming aware of alternative models we can improve safety campaigns within a multi-disciplinary team.

Strong teams form tribes of like-minded people with similar personalities and motivations. These strong tribes are self-affirming and form the strongest cultures. Successful change programmes reinforce those facets of a culture that will deliver a desired function and play down the more toxic elements. By reinforcing facets of a culture that help deliver objectives, a change strategy can successfully shift a deeply held belief by the sustained and long-lived effect. Superficial challenges to behaviours have only superficial effects or do not impact the accident sequence that it is desired to treat. Risk mitigation should be matched to accident type.

Change programmes that mistakenly seek a utopia of an entirely risk-free or accident-free culture can in fact reduce vigilance. Clearly, achieving safety improvements must never be confused as the same thing as achieving another task, but resilient teams adapt existing business delivery cultures and deliver safety as part of the core of systems engineering. A sustainable corporate culture blends individual tribal cultures into larger teams. The more tribes share in common, the stronger the team spirit, especially when those within them share similar background or are allowed to gel (sociological grouping theory). In particular:

- It is counterproductive to drive a single monolithic culture; instead, successful change is formed from alliances between willing tribes guided collectively to best influence the overall desired organisational culture.
- By identifying 'counter-cultures' that oppose some of an organisation's core assumptions (for good reasons), standards, corporate memory and values can be protected.
- Alliances between multiple disciplines and tribes can be made stronger than the sum of the constituent teams (by empathy for the different perspectives).
- Leaders need to understand a tribe's function and why its values are useful to improve corporate memory.

Poor safety cultures look inward, are not self-aware and respond to negative transactional relationships, possibly exacerbated by behavioural safety. The highest-performing system safety companies are the most self-aware and respond to transformational leadership and positive reinforcement. They understand safety is not an end-state but a journey or an upward spiral with many phases where tribes start to share their visions or goals and can slip backwards without leadership driving. It is hoped that some of these concepts can help readers lead their own teams towards a safer world.

References

Bain A (2008) Cultural diversity and careers within defence acquisition: scruffy civvies and poker-stiff matelots. Cranfield University MSc Dissertation

Bain A, De Fossard J (2005) Measuring safety – development of a systems safety management maturity model, with systems readiness levels. Int Syst Saf Conf (ISSC05), San Diego, USA

Bennett G, Wilson I (2010) Achieving excellence in process safety management through people, process and plant. DNV white paper presented at Downstream Asia, Singapore. http://www. theenergyexchange.co.uk/admin/ Accessed 4 October 2011

BHP (2006) Sustainability report. BHP Billiton. http://www.bhpbilliton.com/home/aboutus/ sustainability/reports/Documents/2006%20BHP%20Billiton%20Sustainability%20Report %20documents.pdf. Accessed 17 October 2011

Bird FE Jr, Germain GL (1986) Practical loss control leadership. International Loss Control Institute, Loganville, Ga

Heinrich HW (1931) Industrial accident prevention: a scientific approach. McGraw-Hill

Hewitt, M (2011) Relative culture strength, a key to sustainable world-class safety performance. http://www2.dupont.com/Sustainable_Solutions/en_US/assets/downloads/A_Key_to_Sustain able_World-Class_Safety_Performance.pdf. Accessed 17 October 2011

HSL (2003) Safety climate tool. Health and Safety Laboratory. www.hsl.gov.uk/health-and-safety-products/safety-climate-tool.aspx. Accessed 5 October 2011

Johnson G, Scholes K (1992) Exploring corporate strategy

Massie RK (1991) Dreadnought – Britain, Germany and the coming of the great war. Random House

MoD (2005) JSP 430 MoD ship safety management, part 2: policy guidance. Issue 3. Ministry of Defence

O'Neil D (2006) Processes of change. http://anthro.palomar.edu/change/change_2.htm. Accessed 4 October 2011

Reason J (1997) Managing the risks of organizational accidents. Ashgate, Farnham

Reason J (1998) Achieving a safe culture: theory and practice. Work and Stress 12(3)293-306

Schein EH (1985) Organizational culture and leadership. Jossey-Bass, San Francisco

Schein EH (1990) Organisational culture. Am Psychol 45(2)109-119

Schouwenaars E (2008) The risks arising from major accident hazards, lessons from the past, opportunities for the future. DNV paper presented at Refining Management Forum, Copenhagen

The Need for a Community for System and Functional Safety Professionals

Audrey Canning

Virkonnen Ltd

Reigate, UK

Abstract In March 2011, following several years as the successful Functional Safety Professional Network (FSPN), IET members and others formed a new 'safety community', principally to represent the interests of practicing system safety and functional safety experts. This paper argues that the considerations of safety engineering are additional to both technological and application knowledge and that 'safety' should be considered as a discipline in its own right. In particular the safety discipline is unique, both because of its focus on adverse and unwanted behaviour of a system and by the breadth of its knowledge requirement – involving as it does a broad range of technical, application and management skills and techniques, together with the additional knowledge of failure analyses and control techniques. Engineers and other professionals practicing in these areas have a keen desire for professional recognition of their needs and interests and are keen to support a community in this area. Whilst there are differing views on whether the community needs to be a single body, as a first step system and functional safety experts have set up a community for IET registrants, with the aim of supporting a federated approach to working within and across application and technology divides.

1 Introduction

In March 2011, following several years as the successful Functional Safety Professional Network (FSPN), IET members and others formed a new 'safety community', principally to represent the interests of practicing system safety and functional safety experts. The decision to reform followed several months of discussion and deliberation as to whether there was a demand for professional leadership for system and functional safety professionals. The discussions also addressed whether the needs of engineering and other professionals practicing in system and functional safety could be adequately addressed by sector or technology groupings within their primary fields of expertise. Intrinsic in this discussion is whether those responsible for the design, implementation and deployment of complex systems with a potential impact on safety have professional needs which are distinct from the mainstream engineering and business interests in which they are involved. There is also the consideration of whether, as a result of such distinctions, a cohesive professional identity is required, or whether safety can be addressed purely as an adjunct to a 'matrix' model of technology/application intersection.

This paper argues that the considerations of safety engineering go beyond the normal interests of both technology and application groupings and that 'safety' should be considered as a discipline in its own right. Safety engineering of complex systems (as is the case with other 'non-functional' disciplines, for example EMC and human factors), focuses on how to contain the *adverse* effects of a technology or application, whilst at the same time allowing its benefits to be accrued. This is distinct from the delivery function, which generally focuses on demonstrating that a system or application provides the performance for which it was commissioned in the first place. System and functional safety experts tend to focus on what happens if things go wrong and whether there are undesirable side effects associated with the application, the technology, the manner in which it is realised and the way in which it is deployed. Further, the timescales for 'success' between those focused on delivery as opposed to those focused on safety can be widely different. The benefits of an application or technology normally need to be delivered from the point of deployment – to fail to do so leaves the delivery stream open to criticism of having failed in its task. The adverse effects of an application or technology may not become apparent for many years.

2 What makes a good safety professional?

Those responsible for system and functional safety do require good technical and/or application knowledge relevant to the systems on which they are working. Hazards are normally inherent in the application and the risk associated with existing hazards may potentially be increased so as to achieve improved performance. For example, transport systems continually strive for faster and more efficient behaviour, which is accompanied by levels of energy hazardous to its human passengers. Power generation systems are rarely without side effects hazardous to life (pollution, radiation, global warming). Aspects of technology, particularly novel technologies, can in themselves be hazardous in ways not anticipated when originally developed (cf. use of asbestos, CFCs) and we can expect the hazardous effects of new technologies to emerge over years to come through the introduction of novel technology, e.g. in bio-engineering, green energy or intelligent buildings. Further, technology may be deployed in unsatisfactory ways, e.g. with incomplete understanding of the requirements, or with errors and faults introduced as part of the engineering specification, design and implementation activities (such as would be the case with faulty software codes or compilers). To be effective, those responsible for ensuring a complex system achieves an acceptable level of safety require a thorough knowledge and understanding of the hazards associated with the context of the application, the legal or regulatory regime in which it operates, and how a technology needs to be engineered to avoid intrinsic faults being introduced during development. Safety engineering also requires a wide knowledge of past good practice – whether captured through incidents, codes of practice, standards or legislation – together with an understanding of the context in which they are relevant. Any code of good practice will have its limitations if used beyond the boundaries of the performance for which it was originally devised. Without this knowledge there is a distinct possibility that the criticism often leveled at safety professionals – that of being a 'tick box' functionary, and providing little added value to a project or application – is likely to ring true.

Indeed, the definition of a safety engineer in Wikipedia (Wikipedia 2011) goes further to require:

'To perform their professional functions, safety engineering professionals must have education, training and experience in a common body of knowledge. They need to have a fundamental knowledge of physics, chemistry, biology, physiology, statistics, mathematics, computer science, engineering mechanics, industrial processes, business, communication and psychology.'

as well as specialist knowledge in subjects such as engineering hazards and their control, system and process safety, human factors and the relevant legal and regulatory requirements and standards. It further identifies that safety engineers are likely to have practiced to a senior level in a wide variety of different backgrounds including:

'management and business administration, engineering, system engineering, requirements engineering, reliability engineering, maintenance, human factors, operations, education, physical and social sciences'

It must be acknowledged that it is unlikely that such a skill-set will be found in an individual professional, and therefore that safety will usually need to be managed in the context of a real or virtual organisation, working to a safety management system. Nevertheless a professional with a high safety focus will have some of these skills in depth and a good awareness of the importance and relevance of the other skill-sets, both to recognise the limits of the engineering considerations which *have* been taken into account, and to be able to identify the need for, and to undertake liaison with, a wider body of expertise when appropriate.

Perhaps the key knowledge and behavioural characteristics that set those focusing on safety apart from the delivery expertise is the focus on techniques for limiting the way in which things can go wrong. In particular, a system or functional safety expert will be cognisant of techniques for avoidance of, and/or detection and circumvention of, hazardous behaviour. This type of knowledge will rarely be the delivery team's focus, which, running to strict deadlines, will normally be dedicated to ensuring that the specified requirements are met – often at minimal cost. It is this focus that sets the safety discipline apart from other engineering disciplines, and it is these techniques that form the predominant subject matter of system safety and functional safety standards (e.g. IEC 2010, IEC 2003-2007, IEC 2011,

IEC 2005, RTCA 1992, CENELEC 2007). Typical of the techniques used in the safety discipline will be:

- techniques to elicit information about the nature of hazards, e.g. Hazard Identification (HAZID), Hazard and Operability Studies (HAZOPS) and risk assessments
- techniques to identify how failures might arise and the consequences if they do arise, e.g. functional failure analysis, Failure Mode and Effects Analysis (FMEA), cause consequence analysis, workload analysis
- models to capture the behaviour of a system (though these may also be adopted by the delivery stream, but often from a single viewpoint), including physical and functional descriptions, mathematical models relevant to the particular application domain (e.g. control systems) and relevant to the implementation technology (e.g. discreet logic), environmental and materials properties, etc.
- processes that control the opportunity for defects to be introduced during implementation (e.g. traceability through the various levels of specification, design and test to demonstrate that the required functionality and only the required functionality is present; configuration management to demonstrate that only the intended items and versions of those items are deployed together in the final system; manufacturing methods and software engineering methods that control the opportunity to introduce inconsistent deviations during the realisation process).

A further aspect that sets those involved in safety apart from their delivery colleagues is the nature of the demand on professional integrity and interpersonal skills. That is not to say that all professional engineers will not have committed to deploying such skills – and generally do – but that the level of demand on these skills, arguably, is likely to be more frequent and more onerous for a safety professional than for those concerned purely with delivery. In particular, a safety expert is more likely to be placed in a position where his professional knowledge is contrary to the interests of the project on which he is working compared to that of the delivery team directly trying to satisfy the aims of the project. The particular focus on how and why things go wrong is more likely to place the safety expert in a position where he/she needs to convince others that unpopular problems need to be addressed. The safety professional may need to argue the position effectively to a range of different levels within an organisation, to be able to listen to the counterarguments, and – in the rare circumstances where the problem cannot be resolved locally – to stand their ground in bringing the problem to the attention of the relevant authorities. This can require conflicting skills – flexibility to listen to counterarguments, confidence and independence sufficient to stand one's ground, and the ability to handle isolation from the mainstream interest.

3 The need for a community

Recognising the distinct situation in which those involved in safety find themselves, both in terms of the types of knowledge they need and in terms of their unique position within a project, team or organisation, the author of this paper (and others) have advocated the need for those practicing system and functional safety to have a professional support network distinct from technology and application focused concerns. The author is not alone in arguing that safety engineering should be recognised as a major discipline in its own right. The official inquiry reports into disasters (e.g. Piper Alpha (Cullen 1991), Kings Cross (Fennel 1988), Potters Bar (RSSB 2005)) have repeatedly stressed that safety must be treated as an overarching requirement throughout the product or project life cycle. The legal and regulatory requirements for safety cases, codes of practice and standards that have evolved from these disasters have led to the emergence of safety engineering as a distinct discipline. The pervasive use of computer systems has heightened the perception of the importance of the impact of complex systems on safety. Recommendation 28.4 of the enquiry into the Nimrod disaster (Haddon-Cave 2009) argues the need for a single professional body for safety experts to set professional and ethical standards, accredit members and disseminate best practice, as does a recent paper presented to this conference series (McDermid et al. 2009). Whilst not seeing the need for a single body, the attendees at The Foundation for Science and Technology meeting on 13 July 2011 also advocated that the profile of safety engineering as a discipline needed to be raised and that it should become part of the skill-set and knowledge of all engineers responsible for systems with safety implications.

Indeed the desire for representation is also sought by the body of practicing system and functional safety professionals. In autumn 2010 the IET Secretariat, on behalf of the outgoing FSPN executive, conducted a survey of 3,284 registrants of the Functional Safety Professional Network. The response rate, at 10% of those canvassed, was more than three times that of the average response rate, indicating an unusually high level of interest in the subject of professional representation, with an overwhelming 87% responding that functional safety was a very important aspect of their professional activity. From the feedback received, it is clear that those consulted are united in the view that technical knowledge and specialist expertise in system and functional safety should be retained as a cohesive body of skills and that good practice in functional safety should be shared and harmonised across the UK. More than 60% of the respondents would look to a professional body to provide knowledge and information sharing, with the development of codes of good practice and industry case studies, training, competency standards and support for practitioners being their key areas of interest.

Further, there are important commercial drivers for advocating a cohesive approach to system and functional safety. In particular, the importance of system and functional safety has been recognised only in the last thirty years, driven largely by concerns over the pervasive use of computer-based systems, the huge increase in complexity of the systems that they enable, and the concern to ensure that faults and failures cannot jeopardise human safety. As such, many of the standards and practices are still evolving and there is a risk of widely differing interpretations of the requirements in different organisations, sectors and also internationally. If standards vary, then those involved in development of systems and products run a gauntlet of commercial jeopardy. On the one hand they may over-engineer the system making it expensive and unable to compete in the market place. Or they may meet the requirements of the regulator in one country, but find that they are uncompetitive in an international arena where different standards apply. Alternatively they may develop a product unaware of the standards that apply for a safety application only to find that the product cannot be deployed without extensive re-engineering or safety justification. In this author's experience, this lack of awareness is a common problem for start-up organisations and small to medium sized companies (SMEs). To provide a forum to harmonise emerging technologies and standards presupposes that there are also forums for the exchange of views between those involved in different aspects of the safety discipline.

4 The role of a system and functional safety community

It is argued that to support the professionalism of the system and functional safety expert there are four key needs:

- ability to influence policy affecting their profession
- provision of a forum for a safe exchange of views
- provision of continuing professional development (CPD), training and awareness
- moral and societal leadership and support.

Policy and strategy. Matters of policy and strategy relate to the ability to represent the body of system and functional safety practitioners to government, regulators, employers and others in authority. There is a need to ensure a co-ordinated, professional response to recommendations arising from reports such as the Nimrod review (Haddon-Cave 2009), which raise fundamental issues for the organisation and responsibility of those working in the safety discipline. The question of how to maintain standards of product, process or competence is a recurring discussion amongst safety practitioners. Arguments on how the general market-place can recognise a 'good' safety professional collide with concerns to maintain an open and level playing field and with the need to avoid a 'closed shop' solution. Other aspects of policy which need to be addressed include visibility of, and influence over, emerging standards, as well as developing the industry response to emerging legislation – e.g. the corporate manslaughter act.

'Safe' forum for exchange of views, ideas and questions. Because of the sensitivity of issues arising in the safety community it is often not possible to share problems and concerns in an open discussion. Moreover, even the airing of informal advice might result in exposure to legal claims. Safety professionals therefore need a venue for discrete, technical and authoritative discussions, providing an opportunity to access the knowledge of industry experts and regulators, without jeopardising the interests of either the problem holder or the knowledge provider. Further, for industry to remain competitive on the international stage, it is important that industry is able to meet local regulatory requirements without causing it to become uncompetitive on the international stage. Community discussion provides a good opportunity to explore and identify good practice across a wide cross-section of applications, domains and technologies, as well as to address problems experienced by a broad cross-section of safety practitioners and to set international benchmarks.

Provision of CPD, training and awareness. Safety engineering, requiring as it does a good basic level of engineering and scientific knowledge as well as specialist safety analysis techniques, is not well addressed at undergraduate level. There are a few centres of higher education at Masters or advanced short course level. However, the vast majority of safety practitioners enter the profession by 'being in the right place at the right time' and, probably quite rightly, after several years practicing in their different fields of expertise. The regulatory requirement to provide and maintain formal safety cases in high risk industries has driven many application and technology specialists to need to justify the claims for their products, projects and systems, drawing them into a safety role later in their career. Other organisations (especially SMEs) find themselves deeply committed to a particular product, without having properly appreciated that the level of safety evidence that will be needed to successfully introduce a new product or service into a safety related application. There is a need for a broad awareness of safety practices and constraints to avoid expensive market failures, as well as to ensure adequate training is available for professionals newly entering the profession. Introductory-level training in safety engineering needs to be provided on a cross-sectoral basis, together with ensuring a proper coordination with the evolving functional safety standards and with the more advanced instruction provided by academic institutions.

Supporting the moral and societal obligations of the profession. Given the propensity to be at odds with the main delivery team objectives and perhaps due to poor safety culture at a local level, the safety professional is arguably more likely to need to call upon the support of his professional background. Moreover, it is important that all professional engineers involved in systems using electronic and computer-based systems understand the consequences of failure of their systems. There is a need to ensure that delivery engineers are alert to their obligations to address the consequence of failure, as well as to support those engineers who find themselves in a difficult position due to a conflict between safety and commercial aims.

5 A safety community charter

In response to the need identified above, IET members have drafted a charter for a safety community with the objectives of:

- encouraging and spreading best practice in safety professionalism, including consultation on safety standards and codes of practice
- maintaining a body of knowledge from the community members
- contributing to the development of, and response to, policy and strategy as it affects safety engineering, including the ability to respond proactively on behalf of the community to incidents affecting the safety profession
- liaison with relevant bodies, both inter- and intra-institutional groups and strengthening links on matters of joint interest
- support for networking and experience-sharing between community members
- development of material and structure for CPD for safety professionals.

This safety community is to be taken forward through a dynamic Working Group structure. A Policy and Strategy Working Group has been set up to address matters of policy and public concern as they affect the system and functional safety engineer. The intent is both to be able to respond reactively to incident-driven matters by drawing rapidly on the authoritative body of knowledge within the community, e.g. in developing a well reasoned response to incidents such as the impact of Fukishima on nuclear safety, and also to be proactive in poorly developed areas, e.g. the policing of the community itself and the standards of professionalism that it should adopt. During these initial stages the work of the group is focussing on identifying appropriate *modi operandi* to be able to address policy matters both on an immediate reactive basis and a longer term formulative basis.

A Professionalism and CPD Working Group has been established which recognises that competence, integrity and culture are key ingredients for a safe solution. The required standards of competence and professionalism are both broad and onerous, especially at leadership levels. One of the aims of the Professionalism and CPD Working Group is to support the development and uptake of competency standards through practical interpretation into the industrial context. Another is to solicit feedback for future improvements – which in turn can be fed into CPD and other initiatives.

It is not intended that the working groups are necessarily 'permanent'. Indeed, as an emerging discipline the safety community intends to adopt a dynamic and evolving approach to working groups, establishing them as different needs arise and dissolving their grouping as their task is complete. One of the important features of the community is its intent to 'network' with other bodies in the safety area, thus satisfying the vision of a cohesive body of professionals, without the need to form a new organisation. The dynamic working group structure is ideally suited to such a need, allowing groups to be developed on a short or long term basis for liaison across institutions and between intra-institutional networks as the needs arise.

Governance of the activities of the community lies with a small steering group comprising both of the working group leaders and, unusually for professional networks, of functionary posts responsible for planning, finance, communications and performance monitoring.

6 Concluding remarks

This paper has argued that system and functional safety experts require professionalism support that is distinct from, and not properly served by, traditional technology/application focused networks. The profession is set apart both by its focus on adverse and unwanted behaviour and by the breadth of knowledge and experience it requires. The engineers and other professionals practicing in this area have a keen desire for professional representation of their discipline and are keen to support a community in this area. As a first step IET members and others working in the profession have set up a safety community, with the aim of supporting a federated approach to supporting the interests of the profession.

References

CENELEC (2007) Railway applications – The specification and demonstration of reliability, availability, maintainability and safety (RAMS). EN 50126. European Committee for Electrotechnical Standardisation

Cullen (1991) The public inquiry into the Piper Alpha disaster. HM Stationery Office

Fennel (1988) Investigation into the King's Cross underground fire. HM Stationery Office

Haddon-Cave (2009) The Nimrod review, an independent review into the broader issues surrounding the loss of the RAF Nimrod MR2, aircraft XV230 in Afghanistan in 2006. The Stationery Office, Information and Publishing Solutions

IEC (2003-2007) Functional safety – Safety instrumented systems for the process industry sector. IEC 61511. International Electrotechnical Committee

IEC (2005) Safety of machinery – Functional safety of safety-related electrical, electronic and programmable electronic control systems. IEC 62061. International Electrotechnical Committee

IEC (2010) Functional safety of electrical/electronic/programmable electronic safety-related systems. IEC 61508. International Electrotechnical Committee

IEC (2011) Nuclear power plants – Instrumentation and control important to safety – General requirements for systems. IEC 61513. International Electrotechnical Committee

McDermid J, Thomas M, Redmill F (2009) Professional issues in system safety engineering. In: Dale C, Anderson T (eds) Safety-critical systems problems, process and practice. Springer

RSSB (2005) Formal inquiry, derailment of train 1T60, 1245 hrs Kings Cross to Kings Lynn at Potters Bar on 10 May 2002. Rail Safety and Standards Board

RTCA (1992) Software considerations in airborne systems and equipment certification. DO-178B/ED-12B. RTCA SC-167 and EUROCAE WG-12

Wikipedia (2011) Safety engineer. http://en.wikipedia.org/wiki/Safety_engineer. Accessed 19 September 2011

The Challenge of Technological Change in the Automotive Industry

Roger Rivett

Jaguar Land Rover

Coventry, UK

Abstract   The technology deployed on vehicles, particularly luxury vehicles, has undergone a revolution in the last 10 years. On a modern luxury vehicle, virtually all functionality is delivered via software-based control units, with most communicating over vehicle networks. This is being driven by the availability of the technology and the need to offer the market ever more distinctive and appealing vehicles. The public appetite for such technology seems to know no bounds. The engineering of many of the new features and supporting technologies needs the discipline of functional safety, and a new automotive standard on functional safety is due to be published in October 2011. This paper summaries the recent changes in vehicle features and their enabling technologies, discusses the challenges that these represent to the industry and how the new functional safety standard can help meet some of these challenges while presenting challenges of its own.

1 Technology and feature change in vehicles

The increase in features offered on vehicles over the last ten years is frequently discussed in papers and a brief summary is presented here. One can start by highlighting the fact that nearly all the functionality of modern luxury vehicle involves the use of software-based control units. It has been suggested that rather than thinking of the vehicle as a mechanical machine, with some electrical components, it would be more accurate to think of the vehicle as a distributed computer system programmed for personal transport. While being an overstatement, this does indicate the changed nature of the machine.

The increased use of software in vehicles can be appreciated by considering the following (Charette 2009):

- F-22 Raptor avionics system: 1.7 million lines of code
- Boeing 777 avionics and onboard support systems: 4 million lines of code
- F-35 joint strike fighter onboard systems: 5.7 million lines of code

- Boeing 787 avionics and onboard support systems: 6.5 million lines of code
- modern luxury car: 100 million lines of code.

In fact the radio and navigation systems alone can take up to 20 million lines of code.

It is also worth noting that the development time for a vehicle is of the order of two to three years and the production volumes are often greater than 100,000; this is at least an order of magnitude different to aerospace, which has longer development times and lower production volumes.

The reason for the increase in software over the last ten years is down to a number of factors, some of which are listed here.

To compete in the global market, vehicle manufacturers have to keep up with their competitors and differentiate their vehicles from all the others on offer, so the manufacturers exploit the potential of the software-based systems to add 'customer delight' features to traditional functions. An example is interior lights which come on when the engine stops, and then extinguish some time after the driver has locked the vehicle and walked away. There is also a desire to provide the same facilities in the car as the user has for home entertainment or office working. These technologies are currently undergoing rapid development, feeding an apparently insatiable appetite among the user base for new features.

Both governments and vehicle manufactures need to respond to the widely accepted view on climate change and develop 'green' technologies; this is resulting in the development of various hybrid technologies which is a radical change in the power-train aspect of the vehicle.

Governments are keen to improve traffic management and to see the number of road traffic injuries reduced without the need for too much intervention by the government. They are thus encouraging the development of Advanced Driver Assistance Systems (ADAS) which include:

- adaptive cruise control
- blind spot detection
- lane departure warning
- speed limit monitoring systems
- parking assistance
- night vision systems.

Many of these features are currently available, whilst others are still under development.

Although new features usually first appear on vehicles in the luxury category, those that find favour in the marketplace quickly migrate to other sectors.

This rapid increase in features offered has been possible due the continuing increase in processing power and memory at commercially viable prices, together with the development of communication buses and the availability of new sensing and activation technology. A modern luxury car may have up to 100 individual control units, most of which are nodes on one of the many vehicle networks.

Assuming that we continue to have the energy resources, and that it is still socially acceptable to have mass personal transport in the coming years, this trend in vehicles would seem set to continue with perhaps the next major innovations being in greater connectivity between different vehicles and between the vehicle and external world generally. Currently the connections external to the vehicle are for information and entertainment, for example radio, telephone, satellite navigation and Internet connectivity. Communication between vehicles opens up opportunities for improved traffic management, either through providing more precise information to the driver or, more radically, by having a control system that encompasses many vehicles. The idea of so called 'road trains' has been around for many years and there is currently an EU project, SARTRE, continuing to work on the technology (SARTRE 2011). Another current application, used in Japan, is to use the satellite navigation system to determine when the vehicle is on an official race track and only then allow the full potential of the vehicle to be available to the driver.

As the mobile phone, or other smart device, increasingly becomes an extension of the person, the logical step would be to use the phone as an interface between the driver and the vehicle on those occasions when the driver is not physically present in the vehicle. This possibility opens up a whole Pandora's Box of opportunities which are even now being considered.

2 The challenges for vehicle manufacturers and suppliers

The challenges for vehicle manufacturers and suppliers are both technological and managerial and these are often interlinked.

The huge growth in the use of technology to deliver new features comes at a time when manufacturers and suppliers are seeking to curb costs by exploiting the growing technological ability of countries which hitherto have not had such a technologically capable workforce. From relatively simple tasks the work is now starting to include major innovative engineering. So the traditional multi-tier supply chain, which was largely confined to the Western World and Japan, is increasingly global, adding to the burden of project management.

With their history in mechanical engineering, automotive companies, particular vehicle manufacturers, have traditionally been organised on the assumption that the vehicle is little more than the sum of its parts, and so component areas, e.g. power-train, chassis, body, electrical, have tended to work in isolation. Many of the new features cross these traditional boundaries, and there is often not a part of the company that has the role of system owner with responsibility for everything to do with the features in terms of cost functionality and safety. Rather, each component area will see its responsibilities clearly demarked by some physical boundary in the vehicle. While conscientious staff can overcome the difficulties that may arise, it would clearly be beneficial to have an organisation more suited to the development of the modern vehicle.

This lack of a systems engineering approach, which is not unique to the automotive industry, is recognised and vehicle manufacturers are seeking to change, but they have to do this while continuing with current product development.

Many of the new features being added to the vehicle affect the driver's relationship with the vehicle, so another challenge for the industry is to ensure that the driver is always aware of both what is required of them, and what the vehicle is doing. The Human-Machine Interface (HMI) of the vehicle used to be relatively simple but is now becoming much more complex. The infotainment system with its touch screen and myriad menu levels suffers the same problem as equivalent domestic appliances, but other more traditional features now have functionality which may not be intuitive on first use, for example the park brake (previous known as the hand brake) may apply and release without driver action, and the engine itself may stop and restart when the vehicle is stationary to conserve energy. Understanding what the correct action is during system failures is particularly important. It has been reported to the Department for Transport that in accidents where vehicles have suffered 'brake failure', drivers may not be making full use of the secondary braking system, believing that their vehicle's brakes have completely failed.

With the display technology now used in vehicles, it is possible to tell the driver much more about the vehicle and the state of its systems than ever before. This raises the issue of driver workload and the need to ensure that important information is not missed due to the plethora of other information being presented. This problem is well known and the obvious solution is more technology in the form of a 'workload manager'.

With the automation of some aspects of the driving task, the responsibility of the driver is being reduced but this raises the concern that the driver may become de-skilled. A common approach for coping with failures of these systems is to switch them off and inform the driver that this has happened. The rationale is that by doing this the vehicle has reverted to a standard model which has been sold for many years and the driver too will revert to performing the tasks necessary for such a vehicle. But this rationale may be undermined if indeed the driver has been de-skilled. Something like this seems to be happening with satellite navigation, which has rapidly found favour in the marketplace and has led to drivers becoming dependent upon it and having difficulty finding their way when it is not available.

Clearly many of the issues raised so far will be of interest to those concerned with system safety and functional safety. Some of the changes necessary will be driven by the new automotive standard on functional safety which will be considered next.

3 ISO 26262: an opportunity and a challenge

A new standard for applying the discipline of functional safety in the automotive domain is due, at the time of writing, to be published in October 2011. The work on this standard started at the international level in November 2005 and the first draft for public comment was issued in August 2009. The content is thus broadly known, and already many papers are starting to be published and commercial opportunities are being exploited by tool vendors and consultants.

The assumption behind the standard when it was first drafted was that current production vehicles had been engineered to an adequate level to deal with safety concerns. The purpose of the standard was to bring the whole industry up to the current state of best practice. In reality the standard has brought in several new concepts, which while common in other industries, are new to the automotive industry. However, the standard does not attempt to address some of the challenges now facing the industry as mentioned above, for example system interactions and systems with a larger scope than just a single vehicle.

ISO 26262 (ISO 2011) is an automotive sector-specific version of the generic safety standard IEC 61508 (IEC 2010). It has nine normative parts and one informative guideline part. It has adapted the IEC 61508 safety lifecycle to fit in with typical automotive product lifecycles. In outline the life cycle is:

- Define the system being analysed.
- Determine the hazards associated with the system.
- Classify hazard risk in terms of an Automotive Safety Integrity Level (ASIL).
- Derive the safety requirements necessary to adequately mitigate the hazard risk.
- Verify that the safety requirements have been correctly implemented.
- Validate that the required risk mitigation has been achieved.

There are also requirements concerning the interface between product development and vehicle manufacturing and service.

The safety requirements necessary to adequately mitigate the hazard risk consist of both failure management requirements and failure prevention requirements.

The failure management requirements are in terms of fault detection and reaction, e.g. reducing functionality, transitioning to 'safe' system states, warning the driver. The standard requires this for all values of ASIL, but cannot prescribe what these should be as they are particular to each individual system. Each such requirement inherits the ASIL value from the hazard it is intended to mitigate. In this way a value of ASIL should be thought of as an attribute of a failure management requirement.

The failure prevention requirements are given in the standard and graded according to the value of the ASIL value in terms of:

- process measures for system, hardware and software development
- a target metric for the hardware design in terms of single and multipoint failures and diagnostic coverage.

Although it is not a legal requirement to comply with ISO 26262, it is anticipated than vehicle manufacturers and suppliers will adopt its use, as it will be seen as a definition of best practice and the normal policy of automotive companies is to follow best practice where it is defined. In adopting the standard, automotive companies face a number of challenges to do with both their organisation and the engineering process.

As with addressing the greater interconnectivity in the vehicle, functional safety requires a systems engineering approach and the move to this from the more traditional automotive approach is an ongoing challenge. Skills and training in both systems engineering and functional safety are needed to equip workforces to meet this challenge.

The standard also requires greater formality in project management and document review than is often found in the industry, which typically sees agility and short lead times to market as being desirable characteristics.

The standard also introduces a number of new concepts which the industry will have to formally adopt.

In performance of risk analysis it is acknowledged that risk reduction can be achieved by use of other technologies and external measures leading to the lowering of the ASIL value assigned to the electronic control system; however, no guidance is given as to what is required of the other technologies or external measures in order for the ASIL value to be so reduced.

The standard introduces a set of heuristics for allocating failure prevention requirements to system components in a way that introduces redundancy in implementation, and in doing so allows the value of ASIL to be reduced. This is referred to as 'Requirements decomposition with respect to ASIL tailoring'. This 'ASIL tailoring' affects only the failure prevention process requirements and should not be confused with the more traditional use of redundancy to increase hardware reliability.

When developing a component which implements failure prevention requirements, the process used has to be compliant with the processes requirements prescribed for the highest ASIL value of those requirements. These process requirements are often given as a goal to be achieved, with a level of confidence commensurate with the value of the ASIL. A table is given, in the style of IEC 61508, listing different techniques with various strengths of recommendation. The developer has to choose which of these techniques to use and then justify their selection, or the use of other techniques not included in the table. This need to justify the process used is new to the industry.

The standard also introduces new requirements into the industry regarding the use of software tools, software components, hardware components, proven-in-use arguments and a safety case. The requirements for the latter are not as strong as some would like, but do represent a move towards a practice that is common in other industry sectors. The MISRA organisation is in the process of producing some guidelines on automotive safety cases to encourage the industry to go beyond just meeting the minimum requirement in the standard.

In moving towards compliance with the standard, vehicle manufacturers and suppliers face a number of managerial challenges. Major changes in the way product is developed have to be introduced, taking account of the product lifecycle. Both manufacturers and the different tiers of suppliers have their plans for introducing change in their product and these need to be synchronised in order for the whole vehicle to benefit. At present there are instances where the manufacture is ahead of the supplier and other instances where the supplier is asking for information that the manufacturer has never been asked to supply before.

Another major issue is deciding how to handle the re-application of systems that have been used on previous vehicles to new vehicles. Where the system is unchanged there is no requirement in the standard to re-engineer it for compliance with the standard. However, it is rarely the case that a system is reused without a change of some kind. For minor changes it would seem reasonable to use the design process that was used to create it in the first place, while for major changes it would seem more fitting to fully comply with the standard; the difficulty will be in deciding what is a minor change and what is a major change.

4 Concluding remarks

Given the challenges posed by the rapid deployment of software-based technology and features in vehicles, the publication of the ISO 26262 standard can help provide the impetus to make some of the organisational changes necessary to move towards a proper systems engineering process.

With the introduction of some of the new features and technologies, particularly hybrid vehicles but others as well, we are already seeing the basic functional safety disciplines being used rigorously as part of the system design process and influencing the design at the correct part of the lifecycle, rather than after key decisions have already been made.

Already the standard is having a positive impact, in that the issues are becoming much more widely known and discussed at different management levels within companies, and while at present there is also much confusion and misunderstanding about some of the concepts new to the industry, in time the general level of understanding will only get better.

Assuming that we continue to have the resources, and that it is still socially acceptable to have mass personal transport in the coming years, i.e. we solve the energy and CO_2 challenges, vehicle manufacturers will continue to offer increased customer delight features while responding to the encouragement of governmental bodies to use technology to reduce injury and provide better traffic management. Without legislation, the marketplace will decide which features find acceptance and which become standard aspects of the future vehicle. The engineers will continue to give their best endeavours and cope with the churn that comes with change with a mixture of exasperation and amusement. They will certainly not be bored.

References

Charette RN (2009) This car runs on code. IEEE Spectrum, http://spectrum.ieee.org/green-tech/advanced-cars/this-car-runs-on-code. Accessed 27 September 2011

IEC (2010) Functional safety of electrical/electronic/programmable electronic safety-related systems. IEC 61508 edn 2.0. International Electrotechnical Commission

ISO (2011) Road vehicles – functional safety. ISO 26262. International Organisation for Standardisation

SARTRE (2011) The SARTRE project. http://www.sartre-project.eu/en/Sidor/default.aspx. Accessed 27 September 2011

Safety Process Implementation for Unmanned Aerial Systems

Sirma Celik

TAI-Turkish Aerospace Industries, Inc.

Kazan, Ankara, Turkey

Abstract As Unmanned Aerial Systems' (UAS) operations have increased for both military and civil purposes, UAS have started performing operations over populated areas as well as sharing the airspace with manned aircrafts. For the safety of manned aircraft crew and of people on the ground, the safety assessments of UAS are a vital issue. Safety analyses of UAS become increasingly challenging with newly introduced systems due to their high complexity and intelligent nature. Current system safety processes, however, are mainly based on conventional aircraft and therefore are not fully applicable to UAS. Different approaches and methods can be applied during the safety analysis of UAS design process, according to the operational areas of the UAS. This paper highlights system safety analysis process implemented during the design phase of a Medium Altitude Long Endurance (MALE) UAS. Modifications to the existing methodologies are introduced hereby.

1 Introduction

Their long endurance and cost-saving capacities render UAS advantageous over conventional aircraft (Henderson 2009). Moreover, there is a reasonable demand for using UAS to deal with precarious and risky missions, such as contaminated area monitoring (e.g. nuclear explosion) and natural disaster observations, which are dangerous for pilots. Replacing UAS with manned aircraft in such missions decreases not only the cost of the operation, but also the perils to human life (Henderson 2009). Consequently, there is an increase in UAS usage, including for civil purposes. As the airspace is being shared with manned aircraft while having operations over populated areas, two major dangers that pose high risks to human life arise for discussion: a mid-air collision and an uncontrolled flight termination of the Unmanned Aerial Vehicle (UAV). The former case can be catastrophic for airspace users including crew members and even passengers. In the latter case, an uncontrolled flight leading to a ground impact is dangerous for people on the

43

ground. These risks point out the necessity of UASs establishing at least an equivalent level of safety as manned aircraft of equivalent class or category (Clothier and Walker 2006).

While these issues raised awareness of safety assessments of UAS, certification standard studies for UAS are lagging behind the technological improvements. There are a number of ongoing studies, published regulations and policies world-wide (CAA 2004, CASA 2003, DGA 2005, DoD 2005, NATO 2007, JAA 2004) in order to allow UAS operations in civilian airspace. All these regulatory studies, however, comprise derivations of manned aircraft safety procedures. It might seem adequate to apply the same rules and safety methodology of manned aircraft at first glance, however in practice many of the requirements are not applicable to UAS, and several are missing since there is a huge difference between UAS and manned aircraft.

One of the main reasons for this variance is the complexity of UAS. Generally highly complex systems are present in UAS, such as flight control computer, sensor array, and payload management system (probably another computer) connected via/to assorted busses, embedded in a complicated circuit architecture. Software is another important factor for the variance being responsible for major critical functions such as the coordination of UAS systems with the internal health management, providing blended data from the equipments on the aerial platform to the autopilot and ground station, controlling the UAV autonomously, and interaction of UAV with Ground Control Station (GCS), which can be more than one according to the operation, with piloted aircraft, and with other UAVs (which is important especially in operations of UAV swarms). Using intelligent and complex systems brings the need for sophisticated safety analyses. Additionally, with the integration of new systems like GCS, flight termination systems, and communication data links, these systems and their safety analyses become more exhaustive. Furthermore, the remote controlled nature of the aerial vehicles does not allow detection of failures via pilot sensing, such as noise, smell, vibrations, etc. Therefore, failure cases may not be detected beforehand, which may lead to more critical repercussions.

We conclude that current regulations for UAS are not comprehensive enough and do not satisfy the safety study needs *unless certain adjustments are applied.* Not only the depth of the regulations, but also their span, is inadequate because these regulations are generalized such that they enclose all types of UAS, which is not acceptable according to manned aircraft airworthiness rules. Dedicated regulations for each type of UAS are therefore desired.

Considering the missing parts in current regulations and guidelines, it is clear that the conventional safety assessment methodologies are not appropriate for UAS. An advanced methodology is needed for UAS safety assessments. Indigenous and innovative approaches need to be carried out during the safety analysis of the UAS design process, according to the operational areas of the UAS.

In this study, a methodology with several modifications to the conventional one for a MALE UAS is introduced.

2 System safety process

2.1 Subject UAS

The subject of this study is a MALE UAS, which was designed and manufactured by TAI (Turkish Aerospace Industries, Inc.). Full composite airframe is composed of monocock fuselage, detachable wing and V-Tail, retractable landing gear, equipment bays, service doors and other structural components. The air vehicle is powered by a pusher type piston-prop propulsion system. The airframe is equipped with miscellaneous sub systems like fuel system; de/anti-ice devices; environmental conditioning system for cooling/heating requirements of the compartments.

The avionics system includes a Flight Management System (FMS); integrated to FMS, flight sensors (pitot-static sensor, embedded GPS/INS, magnetic heading, displacement, temperature, pressure transducers), actuators; dedicated communication and identification devices; mission control, record; and other control and interface units.

2.2 Determination of the methodology

For the UAS safety process, first of all, an applicable standard was chosen. Then top level requirements and objectives were defined. Those requirements and objectives are explained in Sections 2.2.2 and 2.2.1, respectively. Then necessary tasks to achieve the safety objectives and meet the requirements were determined and listed together with milestones for those tasks, responsibilities, guidelines, templates, tools etc. in the system safety program plan.

The general safety process was stated in this plan as:

1. determine the requirements and objectives
2. find out the critical points
3. find their possible sources
4. demonstrate the compliance with requirements
5. derive lower level requirements
6. demonstrate the compliance with objectives.

Starting from the top most level, UAS level safety tasks were performed first. Top level requirements and objectives were used. In order to find the critical points, UAS level Functional Hazard Assessment (FHA) document (of which details are given in Section 2.3.1) was prepared. This document was used to assign objectives to the systems. The same assessment was also performed for each system of the UAS to prepare system FHAs (of which details are given in Section 2.3.2). System FHAs were used to define critical failure conditions to be analyzed in Preliminary

System Safety Assessments (PSSA)/System Safety Assessments (SSA) and to assign requirements and/or objectives for sub-contractors.

Once the critical failure conditions were determined, for each system, PSSA was performed (details are given in Section 2.4.1) in order to find out possible causes of those failures. This document demonstrated whether a system was compliant with safety requirements or not. For non-compliant parts, design change was proposed and the analyses were repeated according to new design. According to PSSA documents, hardware and software Development Assurance Levels (DAL) were determined and used as a derived requirement.

In order to show compliance with objectives, SSA (of which details are given in Section 2.4.2) was performed. This assessment included quantitative analyses of critical failure conditions defined in FHA. In SSA, it was checked whether the failure condition probabilities achieved the targets or not. If not, design change was proposed and the analyses were repeated.

Following the analyses, validation and verification process was performed. According to final results, aircraft safety synthesis was performed to show that all objectives were achieved and all requirements were met. It was ensured that necessary design changes or risk mitigation solutions were applied where needed.

2.2.1 Standard Selection and Modifications

For UAS safety analysis, NATO Standardization Agreement (STANAG) 4671 was used. STANAG 4671 is a set of technical airworthiness requirements intended primarily for the airworthiness certification of fixed-wing military UAV systems with a maximum take-off weight between 150 kg and 20,000 kg that intend to operate regularly in non-segregated airspace (NATO 2007). STANAG 4671 is a derivation of European Aviation Safety Agency (EASA) Certification Specifications (CS) 23.1309 (EASA 2003) standard with some particular additional requirements or subparts for UAV systems. In addition to CS-23, 'Command and control data link communication system' and 'UAV control station' subparts are unique to STANAG 4671.

The probability reference system of Acceptable Means of Compliance (AMC)-1309 of STANAG 4671 is similar to that of Class-I of Advisory Circular (AC) 23-1309 of CS-23. For any catastrophic failure condition, acceptable probability is $<10^{-6}$ which is the probability value for 'extremely improbable'. The relationship between probability and severity of failure condition effects defined in AMC.1309 can be seen in Table 1.

For software, DAL allocation in STANAG 4671 for system and portion of the system architecture is given in Table 2.

As seen from the table, STANAG 4671 associates Minor failure conditions with DAL-E which is same as No Safety Effect failure conditions. For the subject UAS, it was decided to allocate DAL-D for Minor failure conditions since they still had an effect on aerial vehicle or on people. DAL-E was only allocated to No Safety Effect failure conditions.

Table 1. Probability vs severity matrix (NATO 2007)

Risk matrix		Severity				
Probability of occurrence (per flight hour)		Catastrophic	Hazardous	Major	Minor	No safety effect
Frequent	$>10^{-3}$					
Probable	$<10^{-3}$					
Remote	$<10^{-4}$	*Unacceptable*				
Extremely remote	$<10^{-5}$		*Acceptable*			
Extremely improbable	$<10^{-6}$					

Table 2. DAL allocation of STANAG 4671 (NATO 2007)

Severity	DAL allocation of STANAG 4671 (for single failures/errors)
Catastrophic	DAL B
Hazardous	DAL C
Major	DAL D
Minor	DAL E
No Safety Effect	DAL E

Aside from these hardware and software targets, 10 Catastrophic failure conditions (i.e. 10^{-5}) were used for UAS system level target, as defined in AMC.1309 of STANAG 4671.

2.2.2 Requirements

Three main requirements were considered for all systems:

- A single failure shall not lead to any Catastrophic or Hazardous effect on the UAS.
- Hidden failures associated with Hazardous or Catastrophic repercussions should be avoided in system design where possible.
- Double failures with one hidden that can lead to Catastrophic failure conditions should be avoided as far as practical.

Especially for the first requirement, it is impossible for engine to comply with it. Probably for this reason, STANAG 4671 also says that USAR.1309 does not apply specifically to UAV engine (NATO 2007). Although there is no chance to duplicate the engine, there is a possibility to see hidden engine failures contributing to Catastrophic or Hazardous failure conditions. For this reason, propulsion system (including engine failures) was assessed as all other systems. Control and monitoring failures of the engine were also assessed and some improvements were made for a 'safer' engine.

2.3 Determining critical points

2.3.1 UAS level FHA

Once UAS level functions were obtained from the systems engineering group, these functions were evaluated. During the analysis, SAE ARP 4761 (SAE 1996) was used as a reference. Risk assessment methodology was in parallel with the Federal Aviation Administration System Safety Handbook (FAA 2000).

For each function, four conditions were considered: total loss of the function, partial loss of the function, inadvertent functioning and malfunctioning. For each failure condition, the effects on the aerial vehicle, on UAS crew, on maintainers, on third parties and on property on the ground were listed for all ground and flight phases. According to the most severe effect, these failure conditions were classified in accordance with AMC.1309 of STANAG 4671 (NATO 2007):

1. **Catastrophic.** Failure conditions that result in a worst credible outcome of at least uncontrolled flight (including flight outside of pre-planned or contingency flight profiles/areas) and/or uncontrolled crash, which can potentially result in a fatality, or failure conditions which could potentially result in a fatality to UAV crew or ground staff.
2. **Hazardous.** Failure conditions that, either by themselves or in conjunction with increased crew workload, result in a worst credible outcome of a controlled-trajectory termination or forced landing potentially leading to the loss of the UAV where it can be reasonably expected that a fatality will not occur, or failure conditions which could potentially result in serious injury to UAV crew or ground staff.
3. **Major.** Failure conditions that, either by themselves or in conjunction with increased crew workload, result in a worst credible outcome of an emergency landing of the UAV on a predefined site where it can be reasonably expected that a serious injury will not occur, or failure conditions which could potentially result in injury to UAV crew or ground staff.
4. **Minor.** Failure conditions that do not significantly reduce UAV system safety and involve UAV crew actions that are well within their capabilities. These conditions may include a slight reduction in safety margins or functional capabilities, and a slight increase in UAV crew workload.
5. **No safety effect.** Failure conditions that have no effect on safety.

Engineering judgment, service experience, and operational experience took an important role during writing down the effects of failure conditions. Possible multiple failures were also included in FHA.

UAS level FHA document was completed very early in the design process. It was used to derive new requirements for systems. It defined system safety objectives and DAL levels of systems. UAS level FHA document was updated when all the system level safety documents had been finalized.

2.3.2 System level FHA

After the UAS level FHA, system level FHAs were performed in the same way. While assessing the system functions, any monitoring, ground-controlling, test, or indication/warning functions dedicated to the main function were associated with the related main function. At the end of the system FHA, detailed system level safety requirements and sub-system DALs were derived. During FHA studies, subcontractors provided assistance for their systems.

2.3.3 Assumptions

Some general assumptions were considered for UAS level safety activities as well as system level safety activities. Some examples of these assumptions are:

- The air vehicle will land on a prepared runway.
- Surrounding area of the runway is cleared of people.
- Manuel override for system controls is available.
- Main procedures for autopilot are available (e.g. link loss procedure, engine failure procedure, electrical loss procedure).
- All the analyses are done considering peace-time environment.

Assumptions about system design were also used in FHA and further assessments. Those assumptions were subject to validation process.

2.4 Assessing the critical points

2.4.1 Preliminary System Safety Assessment (PSSA)

Hazardous and Catastrophic failure conditions stated in system FHAs were analyzed *qualitatively* during PSSA phase. For these assessments, Fault Tree Analysis (FTA) was performed for each critical failure condition in order to demonstrate the sources of those conditions. FTA included equipment failures, other events (such as external events and environmental conditions), and possible combinations that could cause the failure condition. During FTA developing, Failure Modes and Effects Analysis (FMEA) and Failure Modes and Effects Summary (FMES) documents were used as source. Failure modes taken from FMEA and FMES documents were placed in FTAs.

By looking at the FTAs, it was reported whether requirements (from Section 2.2.2 and from UAS level FHA document) were met or not. If the requirements were not met, design change was proposed. When the design team made necessary modifications, PSSA was repeated according to the new design, since any change could affect the fault trees. It was checked again for requirement compliance, and this process was repeated until all requirements were met.

After assuring that the system was compliant with all requirements, DALs were allocated for hardware and software components. From DAL allocation, new requirements were derived and transmitted to software and hardware designers and to sub-contractors. Selection of equipments and/or sub-systems depended on the allocated DAL.

2.4.2 System Safety Assessment (SSA)

SSA included *quantitative* analysis of critical failure conditions. Failure rates from FMEA documents and risk times were placed into FTAs to calculate the probability of failure conditions. Results of calculations revealed whether objectives (from Section 2.2.1) were achieved or not. If the objectives were not achieved, design change or alternative solutions were proposed. The new design was re-assessed to check the objective compliance. If the FTA was affected due to design change, then PSSA was also repeated.

2.4.3 Common Cause Analysis (CCA)

In order to show compliance with safety requirements, FTAs should include independent failure modes and external events. The existence of this independence was analyzed in CCA. Therefore, CCA was used as a means of verification for FTAs. These analyses were used to find and eliminate or mitigate common causes for multiple failures.

CCA was performed in three steps:

- Common Mode Analysis (CMA)
- Zonal Safety Analysis (ZSA)
- Particular Risks Analysis (PRA).

CMA was performed to ensure that *multiple failures in FTAs* were independent. In order to do that, all combinations of events under AND gates were analyzed. Those events were subject to examination for their hardware failure effects on software failures, and vice versa. Apart from hardware and software failures, installation failures, repair failures, environmental influences, etc. were also taken into account. Finally, it was ensured that all events connected to an AND gate were independent of each other.

ZSA was performed to show compliance with safety requirements concerning *equipment installation*. It was used to examine the layout of systems on the aerial vehicle to determine whether a fault at a particular location could affect independence. This analysis was performed for each zone of the aerial vehicle. A checklist for safety requirements was generated and used both on digital mock-up and on real aerial vehicle during production. At the end of this analysis, it was ensured that all necessary precautions were taken such that remaining risks were acceptable.

Similar to ZSA, PRA was performed to find independency violating factors *caused by external events* that were not considered in FTAs. Some external events may affect several zones at the same time. For this reason, PRA was based on selected events; not on systems or zones. PRA demonstrated whether systems on the aerial vehicle were vulnerable to an isolated event such as fire, explosion, tyre burst, high energy devices and lightning strike. For each analysis, first of all, a requirement set was generated for the selected event. Then, affected systems and items were examined due to that event. Risks were reported and precautions were associated for each risk. For unacceptable risks, design change was initiated.

2.4.4 Sub-contractor safety program management

Upon receiving the requirements and objectives (and sometimes related failure scenarios from FHAs in case of need) for the subject system/equipment, the sub-contractor was expected to perform the following tasks:

1. For sub-contractors that were designing system or component:

   – system safety program plan
   – PSSA and SSA (with the demonstration of validation and verification means)
   – list of equipment hazards (caused by intrinsic dangers or environmental conditions) that did not take place in PSSA/SSA.

2. For Commercial Off-The-Shelf (COTS) equipment suppliers:

   – list of equipment hazards (caused by intrinsic dangers or environmental conditions)
   – DAL compliance demonstration.

2.4.5 Validation and verification process

In FHA and SSA documents, demands for validation and verification were addressed. Once the scenarios were written, they had to be validated. Generally, during FHA phase, scenarios were formed according to many assumptions. For example, a safety engineer may think that if there are two identical sensors for the same function, then loss of each sensor might be Major. For such an assessment, there are hidden assumptions such as:

1. both sensors are active during all flight
2. loss of one sensor does not affect the functioning of second sensor
3. there is no common cause for loss of both.

These kinds of assumptions might be written or considered as too obvious that there is no need to write down. For this reason, all scenarios (and assumptions) were validated in UAS safety process. For No Safety Effect, Minor and Major failure conditions of SSAs, validation were performed by ground and flight test. For critical failure conditions, however, it was decided not to have a flight test because there was a risk of serious injury for people and a risk of damage to aerial vehicle. Such critical failure conditions were validated by simulator and lab tests. With this methodology, it was possible to validate whether a certain scenario was Major or not, for example. Any ignored common failure was also observed.

For verification of scenarios, FTA, CCA, studies, analyses of flight sciences and procedures were used.

2.4.6 UAS level safety synthesis

Finally, aircraft safety synthesis was performed to show that UAS level failures achieved the UAS level target.

3 Conclusion

UAS have been expected to demonstrate the equivalent level of safety with manned aircraft due to increase in their operations in civil airspace. Several restrictions are being implemented to ensure the safety of people on the other aircraft in the shared airspace and people on the ground. These restrictions, however, limit the potential advantages of UAS. Therefore, demonstration of UAS safety is crucial to reduce the number of the restrictions.

An alternative way to get rid of the restrictions might be using of Optionally Piloted Vehicles (OPV): pre-certified aircraft that are converted to UAVs in order to access civil airspace easily (Lake and Withington 2010). This idea, however, could be applied only for those previously manufactured manned aircrafts. A new generation of UAV still needs to satisfy the requirements of public safety.

In order to access a shared airspace, the UAS have been forced to follow the regulations that were set for the needs of manned aircrafts. Moreover, the studies that were done on safety of UAS are not only limited in number but also lack the records of the vehicle. The lack of regulations and studies forces UAS manufacturers to define their own methodology. This paper was prepared aiming to be a guide for future UAS safety studies. The main different approaches in this study can be listed as:

- DAL allocation approach

- engine safety analysis
- assessing monitoring and control functions in system FHAs
- validation and verification process.

Overall, the findings of this paper are expected to reveal insights to future UAS safety analyses and, therefore, to decrease the limitations and restrictions applied for UAS in civil airspace.

References

CAA (2004) CAP 722 – Guidance for Unmanned Aerial Vehicle (UAV) operations in UK airspace. UK Civil Aviation Authority
CASA (2003) Unmanned aircraft and rocket operations. CASR Part 101. Civil Aviation Safety Authority, Australia
Clothier R, Walker R (2006) Determination and evaluation of UAV safety objectives. Proc 21st Int Unmanned Air Veh Conf, Bristol, UK
DGA (2005) UAV Systems Airworthiness Requirements (USAR). Délégué Général pour l'Armement, Ministre de la défense, France
DoD (2005) Unmanned aircraft systems roadmap 2005-2030. Department of Defense, Office of the Secretary of Defense, USA
EASA (2003) CS-23 Certification Specifications for normal, utility, aerobatic, and commuter category aeroplanes. European Aviation Safety Agency
FAA (2000) System Safety Handbook. Federal Aviation Administration, USA
Henderson A (2009) A promising year ahead? Unmanned Veh J 14(6)
JAA (2004) A concept for european regulations for civil Unmanned Aerial Vehicles (UAVs). UAV Task-Force Final Report. The Joint JAA/EUROCONTROL Initiative on UAVs
Lake D, Withington T (2010) Dropping the pilot. Unmanned Veh J 15(6)
NATO (2007) STANAG 4671 UAV Systems Airworthiness Requirements (USAR). Draft Edn 1
SAE (1996) SAE-ARP 4761 Guidelines and methods for conducting the safety assessment process on civil airborne systems and equipment. S-18 Committee

Risk Analysis and Development of an IP-Network-based Railway Signal Control System

Reiji Ishima[1] and Minoru Mori[2]

[1]East Japan Railway Company, Omiya, Japan

[2]Toshiba Corporation, Tokyo, Japan

Abstract   This paper describes risk analysis and development of an IP-network-based railway signal control system that East Japan Railway Company has developed for important railway operation lines in the Tokyo metropolitan area. The system controls railway signals to maintain safety for running trains and is one of the safety-critical systems. High availability is also a requisite because of railway customer needs and consideration of the social effects of a stoppage of operation. Several methods for safety and high availability which replace old methods (those with relays) and respond to networking technologies are proposed and applied to equipment and transmission between equipment. The development was based on those methods and risk analysis. Maintaining safety, the system has redundant structure for availability and transmission between equipment has quadruple redundancy. FTA and FMECA were used for risk analysis for the equipment. It was verified that the system can prevent the top event with sufficient measures having been taken. The transmission between equipment fulfils IEC62280-1, and its fulfilment was examined through risk analysis.

1 Introduction

The Railway Signal Control System (RSCS) has an extremely important role to play in the safety of train operation. If a train collision happens, the lives of hundreds of train passengers will be jeopardized. The RSCS should maintain normal train operation and keep all running trains safe. RSCS is, of course, one of the safety-critical systems.

RSCS is based on the fail-safe concept. According to the definition in IEC62425, fail-safe is a concept which is incorporated into the design of a product such that, in the event of a failure, it enters or remains in a safe state. If a failure occurs, the system immediately detects it and activates a safe-side control. Relays have been used to create RSCS since the early days. Relays using gravity and/or springs are designed appropriately for fail-safe.

Recently, rapid computerization and spread of Information and Communication Technology (ICT) has had a big impact on RSCS. The logic circuits of relays are replaced with processes of a computer. ON/OFF control by voltage through a metal wire is also replaced with data transmission. The method of fail-safe for relay circuits, however, cannot be applied to computer processing and data transmission. In those areas, therefore, new methods are necessary which can equal or improve upon the level of safety of the old methods with relays.

High availability, as well as safety, is required for RSCS especially for important lines with high-density train operation. If, in a rush hour, a RSCS detects a failure and turns into safe state which makes all running trains stop, many people may rush on to station platforms, panics may occur everywhere, and certainly many train customers will complain about the operation suspension. Social influence is pretty big and even the people's safety may be threatened. Considering this social influence and train customer satisfaction, we must cope with both safety-critical and high availability for RSCS for high-density train operation. IEC62278, the international standard of RAMS for railway, treats Reliability, Availability, and Maintainability as well as Safety. Availability is also handled in the railway industry under the international standard.

East Japan Railway Company (JR East) has developed a new RSCS using IP network technology. It controls railway signalling devices such as signals by data transmission through optical fibres instead of metal wiring which is very complicated and may cause human error. JR East has developed two types of the new RSCS, one of which controls signals and point machines in a station yard, and another of which controls Automatic Block Signals (ABS) and train detection circuits between station yards. The first system for a station yard has already been in operation since February 2007 (JR East 2006). The first system for ABS is to be in operation in 2013 under a project which replaces RSCSs on the Keiyo line between Tokyo and Soga. Both types of the new RSCS are safety-critical systems with high availability.

Various methods for both safety and availability are used, and careful risk analysis was done in the phase of development. In this paper we focus on the new IP-network-based RSCS for ABS, introduce methods coping with both safety and availability, and discuss risk analysis.

2 Overview of the system

2.1 Fundamental function

A fundamental function of the IP-Network-based RSCS for ABS is to detect train location and to control ABSs so that the system can maintain safety of all the trains running in a covered section. The aspect of a signal is to be red if a train is detected in the inner section of the signal in order that a following train will not proceed beyond the signal. The fundamental railway rule that only a single train can run in a section prevents train collision. The aspect of a signal preceding the red-aspect signal is to be yellow so that a train can decrease its running speed and stop at the next red-aspect signal. In Figure 1, a train is running in section 4 and another train is running in section 1, so the aspects of signal 4 and signal 1 are red and the aspect of signal 2 is yellow.

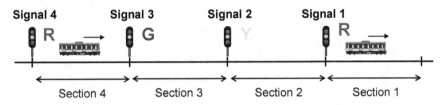

Fig. 1. Fundamental function

The system also has a function of ATS-P (Automatic Train Stop with Pattern, i.e. Automatic Train Protection). The system decides ATS-P data corresponding to the aspect of a signal. Speed limitation corresponding to the aspect of a signal is automatically activated if the speed of a running train is beyond the designated speed.

In order to cover high-density train operation in the Tokyo metropolitan area, the system needs to simultaneously process several trains and exchange information with interlocking equipment at a station yard, all of which makes the detailed functions more complicated.

2.2 System configuration

The basic system configuration of the IP-Network-based RSCS for ABS is shown in Figure 2 (Ishima et al. 2008, Hayakawa et al. 2010). The system consists of Logic Controllers (LC), Field Controllers (FC), IP networks, and other parts such as supervision and maintenance.

2.2.1 Logic Controller (LC)

An LC is a dual system which consists of fail-safe units. It has the role of logic processing. It receives result messages including train detection information from FCs, decides appropriate aspects of signals and ATS-P data using train detection information, and sends control messages including aspects of signals and ATS-P data. The duration of control is 200ms. It sends a control message to FCs and receives a result message from FCs every 200ms. It exchanges control and result information with interlocking equipment in a station yard through the FC for signal control at the system boundary to a station yard. Furthermore, an LC can even exchange necessary information with an adjacent LC. One LC and an adjacent LC can control signals in the designated section together.

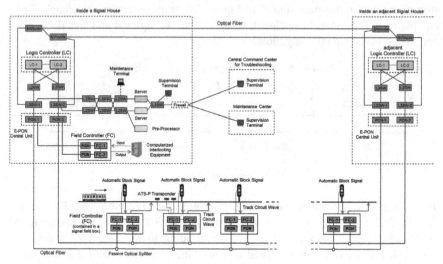

Fig. 2. System configuration

Two suppliers concurrently developed the LC under the same requirement specification provided by JR East. One supplier developed a new hardware for LCs improving the hardware of computerized interlocking equipment. The other supplier created an LC using the same hardware as computerized interlocking equipment. In this paper we mention the former only. Figure 3 shows the appearance of an LC with the newly developed hardware.

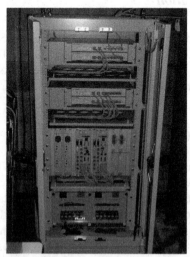

Fig. 3. Appearance of LC

2.2.2 Field Controller (FC)

An FC is a hot-standby duplex system which consists of fail-safe units. It has a role of Input and Output (I/O) with signal field devices connected. The FC receives a control message from an LC and electrically controls signal field devices such as signals and ATS-P transponders together. The FC also transmits train detection signals into rails, judges the existence of trains by the level of return signal received, and sends a result message to an LC. The duration of control is 200ms. It sends a result message to an LC and receives a control message from the LC every 200ms. Many FCs belong to one LC. The FC is placed near an automatic block signal along the railway field. Figure 4 shows the appearance of an FC placed in an actual railway field for a long-term field test.

Field
Controller
(duplex)

Fig. 4. Appearance of FC

2.2.3 IP network

IP networks are used for transmission in the whole system. All the transmission routes in the system have redundant structure in order to keep high availability.

Ethernet Passive Optical Network (E-PON) is used for transmission through optical fibres between LCs and FCs. E-PON is suitable for RSCS, because its optical signal can be split at a passive optical splitter with high environment-resistance.

For transmission between one LC and the adjacent LC through optical fibres, switching nodes are used. Here, I would like to mention only transmission between LCs and FCs after Section 3 regarding the methods for both safety and high availability because the methods and the results of risk analysis can equally be applied to transmission between an LC and an adjacent LC.

3 Methods for safety and high availability

3.1 Redundancy

High availability is mandatory for the IP-network-based RSCS for ABS because it is to be installed in the Tokyo metropolitan area. Therefore, as mentioned in Section 2.2, the system has redundant structures of LCs, FCs, and transmission routes. The failure rate of the system with one LC and twenty dependent FCs is less than 10^{-6} per hour.

An LC doesn't need complicated configuration management because the two sub-systems of the LC simultaneously receive result messages, execute logic processes, and send control messages as a dual system. Configuration management for real-time systems requires a detailed review of system change modes and extra hardware and software, which sometimes causes trouble. Several system troubles caused by a system change failure have happened in computerized interlocking equipment in JR East. From the point of view of availability, the absence of necessity for complicated configuration management is one advantage.

We use User Datagram Protocol (UDP)/IP as a transmission protocol between LCs and FCs. UDP/IP is more suitable for simultaneous transmission and real-time control compared to Transmission Control Protocol (TCP)/IP. In order to optimize traffic and transmission time, an LC sends a control message as a broadcast message to dependent FCs and each dependent FC sends a result message as a unicast message to the LC.

Furthermore, as shown in Figure 5, both LC-1 and LC-2, the two sub-systems of an LC, send a control message to both FC-1 and FC-2, the two sub-systems of each FC, and then both FC-1 and FC-2 send a result message to both LC-1 and LC-2. Therefore there are four transmission paths between LC and FC. Since normal control can be kept with only one path, the whole system has quadruple redundant transmission between LC and FC (Ishima et al. 2008, Saiki et al. 2010). This transmission redundancy by multiple transmission of networking technology surely contributes to high availability of the whole system. However, appropriate methods to maintain safety are necessary for the quadruple redundant transmission and sufficient risk analysis should be done.

3.2 Methods for LC

3.2.1 Fundamental policy

Each sub-system of each LC must maintain safety independently. The fundamental policy for the safety of each sub-system is as follows.

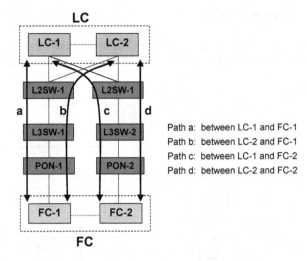

Fig. 5. Quadruple redundant transmission between LC and FC

1. **Comparison by two processors.** Since one processor itself can't maintain safety independently, each sub-system of an LC has the two processors which process in parallel with synchronicity and compare their own result with that of the other in order to find discrepancy and to maintain safety.
2. **Self-checking.** Each processor checks the health of its own units by itself. It also checks the status of the other processor. If the processor detects any failure, then it immediately activates safe-side control.
3. **Stop of output in the case of detecting failure.** If one of the sub-systems of an LC detects failure by comparison or self-checking, then it immediately makes itself halt and stops output of control messages by force. Stop of output of control messages by an LC makes dependent FCs detect the failure of receiving control messages and activate safe-side control for signal field devices. Details are shown in Section 3.3.3.

LC, as a dual system, makes its two sub-systems process in parallel for availability. The required fundamental policy for the dual system of an LC is as follows.

1. **Synchronicity of the two sub-systems.** It is necessary for the two sub-systems to process in parallel with synchronicity and to output control messages simultaneously.
2. **Accordance of four input messages.** If transmission paths are all normal, an LC receives four result messages in total from each FC (see Figure 5). While the four result messages are supposedly the same, LC makes the four result messages accord, considering the case that the four are not the same.
3. **Accordance of four output messages.** In order to make the output of four control messages of an LC accord, the LC makes its internal process information accord, in addition to the accordance of the four input messages.

3.2.2 System configuration of LC

We have newly developed the hardware of LC following the fundamental policy mentioned in Section 3.2.1 (Mori et al. 2008). Figure 6 shows the system configuration of LC.

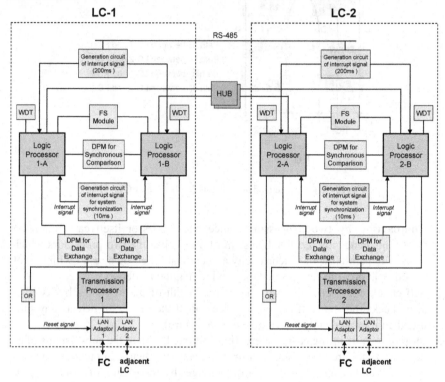

Fig. 6. System configuration of an LC

Two logic processors are parallel equipped in each sub-system of an LC. The two execute parallel process with synchronicity, exchanging data through Dual Port Memory (DPM). The two receive the interrupt signal at every 10ms for synchronization. Each logic processor notifies its state to the other using a fail-safe (FS) module. Each sub-system of an LC also notifies its state to the other sub-system with a FS module.

The transmission processor has the role of exchanging messages with outside equipment through LAN adaptors. DPM is equipped between each logic processor and the transmission processor for data exchange.

The LC also has the 200ms interrupt for the synchronization of the two sub-systems. Data exchange between the two is through a redundant Ethernet link with HUB.

Each sub-system of an LC has control modes of master and slave. If the one is in master mode, then the other is in slave mode. If the slave sub-system cannot receive information from the master through the HUB link and the slave confirms that the master is alive, then the slave turns into halt.

3.2.3 Comparison and accordance processes

The two logic processors compare output control messages, input result messages, and internal data with each other. These comparison processes are executed every 200ms of the control duration. If they detect a failure, then they activate safe-side control.

The two sub-systems of an LC also compare input result messages and internal data with each other and make them accord because the LC receives four result messages in total by quadruple redundant transmission and needs accordance of the four.

The process of accordance of four result messages is as follows. First, for the selection of two result messages from an FC received by each sub-system of an LC, the result message from sub-system 1 of the FC is to be selected. Second, for the selection of the two result messages between the two sub-systems of the LC, the message of the master sub-system of the LC is to be selected. The master has priority for selection of the messages. Finally, the LC is able to make the four result messages accord as the selected message.

3.2.4 Self-checking process

The self-checking processes of an LC are as follows:

- memory read-write check
- program CRC check
- check of Error Checking and Correction (ECC) circuits
- check of synchronization of the two logic processors
- check of comparison command of CPU
- output signal read-back check
- input signal OFF check
- WDT check
- check of the other logic processor's healthy signal
- check of the other subsystem's healthy signal
- run-time check.

3.2.5 Stop-of-output process

If one of the subsystems of an LC detects failure by comparison or self-checking processes, then it immediately turns into halt and stops output of control messages.

For stop of output in the case of detecting failure, each logic processor sends a reset signal to LAN adaptors and makes them stop. It also zeros the transmission buffer area of DPM. Therefore, even if the logic processor cannot stop LAN adaptors and control messages are sent to the IP network, the contents of the messages are all zero and they are disregarded thanks to the FC's check.

3.3 Methods for transmission between LCs and FCs

While both LCs and FCs are fail-safe systems, the IP network for transmission between LCs and FCs is not fail-safe. The IP network consists of COTS products such as E-PON, L3SW and L2SW. In order for the new RSCS to maintain safety, we have developed the system to meet the requirements of IEC62280-1: Safety-related communication in closed transmission systems (Endo et al. 2008, IEC 2002). Quadruple redundant transmission should also be considered in the safety-related transmission.

3.3.1 Protocol for the safety-related transmission

A special protocol for the safety-related transmission between LCs and FCs is as follows.

1. **Sequence number.** In order for both LCs and FCs to supervise the continuousness of received messages, a sequence number is added to the message. The LC adds the sequence number to a control message. The FC adds the same sequence number to a result message. In the same control duration, the LC and the FC exchange messages with the same sequence number.
2. **Time-out.** LCs and FCs supervise time-out in order to exchange messages of the same sequence number in the same control duration. With the non-reception of one control duration, an LC and an FC keep their control state as they were. With the non-reception of two control durations, the LC and the FC activate the safe-side control.
3. **Redundancy code.** Distinct from the Frame Check Sequence (FCS) of the Ethernet frame, LCs and FCs add Cyclic Redundancy Code (CRC) and reversed data to the UDP data area as redundancy codes in order to check the correctness of a message. Since both LCs and FCs are themselves fail-safe equipment and CRC and reversed data are created by fail-safe equipment, we can keep the correctness of a message.
4. **IP addresses of source and destination.** Distinct from the source and destination of the Ethernet frame, LCs and FCs add IP addresses of source and destination to the UDP data area. Since both LCs and FCs are themselves fail-safe equipment and the source and the destination are both created by fail-safe equipment, we can keep the correctness of the IP addresses.

5. **Non-reception flag.** LCs adds the non-reception flag to the UDP data area in order to tell FC the validity of control messages. An LC uses the non-reception flag '1' to stop the FCs' control of signal field devices in the case of the reception failure of result messages. No FC uses control messages with the non-reception flag '1'.

Figure 7 shows an example of the message transmission sequence between an LC and an FC in the case of transmission delay and termination. Message transmission sequence is almost the same as in the case of detecting message error and message sequence failure.

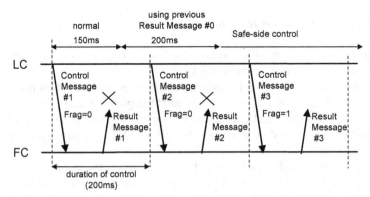

(a) Detection of transmission delay and termination by LC

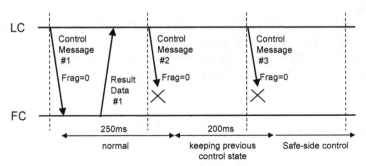

(b) Detection of transmission delay and termination by FC

Fig. 7. An example of the message transmission sequence between LCs and FCs

3.3.2 Processes for redundant transmission

Transmission between LCs and FCs is quadruply redundant with four transmission paths (see Figure 5). The processes required to achieve this redundant transmission are as follows.

1. LCs and FCs supervise received messages by the protocol mentioned in Section 3.3.1 independently for each transmission path.
2. The four control messages an LC sends at the same control duration are to be all the same.
3. Each FC sends a result message only to the source of the control message received at the same control duration.
4. If the sub-system of an FC receives the two normal control messages from the subsystems of an LC, it chooses the first arriving control message.

3.3.3 Safe-Side control for transmission failure

LCs and FCs activate safe-side control if they detect transmission failure for more than two control durations, as mentioned in Section 3.3.1.

The safe-side control of an LC is that the LC turns train detection information into the state 'Fault' and considers 'Fault' as 'Occupied' which means that a train is in the track section. The LC executes the logic processes using train detection information as usual, and consequently the aspect of the signal corresponding to the track section is fixed 'Red'.

The safe-side control of an FC is that the FC turns off the signal, outputs ATS-P data corresponding to the stop aspect of signal, and turns train detection information in its result message into the state 'Fault'. It is an operation rule that a train driver must stop in the case of a signal turned off. If an LC receives the result message with train detection information 'Fault', then the LC interprets 'Fault' as 'Occupied'.

After safe-side control is activated in the case of transmission failure, both LCs and FCs supervise the state of transmission and, if the state turns normal, they immediately, in order to keep high availability, execute a recovery process and recover normal message exchange between LCs and FCs.

3.4 Safety for FCs

Similar to LCs, FCs have a fail-safe duplex system, but FCs have the role of I/O control of signal field devices. We have developed FCs based on the hardware and the software of the I/O control equipment which has a long track record in JR East. We have followed the traditional method. Since FCs are placed along the railway field, the influence of EMC should be examined in order that FCs remain safe despite electro-magnetic fields radiated from passing trains. I would like to omit the details in this paper.

4 Risk analysis

4.1 Risk analysis for LC

To the safety methods for LC mentioned in Section 3.2, we performed risk analysis using Fault Tree Analysis (FTA) and Failure Mode, Effects and Criticality Analysis (FMECA) methods.

4.1.1 FTA for LC

First, we performed an FTA for the IP-network-based RSCS for ABS as shown in Figure 8. 'Train collision' was chosen as the top event. 'Wrong signal aspects' was selected as the top component of elements that the system can cause. 'Control of wrong signal aspects by FC' was chosen as the second layer of component. While 'malfunction of signal field device itself' and 'insulation failure of metallic field cable' can also cause 'wrong signal aspects', they are considered as exception because of long track records over the past years in the actual railway field conditions.

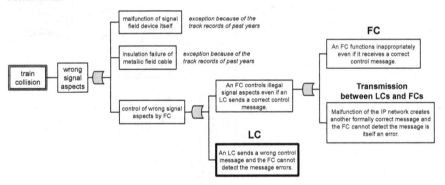

Fig. 8. An extract of FTA for the IP-network-based RSCS for ABS

The components for 'control of wrong signal aspects by FC' are the following three.

1. An LC sends a wrong control message and the FC cannot detect the message errors.
2. Malfunction of the IP network creates another formally correct message and the FC cannot detect the message is itself an error.
3. An FC functions inappropriately even if it receives a correct control message.

Item 1 is considered as the top component of the FTA for LC. Item 2 leads to the FTA for transmission between LCs and FCs. Since the transmission satisfies the requirements of IEC62280-1 as mentioned in Section 3.3, the system can prevent the occurrence of item 2 (details mentioned later in Section 4.2). Item 3 leads to the FTA for the FC itself. I would like to omit the details of the FC in this paper.

Second, we performed an FTA for an LC as shown in Figure 9. In the case of the components of 'wrong output from transmission processor' and 'data transfer failure from logic processor to transmission processor', they cause the destruction of data or the failure of increments in the sequence number and the resulting wrong control message is to be disregarded thanks to the FC's check of error messages (see 'a' in Figure 9). Similarly, in the case of components of 'transmission errors of a result message' and 'message delay or sequence inversion', the resulting wrong message is to be disregarded because of the LC's check of error, time-out, and sequence (see 'b' in Figure 9).

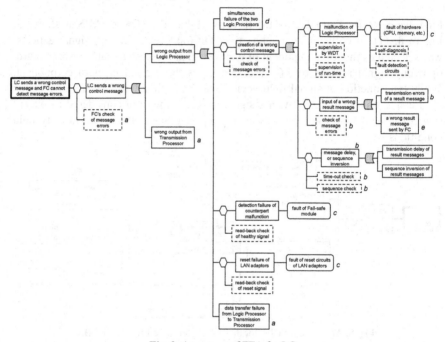

Fig. 9. An extract of FTA for LC

As for the components of 'fault of hardware such as CPU and memory, etc.', 'fault of fail-safe module', and 'fault of reset circuits of LAN adaptors', they are analyzed in detail later in Section 4.1.3 about fault modes and countermeasures following FMECA. Various kinds of check processes of the LC prevent upper layer of component from occurring (see 'c' in Figure 9).

As for a component of 'simultaneous failure of the two logic processors', the probability of the component is extremely small and even if it happens, the FC's check of error messages detect errors except in the case that the two logic processors fail in the exact same way and create the same wrong messages. The probability of the upper layer of component can be extremely small with a relevant checking process (see 'd' in Figure 9).

As for a component of 'A wrong result message sent by FC', several checking processes of the FC itself as safety-related equipment can detect errors of a wrong result message before the FC sends the message (see 'e' in Figure 9).

As mentioned above, the LC prevents the occurrence of the upper layer of components by various checking processes and covers checking even for a component with quite a low probability.

4.1.2 FTA for availability

An LC makes its master and slave sub-systems process in parallel as a dual system for availability. The LC also processes quadruple redundant transmission. Risk analysis should also be done for availability.

We performed an FTA for availability as shown in Figure 10 focusing on accord of four output messages mentioned in Section 3.2.1 as a required policy of the LC.

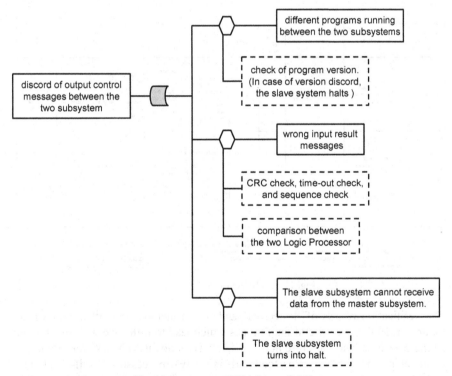

Fig. 10. An extract of FTA for availability

We chose a component of 'discord of output messages between the two sub-systems' as the first layer. There are three second-layer components as follows:

1. different programs running between the two sub-systems
2. wrong input result messages
3. slave system unable to receive data from the master sub-system.

Item 2 can be checked because of the LC's various checks. Items 1 and 3 can also be processed by selecting the master-sub-system's message under the policy that the master sub-system has priority over the slave (see Section 3.2.3). Therefore, we verified that the LC prevents the occurrence of discord of output messages between the two sub-systems and that accord of four output messages can be kept.

4.1.3 FMECA for LC

As FMECA for LC, we listed up 'Fault mode', 'Influence', and 'Fatality' of each part of the hardware of LC, and verified that 'Evaluation' of all parts keeps a good level after taking 'Measures'. Figure 11 shows an extract of the FMECA for an LC.

No.	part	Fault mode	Influence	Fatality before taking mearures	Frequency	Method of fault detection	Measures	Evaluation after taking measures
1	Processor	1. internal device fault 2 address bus fault 3. control signal fault 4. data bus fault	- cannot boot - illegal logic calculation - indefinite process time (to all of 1-4)	A	medium	- self-diagnosis by comparison order - WDT detection - failure detection by FS module - comparison of input, output, and internal data between the two Logic Processors - synchronous check between the two Logic Processors	- redundant system configuration with function of fault detection - If it detects fault, Logic Processor (A or B) stops alternating signal to FS module and sends stop signal to LAN adaptor in order to stop transmission to FC	B in case of a single system C in case of a dual system
2	Main memory circuit (SDRAM)	1. malfunction of memory element bit 2. malfunction of access size 3. address bus fault 4. control signal fault 5. data bus fault	- failure of program run - failure of input, internal, and output data	A	medium	- parity check - write and read check - program CRC check - WDT detection - failure detection by FS module - data CRC check - comparison of input, output, and internal data between the two Logic Processors - synchronous check between the two Logic Processors	- redundant system configuration with function of fault detection - If it detects fault, Logic Processor (A or B) stops alternating signal to FS module and sends stop signal to LAN adaptor in order to stop transmission to FC	B in case of a single system C in case of a dual system

Fatality	Frequency	Evaluation
A: system down with risk	medium: a hundred to several hundreds fits	A: product mission lost with risk
B: system down with safe-side control	small: ten to several tens fits	B: product mission lost without risk
C: system running with limited function	extreme small: several fits	C: product mission kept by redundancy
D: not related to safety		D: product mission kept without degradation

Fig. 11. An extract of FMECA for LC

The verification results of 'Processor' and 'Main memory circuit' are shown in Figure 11. Both have several fault modes which lead to influence with risk before taking measures, and therefore both get 'A: system down with risk' for 'Fatality'. After taking measures such as 'comparison by two processors', 'self-checking', and 'Stop of output in the case of detecting failure' mentioned in Section 3.2.1, both 'Processor' and 'Main memory circuit' are evaluated as 'B: product mission lost without risk' in the case of a single system, and as 'C: product mission kept by redundancy' in the case of a dual system. By applying such analysis to all safety-related parts of the hardware of LC, we clarified the fatality of the hardware of an LC and verified its safety.

4.2 Risk analysis for transmission between LCs and FCs

4.2.1 Fulfilment of IEC62280-1

As a part of risk analysis, we checked whether or not the methods for safety for transmission between LCs and FCs mentioned in Section 3.3 satisfy the requirements of IEC62280-1.

First, the system architecture of the IP-network-based RSCS for ABS has the following features.

1. Both the LCs and the FCs are fail-safe equipment.
2. Transmission paths between LCs and FCs are closed with exclusive lines used.
3. The maximum number of FCs controlled by any single LC is defined.
4. The physical characteristics of the transmission paths are fixed.

These features satisfy the preconditions Pr1, Pr2 and Pr3 of IEC62280-1 respectively for the exchange of safety-related messages. Therefore, IEC62280-1 can be applied to the whole system.

Second, in order to maintain safety for communication between safety-related equipment, the whole system has the following features mentioned in Section 3.3.

5. Both LCs and FCs add IP addresses of source and destination to the UDP data area.
6. Both LCs and FCs add CRC and reversed data to the UDP area as redundancy codes. This process doesn't depend on the transmission system.
7. Both LCs and FCs add a sequence number to the UDP area and provide timeliness of control and result messages.
8. Both LCs and FCs check the continuousness of control and result messages by checking a sequence number.
9. Safety-related processes in LCs and FCs are functionally independent of the process of transmission paths.
10. Both LCs and FCs always supervise the features 5 to 9 mentioned above at message receiving and check the correctness of a message. If they detect message error, they recognize transmission failure, activate the safe-side control, and turn into safe state in two control durations (see Figure 7).

These features satisfy the safety procedure requirements for communication between safety-related equipment R7, R8, R9, R10, R11, and R12 of IEC62280-1 respectively.

Third, in order to fulfil the required safety integrated level, the whole system has the following features.

11. The whole system needs to detect typical faults which occur in non-safety related transmission lines. The system can detect typical transmission faults such
as 'interrupted transmission line', 'all bits logical 0', 'all bits logical 1', 'message inversion', 'synchronization slip', etc. with the check of time-out, redundancy codes, and sequence number mentioned in Section 3.3.
12. The whole system needs to detect typical errors. The system can detect typical
transmission errors such as 'random errors', 'burst error', 'systematic error',
and 'combinations of the above' with the check of redundancy codes.
13. Redundancy codes are added to the UDP data area. They are functionally independent of transmission codes.
14. CRC and inversion data are used as redundancy codes. Since they are sufficiently complicated, the probability that transmission lines create redundancy
codes is extremely small.

These features satisfy the safety code requirements for communication between
safety-related equipment R15, R16, R17, and R18 of IEC62280-1 respectively.

As mentioned above, the whole system fulfils architecture preconditions, safety
procedure requirements for communication between safety related equipment, and
safety code requirements of IEC62280-1. Therefore, we verified that the whole
system fulfils IEC62280-1.

4.2.2 FTA for transmission

We also performed an FTA for transmission between LCs and FCs as shown in
Figure 12 as a part of risk analysis, extending Figure 9 and focusing on failures of
result messages. A component related to LCs and six components related to IP
networks are listed for three types of transmission faults. The six components related to IP networks are further examined through five lower-layer components.
We examined to ensure that all possible components related IP networks and LCs
result in only the three types of transmission faults which can be detected thanks
to the LC's checks of message error, time-out, and sequence inversion.

5 Development

5.1 Development and test

We have developed the IP-network-based RSCS for ABS based on the methods
mentioned in Section 3 and on the risk analysis mentioned in Section 4. In the case
of any change of specifications, we performed risk analysis again for related parts
and made development and risk analysis get feedback from each other. As for
software, we utilized the software which has a good track record in actual RSCSs
as much as possible.

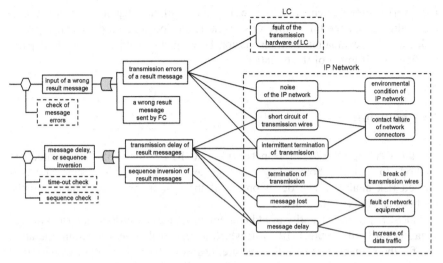

Fig. 12. An extract of FTA for transmission between LCs and FCs

JR East made the interface requirement specification between LCs and FCs, and showed it to the suppliers, expressing methods for transmission between LCs and FCs mentioned in Section 3.3. Since the suppliers of LCs and FCs are different and products for transmission paths such as E-PON, L3SW and L2SW are COTS of another supplier, JR East didn't ask a specific supplier to create the interface specification, but made the interface requirement specification on its own for impartial development. JR East and the suppliers of LCs and FCs jointly created the detailed interface specification between LCs and FCs, and the suppliers of LCs and FCs built functions for safety-related transmission.

Since the whole system consists of equipment from different suppliers, we performed many tests for the whole system in addition to the tests of equipment at each supplier's factory. Furthermore, we accomplished a field test of about three and a half years where FCs were placed along an actual railway field and the whole system was running parallel to an actual RSCS. We evaluated reliability and environment-resistant ability as well as control and transmission functions under the long-term running of the system. The result of the field test was good.

5.2 Safety evaluation by a third party

The IP-network-based RSCS for ABS was evaluated by a third party in Japan during development. The third party evaluated the system and judged that the policies and concrete methods of the system for safety are good. We decided to take the step of manufacturing the system based on this evaluation. For evaluation of the LC, the supplier performed FTA and FMECA as risk analysis and proved that sufficient measures to prevent failure of the system have been taken, and the third party verified the contents one by one. In the case of any change of specifications, the evaluation by the third party was taken again, focusing on the change and its influence. For evaluation of transmission between LCs and FCs, the third party verified its fulfilment of IEC62280-1.

6 Conclusion

For the development of an IP-network-based RSCS for ABS, we created the methods to maintain both safety and high availability for the system and performed risk analysis. The development of the system progressed based on the methods and the risk analysis.

In RSCSs, a large quantity of old equipment such as relay-logic interlocking for a station yard still remains. JR East, which is responsible both for train operation and for the management of infrastructure, has to replace old equipment with new over a short period and at small cost, utilizing the newest technology. Old electric parts and products may go out of production soon and JR East will be forced into system change toward new technologies.

The methods discussed above to maintain both safety and high availability are response to networking technology and we believe that the concept will be applied long into the future. In particular, the quadruple redundant transmission is new to conventional RSCSs and further application is widely expected and highly likely. With the growth of ICT, we must continue to cope with the transition from old technologies to new ones in all the railway fields in the future. We will adapt to new technologies based on the discussed methods.

References

Endo M, Okada T, Watanabe D et al (2008) A safety-related transmission method for a new railway signalling system based on IP-Network. 11th Int Conf Comput Syst Des Oper Railw Transit Syst (COMPRAIL 2008), Toledo, Spain
Hayakawa K, Miura T, Ishima R et al (2010) An IP network-based signal control system for automatic block signal and its functional enhancement. 12th Int Conf Comput Syst Des Oper Railw Transit Syst (COMPRAIL 2010) , Beijing, China
IEC (2002) Railway applications – communication, signalling and processing systems – Part 1: safety-related communication in closed transmission systems. IEC62280-1
Ishima R, Fukuta Y, Matsumoto M et al (2008) A new signalling system for automatic block signal between stations controlling through an IP network. 8th World Congr Railw Res (WCRR2008), Seoul, Korea
JR East (2006) Installation of the first network signal control system. East Japan Railway Company press release. http://www.jreast.co.jp/e/press/20061102/index.html. Accessed 20 September 2011
Mori M, Hideo T, Ando H, Ishima R (2008) Logic controller for automatic block signal between railway stations. Toshiba Rev 63(1)
Saiki Y, Masutani S, Kunifuji T et al (2010) Reliability of the IP network-based signal control system and the integrated logical controller. 8th Symp Form Methods Autom Saf Railw Automot Syst (FORMS/FORMAT 2010), Braunschweig, Germany

Taking Safe Decisions in the GB Railway Industry

George Bearfield

RSSB

London, UK

Abstract   The railway industry in Great Britain has accepted processes for taking decisions that impact upon safety which have been in place for a number of years. This paper provides an overview explanation of the processes. The UK railway industry now has some practical experience around the use of its agreed safety related decision making processes. This paper includes a review of some of the practical problems and difficulties that can be experienced in applying the processes. The industry's experiences have clarified that safety appraisals are more complex in nature than was perhaps appreciated when the guidelines were drafted by RSSB and the ORR. It has also highlighted the importance of intelligent interpretation of the results of the CBA. This information is being used to feed into an ongoing review and update of the guidance to support its wider use in the industry.

1 Taking safe decisions – the industry consensus

Historically in the GB railway industry, the interpretation of health and safety law has been a matter for significant debate. In particular there was little guidance from case law to explain how the general duties to manage safety so far as is reasonably practicable, in the Health and Safety at Work etc. Act 1974 (HM Government 1974) could be made specific for the purposes of deciding how to invest in or manage safety. When considering risk estimation and management this general duty is considered to be discharged by showing that risk has been reduced to a level that is as low as is reasonably practicable (ALARP). As a result of this, RSSB, the GB rail safety and standards body, and the wider railway industry initiated a programme of research and consultation to develop guidance targeted specifically at the companies with the legal responsibilities under that regulation, namely the duty holders (train operating companies and the infrastructure manager, Network Rail). The resulting guidance, 'Taking safe decisions' (RSSB 2008), acknowledges that different types of decision are taken in the railway industry. For example:

- Duty holders may decide to take a decision because they judge that it is necessary in order for the company to meet its legal duty.

- Duty holders may decide to take a decision that is not legally required because they believe that it makes commercial sense for their business.
- Policy-makers may choose to undertake policy decisions.

Figure 1 shows how these different types of decision relate to each other. It is important to differentiate between these types of decision, as each entails different considerations, and each has different legal implications. Figure 1 summarises the various considerations that duty-holders need to take into account when determining what is legally required (as shown in the first two boxes of the diagram of Figure 1). It highlights that the industry is not responsible for policy decisions. Policy decisions are taken by government (or initiated by a regulatory body) as the legitimate proxy of society. If these decisions are taken then they will be mandated upon the railway industry via legislation. It also highlights that often railway duty-holders voluntarily take decisions which impact upon safety that are not legally mandated.

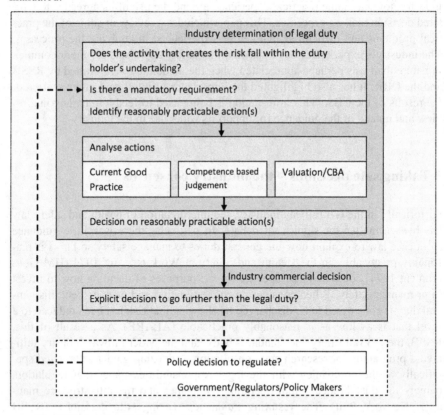

Fig. 1. The relationship between different decision criteria in the GB railway industry

2 Industry determination of legal duty

There are different ways in which a duty holder can demonstrate that they are doing all that is reasonably practicable to reduce risk. Where good practice exists in the GB railway industry, this is a good indicator of what measures are likely to be reasonably practicable. However, there are many risks where that which is good practice is not yet agreed. In the modern railway industry, where there is increasing technological change, good practice may need regular review. In such cases a decision must be made from first principles. Whether the decision is a simple judgment or based on detailed analysis, the same principles should apply. Determination of whether an action is reasonably practicable involves balancing its risks, costs and benefits. The principle was set out in a Court of Appeal judgment in the case of Edwards (Asquith 1949):

> '…a computation must be made…in which the quantum of risk is placed on one scale and the sacrifice involved in the measures necessary for averting the risk (whether in money, time or trouble) is placed in the other, and that, if it be shown that there is a gross disproportion between them – the risk being insignificant to the sacrifice – the defendants discharge the onus on them.'

In 'Taking safe decisions' the GB railway industry has set out a clear process for determining whether measures are reasonably practicable. There are three approaches which a duty-holder might apply, individually or in combination, to determine whether a measure is legally required: good practice, judgment and cost-benefit analysis (CBA).

The GB railway has many conventions of good practice, such as Railway Group Standards, codes of practice and British and Euronorm standards. Good practice can be important in determining whether a particular decision meets the legal duty with respect to safety. Its correct application removes the need to assess safety risks from first principles as well as providing quick and effective guidance about how to proceed in a particular set of circumstances.

In other circumstances, where there is no time for rigorous analysis or it is not considered appropriate, decisions might be made on the basis of judgment and experience. In such cases it is appropriate for professionals with the right levels of confidence and experience to take the judgment. However, in many cases where risks and options are complex it is necessary to undertake an analysis from first principles. In such cases a CBA might be undertaken, supported by quantitative risk assessment. This process follows an explicit application of the test of reasonable practicability as outlined previously in the Edwards judgment. Comparison of the risk associated with an action and its cost, as implied by the Edwards judgment, is not simple because risk and cost are not measured in the same units. In the GB railway industry, risk is generally estimated in fatalities and weighted injuries (FWI) per year. In order to make a comparison of risks with costs, the risk needs to be translated into a financial value. This is done using the industry 'value of preventing a fatality' (VPF), a figure endorsed for use by the Department for Transport (DfT 2004), which is currently approximately £1.76 million per statistical fatality averted. This figure was originally developed from studies of what a selection of members of the public said that they would be willing to pay for reduction in risk levels. It is a measure of what the average member of the general public is willing to pay to reduce the level of risk to the average victim.

'Taking safe decisions' describes how this test is applied:

> '...where the cost [of the measure] is above the monetary value of the safety benefit [of the measure], we apply professional judgment in determining whether the cost is grossly disproportionate to the safety benefit and it is reasonably practicable to implement the improvement. In making this judgment, we pay particular attention to:
>
> - the degree of uncertainty in the assessment of costs and safety benefits
> - the range of potential safety consequences.'

The document confirms that the safety benefit is calculated using the VPF, not a multiple of it. Edwards use of the term 'gross' is taken as an acknowledgement that, as accidents and their consequences are difficult to predict, the estimation of risk is an inherently uncertain process, and in some circumstances wide confidence limits may need to be applied to risk estimates. Uncertainty is particularly likely when trying to estimate the risk associated with high-consequence, low-frequency events such as train collisions. There are two reasons for this:

- These incidents are rare so there is by definition little past data to use to develop estimates of future risk.
- These types of incidents can result in a wide range of consequences the severity of which can vary greatly. For example, the Ladbroke Grove accident resulted in 31 fatalities. The accident at Southall was similar in many ways, and resulted in the occurrence of seven fatalities.

Conversely, the risk associated with high-frequency, low-severity incidents can be much more easily ascertained because there should be more historic data available to support risk estimation. The degree of uncertainty in risk estimates should be considered and factored into any judgment that the risk estimates are used to inform.

Recent legal judgments, such as Baker v Quantum, and R v Tangerine Confectionary, have served to support the position taken in 'Taking safe decisions' with an emphasis on disproportion, rather than gross disproportion between costs and benefits as the margin in the legal test of whether or not a measure is required.

'Taking safe decisions' was published by the industry in 2008. At about the same time the Office of Rail Regulation (ORR), the railway industry's joint economic and safety regulator, published its own guidance on the use of CBA to support safety related appraisals (ORR 2008) and this guidance was closely related to 'Taking safe decisions'. Since this time the principles described in both documents have been applied to a wide range of projects and a number of practical issues have emerged which warrant discussions and wider review.

3 The four ALARP quadrants

A key point of the clarification in 'Taking safe decisions' and the related ORR CBA guidance, is that the safety benefits and costs are net values and should be calculated as such. Costs and benefits accrue over a number of years, and in order to make valid comparisons of them they need to be discounted to net present values. 'Taking safe decisions' describes which costs and benefits are relevant, or potentially relevant, to the legal criteria (an ALARP decision) and the ORR guidance gives general guidance on the financial aspects of such appraisals including what discount rates to use, for example. In practice net values can be positive as well as negative and this throws up a number of different possible outputs of a CBA appraisal to evaluate whether measures are required in order to reduce risk ALARP. The four quadrants of the diagram of Figure 2 show the possible different outcomes and the subsequent sub-sections of this paper describe each quadrant in detail.

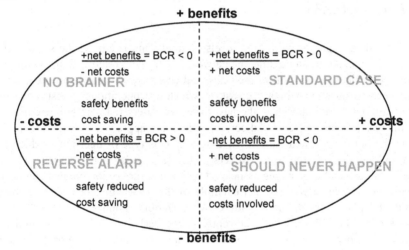

Fig. 2. The four ALARP CBA quadrants

3.1 The standard case

In general, when ALARP decisions are considered, most people seem to consider the weighing up of some improvement in safety (a positive safety benefit) with some financial cost. An example of this might be a decision about whether or not to fit sander systems to a particular fleet of trains. Sanders are train borne systems which release sandite onto the track in front of train wheels in the event of emergency braking to increase adhesion in situations where it is poor (such as where there is leaf fall or other contaminants on the track). There will be a net financial cost of the fitment of such systems, but there will also be a safety benefit associated with improved braking in certain potentially hazardous scenarios. The question then is: does this money need to be spent given the safety benefit that it will achieve? The standard approach outlined in Section 2 is followed and the measure should be required unless the duty holder judges that the costs calculated are sufficiently disproportionate to the benefits, taking into account the uncertainties in the analysis undertaken. It should also be noted that the ALARP appraisal must be conducted over the lifetime of the measure. For railway assets this is typically of the order of 25 years, however in the train sander case it would be sensible to use the remaining life of the rolling stock as this is the period over which the measure will be in use. It does not make sense to use the remaining period of the train operator's franchise as whether or not a measure is required to reduce risk to a level that is ALARP is unrelated to its affordability.

3.2 Reverse ALARP

The GB railway operates with high levels of safety and is among the safest railways in Europe. At the same time, the network is very congested with many routes operating services at the limit of their physical capacity. There is therefore a continual need to question whether measures which are operationally restrictive in some way, but were imposed in the past to reduce safety risk, are still necessary. For this reason many systems and controls which are appraised by CBA are actually in the bottom left quadrant of the diagram. This type of decision – which is often colloquially referred to as 'Reverse ALARP' – relates to situations where there is a significant cost saving associated with a measure or its removal and only a small increase in safety risk. An example of this is whether or not to remove lineside telephones from areas with GSM-R (mobile phone) coverage in the driver's cab. The GB railway is currently in the early stages of a transition to GSM-R, the railway's own dedicated GSM mobile network, to support train and signaller communications. This system, when fully implemented, is expected to have much higher availability than current train radio systems. This means that there is less dependence placed on lineside telephones, such as signal post telephones, as a redundant communication medium in the event of a train radio failure. However, even though there is less dependence on them they still do provide a level of risk reduction in the event that GSM-R systems fail. The question then is: is it worth continuing to install and maintain such phones given that GSM-R has now been installed? There is guidance in 'Taking safe decisions' which explicitly acknowledges the potential need to take such decisions which says:

'It is permissible to remove/reduce risk controls that can no longer be shown to be reasonably practicable. This situation could arise if:

- The cost of the control increased (due to obsolescence, for example).
- The safety benefits reduced (due to the effect of other controls).

- It was found that the control had never been justified under the ALARP principle.

Decisions to remove risk controls should be justified by a thorough assessment of the risks and a carefully considered ALARP case.'

ORR guidance similarly says:

'removing existing control measures is usually only acceptable where circumstances have changed (for example, where risks have been removed or controlled by other measures), there are changes in the understanding of the hazard, or the costs of continuing the measure are clearly grossly disproportionate to the risk reduction it achieves.'

This guidance leads the decision maker to a consideration of some hypothetical arguments such as: 'If the control measure I just put in existed before, would it have been ALARP?' In the case of the GSM-R/lineside phones example this would entail consideration of the question: 'Assuming I already had GSM-R would installation of lineside phones be reasonably practicable?' Ultimately the results of any analysis will need to be ratified by appropriate senior level decision makers in a company. Experience with application of the process shows that these types of decision maker may not be convinced by the hypothetical nature of these types of argument. When this is coupled with the fact that these types of decision involve increases in safety risk, it has been found that it can be difficult for high level decision makers to 'buy into' CBAs of this type as sufficient demonstration that the legal duty has been discharged. However, experience has also shown that if such safety arguments are to be used to support the removal of controls in this way, it is sensible to include an alternative CBA showing that the net financial benefits of removing a control are significantly more than the monetised increase in safety risk (the 'reverse ALARP' argument shown in the diagram). The problem with this type of assessment is that it is difficult to know when to stop removing controls on the basis of analysis. Consideration of absolute, rather than relative, levels of risk becomes necessary in order to ensure that the residual risk remains tolerable when controls are removed.

Another relevant consideration is that when these types of appraisal are undertaken it is generally the case that the financial benefits are significantly driven by reduced train delays. Such delays have secondary safety risk implications of their own, e.g. crowding on trains or at stations may cause increased risk of slips and falls of passengers, or of passenger assaults. Train evacuation might also become necessary, with a range of associated risks. Delays may also cause increased numbers of red signals on the network and hence increased opportunity for signals to be passed when they are at danger. Raising the awareness of these secondary safety risks provides a complement to the financial arguments for the removal of other operationally restrictive safety controls.

3.3 The no-brainer

The upper left hand quadrant of the diagram refers to decisions where there is a cost saving associated with a particular measure, and a safety benefit. This would seem to be clearly a decision where a measure must be applied. One example of this would be consideration of the removal of fire extinguishers from the public areas of trains. Previously, on some rolling stock, a requirement existed for fire extinguishers to be provided in each train carriage. However, this was expensive, particularly as in some areas the extinguishers were regularly vandalised, and there were risks associated with such behaviour. The provision of multiple fire extinguishers was also found to create risks as passengers might injure themselves if they tried to put out fires themselves. As a result of this the requirement was changed to provide a single fire extinguisher in each train, which is accessible to staff only. This changed measure therefore reduced both cost and safety risk.

However, there are some decisions which, although technically within the 'no-brainer' category, do require further judgment and consideration. 'Taking safe decisions' states:

> 'where the gross cost of a measure (excluding any performance benefits) is substantially higher than the safety benefit then this would indicate that safety is not the key driver for the measure'.

An extreme example of this is the industry decision to implement the European Rail Traffic Management System (ERTMS) in the UK. This is a European standard for automatic train protection. The nationwide programme of work has a positive business case and is predicted to improve safety. However, it is accepted that the implementation of ERTMS is a business decision and has not been taken on the basis that it was a reasonably practicable measure. The expenditure is far in excess of the financial value of any safety benefit and therefore it is accepted that the safety benefit should not drive the decision making process in these circumstances. However, what has not yet been established is the degree to which the gross costs must be higher than the safety benefits for the decision not to be one based on reasonable practicability criteria.

3.4 Should never happen

The final category, in the bottom right quadrant of Figure 2, concerns a situation that would never be expected to warrant serious consideration, namely where a measure both increases safety risk and costs money. However, there may be some decisions in the UK railway industry that, by a strict application of the guidance, result in CBA output which falls into this category. One project that has been considered for the railway is the development of 'wayfinding' systems to help the blind and partially sighted to navigate their way around railway stations. These systems would obviously require financial investment, and there is an argument that, by encouraging more use of stations by blind people, the absolute levels of risk at stations with such systems in operation would be expected to rise. Strict interpretation of the guidance would mean that such systems would be inconsistent with the ALARP principle and therefore could not be implemented. A more rounded view of the issue would surely lead to the conclusion that such systems would benefit the blind and that perhaps the individual risk levels of blind passengers both with and without the system in place would be more useful as a measure of its comparative safety benefit. There may well also be other legislative drivers to consider. This case therefore illustrates the subtleties around ALARP decision making and the fact that complex decisions cannot be simplified purely to a benefit to cost ratio. CBA can be a blunt tool, but its benefit is in forcing the analyst to consider the objective data so that the eventual judgment can be properly informed.

4 Conclusions

The GB railway industry now has some practical experience around the use of its agreed safety related decision making processes. These experiences have clarified that safety appraisals are more complex in nature than was perhaps appreciated when the guidelines were drafted by RSSB and the ORR. It has also highlighted the importance of intelligent interpretation of the results of the CBA. This information is being used to feed into ongoing review and update of the guidance to support its wider use in the industry.

Acknowledgments The author would like to acknowledge the essential contribution made to this work by a wide cross section of individuals from across the GB railway industry and community. Key support was provided in particularly by members of ATOC and Network Rail. The author would also like to thank Wayne Murphy of RSSB for devising Figure 2, the representation of the ALARP quadrants, as a way of helping to explain the possible outputs of an ALARP CBA in a succinct and easy to understand way.

References

Asquith LJ (1949) Edwards vs National Coal Board. 1 AER 743
DfT (2004) Highways economic note no. 1. http://webarchive.nationalarchives.gov.uk/+/http://
    www.dft.gov.uk/pgr/roadsafety/ea/highwayseconomicnoteno12004. Accessed 26 September
    2011
HM Government (1974) The health and safety at work etc. act 1974. HMSO, London
ORR (2008) Internal guidance on cost benefit analysis (CBA) in support of safety-related investment decisions. http://www.rail-reg.gov.uk/upload/pdf/risk-CBA_sdm_rev_guid.pdf. Accessed 26 September 2011
RSSB (2008) Taking safe decisions. http://www.rssb.co.uk/safety/Pages/safetydecisionmaking.
    aspx. Accessed 26 September 2011

CyberSafety: CyberSecurity and Safety-Critical Software Engineering

Chris Johnson

Department of Computing Science, University of Glasgow

Glasgow, UK

Abstract A range of common software components are gradually being integrated into the infrastructures that support safety-critical systems. These include network management tools, operating systems – especially Linux, Voice Over IP (VOIP) communications technologies, and satellite based augmentation systems for navigation/timing data etc. The increasing use of these common components creates concerns that bugs might affect multiple systems across many different safety-related industries. It also raises significant security concerns. Malware has been detected in power distribution, healthcare, military and transportation infrastructures. Most previous attacks do not seem to have deliberately targeted critical applications. However, there is no room for complacency in the face of increasing vulnerability to cyber attacks on safety-related systems. This paper illustrates the threat to air traffic management infrastructures and goes on to present a roadmap to increase our resilience to future CyberSafety attacks. Some components of this proposal are familiar concepts from Security Management Systems (SecMS), including a focus on incident reporting and the need for improved risk assessment tools. Other components of the roadmap focus on structural and organizational problems that have limited the effectiveness of existing SecMS; in particular there is a need to raise awareness amongst regulators and senior management who often lack the technical and engineering background to understand the nature of the threats to safety-critical software.

1 Introduction

In the past, the specialized nature of infrastructure engineering has limited the failure modes that could cross multiple systems boundaries. The future looks very different. The increasing integration of critical infrastructures creates new opportunities, for instance through the development of smart grids for the generation and distribution of electricity or through the use of EGNOS satellite based timing and location services for railway signaling (Pederson et al. 2006). However, this integration creates new vulnerabilities. Safety-critical applications increasingly rely on a small number of common operating systems and network protocols. Very similar algorithms are being used by the same suppliers across both primary and secondary systems. For example, Voice Over IP (VOIP) communication technologies are being used for backup and principal systems in areas ranging from air traffic management to emergency response.

The increasing use of common software components across many different safety-critical industries creates concerns that the consequences of any bugs might extend across multiple applications. For instance, previous work has shown that design flaws have been carried between the GPS applications that were initially developed for aviation and then were subsequently integrated into maritime bridge information systems (Johnson et al. 2008). There are also significant security concerns where safety-critical systems rely on Commercial Off The Shelf (COTS) operating systems and network infrastructures. This brings significant savings to the developers and operators of safety-critical systems. However, they also attract a host of 'mass market' viruses. For instance, Linux variants are increasingly being used in Air Traffic Management (ATM). There have been several recent cases where engineering teams have discovered malware affecting these systems; typically introduced by contractors using infected USB sticks. These incidents illustrate the problems that Air Navigation Service Providers (ANSPs) face in implementing their existing security policies. The Linux attacks have not yet had significant safety implications; Air Traffic Control Officers (ATCOs) maintain sufficient situation awareness to continue service provision even when primary systems have been compromised. However, with increasing traffic loads and greater systems integration planned by the US NextGen and European SESAR programmes, there is no scope for complacency over the consequences of future security threats (Johnson, 2011).

2   Assessing security threats to ATM safety

The increasing reliance on common software components leaves us unprepared for the consequences of coordinated attacks on safety-critical infrastructures. These vulnerabilities are compounded by the problems that arise when determining who is responsible for meeting the costs associated with national resilience. Government security agencies rely on support from industry. However, few companies can afford to meet the costs of design diversity and redundancy that provide higher levels of assurance. Further problems arise when commercial organizations fail to monitor the effectiveness of their security management systems. Many policies and procedures only exist on paper and are never used in daily operations. In consequence, many safety-related applications remain highly vulnerable to a wide range of cyber security and cyber defense threats.

These arguments can be illustrated by the General Accounting Office review of CyberSecurity in US air traffic management (GAO 1998). They found that the FAA was 'ineffective in all critical areas including operational systems information security, future systems modernization security, and management structure and policy implementation'. They further concluded that the 'FAA is similarly in-effective in managing systems security for its operational systems and is in viola-tion of its own policy'. They had 'performed the necessary analysis to determine system threats, vulnerabilities, and safeguards for only 3 of 90 operational ATC computer systems, or less than 4 percent'; only one of the nine telecommunica-tions networks had been analysed for security vulnerabilities. The GAO also found that the FAA 'does not consistently include well formulated security requirements in specifications for all new ATC modernization systems, as required by FAA pol-icy'.

Many of the same concerns were again raised by the US Department of Trans-port (DoT 2009). This identified problems in both corporate information systems and operational infrastructures. In February 2009, an intrusion compromised the social security details of more than 48,000 staff held on FAA servers. In other at-tacks, the administrators' passwords were obtained for FAA networks in Oklaho-ma and Alaska. These intrusions focused on web-based information systems but the interconnected nature of FAA operations created significant concerns for the operational networks where surveillance, communications and flight information is processed. It was hard for the systems engineers to guarantee that these attacks could not have any impact on service provision. The Department of Transport re-port argued, 'In our opinion, unless effective action is taken quickly, it is likely to be a matter of when, not if, ATC systems encounter attacks that do serious harm to ATC operations.'

The DoT report went on to reiterate many of the arguments that have been made in the opening sections of this paper. The introduction of commercial soft-ware and Internet Protocol technologies has provided significant cost savings to FAA modernization initiatives. However, they also introduce greater security risk compared to previous generations of proprietary software: 'Now, attackers can take advantage of software vulnerabilities in commercial IP products to exploit ATC systems, which is especially worrisome at a time when the nation is facing increased threats from sophisticated nation-state-sponsored cyber attacks.' (DOT 2009) Their concern was exacerbated by the inadequate response to previous inci-dents. In 2008, there were more than 870 cyber incident alerts. By the end of the year, 17% (150) of these had not been resolved, 'including critical incidents in which hackers may have taken over control' of the computational infrastructure for ATM operations.

Europe lags behind the United States in this area. There are no surveys of ATM security practices, which might be compared to those produced by the GAO and DoT. We lack detailed evidence about the extent of CyberSecurity vulnerabilities across member states. As part of the preparation for this paper, the author visited engineering teams in more than a dozen ANSPs across Europe. Every centre re-ported having experienced problems from malware. In several cases, these intru-sions had forced them to rely on secondary communication systems or flight data processing systems.

The vulnerabilities are likely to increase. For example, EUROCONTROL's CASCADE programme has considered a range of security concerns associated with the unauthorized use of Automatic Dependent Surveillance – Broadcast (ADS-B) information. ADS-B relies on aircraft transmitting their identity, position etc., to support ground surveillance by ANSPs. The data can also be used by on-board avionics to improve the situation awareness of other aircraft. However, the increasing use of this technology creates the potential to deliberately introduce false targets into the system or to use aircraft identity and position information for malicious purposes.

There is an urgent need for more information about existing vulnerabilities and future threats. It is, therefore, important for the European Commission to review the CyberSecurity of air traffic management across member states. This should be completed before the SESAR programme for the modernization of ATM infrastructures further increases our reliance on software systems.

3 A roadmap for CyberSafety engineering

Previous sections have described the security vulnerabilities that permeate software infrastructures in some safety-critical applications. We have also argued that these vulnerabilities will increase as common software components, including network management tools and operating systems, are used across multiple systems in many different industries. These concerns have motivated the development of a roadmap to increase resilience against cyber-attacks on safety-critical systems (Johnson and Holloway 2011). Figure 1 provides an overview of the approach advocated in the remainder of the paper.

3.1 Addressing managerial and regulatory complacency

In the past, operational staff could intervene if they had concerns about problems in the underlying software infrastructures. Air Traffic Control Officers (ATCOs) retain the right to 'close the skies' or adjust the amount of traffic in response to periodic malfunctions or if there is evidence of an intrusion in networked systems. However, this position cannot be sustained. The next generation of automated systems will stretch the ability of operational staff to directly intervene without decision support tools. It is also becoming increasingly difficult for ATCOs to distinguish malicious behaviours from more benign bugs or from 'normal operation' in complex, integrated systems. This significantly increases the consequences of any breach in the security of underlying software infrastructures by delaying the time before an intrusion is detected.

These problems are exacerbated by a lack of strategic leadership in CyberSecurity. Most regulatory organisations do not understand the security threats that are posed to software architectures. Very few regulators have expertise in software engineering or the integration of complex distributed systems; there are few incentives for leading technical staff to join regulatory bodies where the salaries and career prospects may be less attractive than in many companies. These problems are compounded by the under-representation of engineers at higher levels of management in safety-critical industries. The appointment of operational and financial experts deprives engineering teams of the strategic guidance needed to address CyberSafety concerns. This creates a situation in which many governments across Europe and North America have identified the potential threat and taken action to create specialist agencies, such as the UK's Centre for the Protection of National Infrastructures. However, their warnings about the vulnerabilities of technologies such as the Internet Protocol for safety-critical applications have not been acted upon. These criticisms extend well beyond the field of air traffic management.

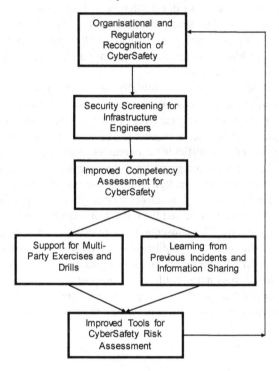

Fig. 1. A Roadmap for CyberSafety Engineering

3.2 Security screening for infrastructure engineers

Our roadmap includes improvements to the security screening of technical staff across safety-critical industries. Most attention has focused on external cyber threats. The 'insider threat' has been ignored. In consequence, air traffic management security management systems often do not require background checks on the staff employed by sub-contractors. There is minimal vetting for the engineers and technicians who work on critical infrastructures in Europe and North America. These limitations are compounded by a lack of guidance on how to mitigating vulnerabilities to insider attacks within existing security standards, such as ISO 17799 (Theoharidoua et al. 2005).

It is important to stress that these are not hypothetical concerns. NIST's Industrial Control System Security project reports how a disaffected worker used their knowledge of the underlying software infrastructures to attack SCADA controlled sewage equipment (Abrams and Weiss 2008). On at least 46 occasions, he issued radio commands that caused 800,000 litres of raw sewage to contaminate local parks and rivers. When he was arrested, he was found to possess a laptop that ran a version of the sewerage control application. This was connected to a Motorola M120 two-way radio; the same device that was used to send 'legitimate' commands to the equipment. The serial numbers showed that the radio had been ordered by the operating company. He also had a PDS Compact 500 computer control device with an address that mimicked a spoof pumping station enabling him to test out the impact of his commands.

The perpetrator of this attack was initially employed by an IT subcontractor to the sewage company. His everyday work provided him with a good understanding of the underlying software infrastructures. This has strong parallels in air traffic management. Many ANSPs have outsourced IT infrastructure provision. In such cases, it can be particularly difficult for operators to identify and diagnose potential attacks. In this incident, the perpetrator took steps to disguise his actions, interspersing them between less malign system failures. It was difficult to distinguish the impact of the malicious attacks from design flaws and malfunctions.

Most ANSPs have not considered the impact of a similar 'insider' attack on the systems that they operate. The consequences are difficult to exaggerate. For most service providers, the threat of a deliberately introduced bug would be enough to halt service provision with no immediate way to trace whether safety requirements continue to be met across many millions of lines of code (Haley et al. 2008). In Europe, many military air traffic management systems share the same machine rooms as their civil counterparts. In some states, they share a common network infrastructure.

3.3 Competency assessment for CyberSecurity

The roadmap in Figure 1 also includes the need to improve the competency of engineering teams in dealing with cyber threats. For instance, very few technical staff are aware of recent developments such as Maddalon and Miner's work on intrusion tolerance for computational systems in air traffic management (Maddalon and Miner 2003).

There has been some progress in considering security requirements within the modernisation programmes mentioned in previous sections. For instance, the FAA's System Wide Information Management programme distinguishes between security mechanisms to be implemented at the application layer and those that are implemented at lower levels within a prototype secure service gateway. These plans will have little impact if existing engineers lack the skills to configure and maintain the new security infrastructures. Today, many Linux installations are not protected by anti-virus programs because technical staff remain unaware of the potential threats. Operational pressures have 'forced' staff to cut corners by instal-ling updates using unverified media. Security patches are not always introduced in a timely manner across the many different systems that support ATM services.

The lack of CyberSecurity competency contrasts with the detailed training re-quirements that have been developed for operational staff, such as air traffic con-trollers (EUROCONTROL 2004). The site visits that motivated this paper re-vealed that none of the engineers in the twelve European countries had any formal training in computational forensics. When malware was detected, it was often through chance rather than the result of coherent security monitoring techniques. For instance, previous attacks have been detected as an indirect consequence of ef-ficiency concerns by ANSP engineers trying to understand where additional CPU cycles were being lost.

3.4 Supporting multi-party exercises and drills

Figure 1 identifies three further requirements in the roadmap for CyberSafety. The first advocates multi-party exercises and drills to assess the potential consequences of a cyber-attack. The Idaho National Laboratory launched a well-publicised at-tack on a SCADA system to show that this could result in physical damage to electricity infrastructures. Questions have since been raised about the veracity of these tests. Other simulated attacks have identified vulnerabilities in the SmartGr-ids proposals for energy distribution in Europe and North America. There have al-so been attempts to rehearse large scale attacks across infrastructures; these are il-lustrated by the US Cyber Storm and CyberEurope exercises. Such initiatives have had little impact on ANSPs; there has been minimal involvement in previous stu-dies.

Significant advances have been made in helping promote cooperation between operational users – for instance through the use of simulation tools and training in the management of critical events. However, these techniques are not used to pre-pare engineers for the demands that are placed on them during cyber-attacks. Very few training exercises or drills have been held so that technical staff can practice their response to malware or an intrusion into the underlying systems and net-works that support air traffic management. It is, therefore, unsurprising that sys-tems engineers often find it difficult to coordinate their response when a threat is discovered.

It is particularly important to rehearse the response to a potential attack because cyber-threats affect many different stakeholders. Engineering teams must integrate their response with the ATCOs and managers who are responsible for maintaining service provision. Additional help may be required from external experts, for example in computational forensics. In some circumstances, the operational consequences of an attack must be communicated to neighbouring states. It is also important to involve a range of national bodies, including regulators as well as police and investigatory agencies. Very few ANSPs have integrated their plans with the support provided by national Computer Emergency Readiness Teams, including US-CERT.

In air traffic management, the sophistication of software infrastructures has stretched the engineering capabilities of most service providers. In consequence, many states rely on external support for the operation of their network infrastructures. This creates a situation in which ANSPs depend upon the security management practices of a small number of contractors. In an ideal situation this might increase resilience by providing a pool of committed engineers with significant expertise in detecting and mitigating threats. In reality, the quality of external personnel and their ability to implement the principles of security management is variable. Sub-contractors often share the lack of interest that many ANSPs show in CyberSecurity until they become victims. In contrast, our roadmap argues for increased investment in multi-party exercises and drills that help develop team resource management skills in response to a range of simulated attacks.

3.5 Sharing lessons learned

Site visits to ECAC ANSPs revealed considerable reluctance to let anyone outside of their own company know that they had been the victims of an attack. In some cases this information was not passed to senior management or to the national regulator. None of the incidents were passed to the European agencies responsible for exchanging 'lessons learned' across member states.

Political, economic and regulatory concerns limit the extent to which security information is passed within industries. This forms a strong contrast with the growing use of reporting sites for the exchange of information about safety concerns and operational problems. In consequence, many companies remain completely ignorant about the attacks the have been suffered by their neighbours and colleagues (DoT 2009).

The need to share lessons from previous attacks is apparent when discussing cyber threats with engineers and senior management across many European states. None of the sites visited in the review phase of this project had read the studies of US security in air traffic management. This had important implications. For example, the DoT 2009 review identified that intrusion detection systems had only been deployed in eleven out of three hundred ATM facilities. If these reports were more widely disseminated then service providers might be encouraged to consider the possible consequences of CyberAttacks on their infrastructures.

3.6 Tools for CyberSafety risk assessment

The final element of the roadmap uses the insights from drills and exercises together with the lessons learned from previous incidents to revise security risk assessments in safety-related applications. This is non-trivial. In previous work we have considered the potential consequences that a CyberAttack might have on service provision (Johnson and Atencia Yepez 2011). This has demonstrated that most of the evidence gathered to support safety cases can be undermined by the detection of malware or unauthorised access. For instance, it can be difficult to guarantee response times given the potential impact on processor and memory resources.

Existing software architectures lack many of the security features being considered, for instance within the FAA's SWIM program. Intrusion detection programmes and access control techniques have been installed in a piecemeal fashion. In consequence, it is very difficult to create convincing arguments that safety can still be maintained once an attack has been detected. Typically, the affected systems are shut down and engineering teams assume that secondary applications are unaffected. This assumption can be difficult to support when common infrastructure components are increasingly being used across multiple redundant systems. In some cases, ECAC states have created secondary systems that rely on identical software to their primary applications. This reduces the costs associated with design diversity and helps to mitigate the risks of introducing errors by trying to maintain two different applications. However, this approach creates enormous concerns when security vulnerabilities are common to primary and secondary systems. Risk assessment tools help to identify the likelihood and consequences of attacks that exploit the vulnerabilities created by common software components.

The final stage in the roadmap communicates the insights from revised risk assessments back to senior management and regulators. The lack of strategic leadership can only be addressed if information is provided to senior management about future forms of attack.

4 Conclusions

Common software components are gradually being integrated across many safety-critical infrastructures. These include network management tools, operating systems such as Linux, Voice Over IP (VOIP) communications techniques, satellite based augmentation systems for navigation/timing data etc. The increasing use of these common components creates concerns that bugs might affect multiple systems across many industries. It also raises significant security concerns. Malware has been detected on a range of safety-related systems in the power distribution, healthcare, military and transport industries (Anderson 2008). Previous attacks have not been targeted on critical applications. However, there is no room for complacency in the face of increasing vulnerability to cyber attacks on safety-related systems. In order to illustrate the vulnerabilities, we have identified security threats to air traffic management infrastructures.

This paper has presented a roadmap for increasing resilience to future CyberSafety attacks. We must raise awareness about the potential threats to safety-related systems amongst regulators and senior management. Without greater strategic leadership there is a danger that ANSPs will continue to respond to security breaches in a piecemeal way that leaves major vulnerabilities in our underlying infrastructures.

A second element of the roadmap focuses on improved screening, competency assessment and training for engineering staff. Most ANSPs continue to ignore the 'insider threat' and lack the expertise either to diagnose or resolve potential attacks. It is for this reason that organizations including the FAA and EUROCONTROL should promote and provide training in anticipation of future incidents.

Other areas for action include the use of drills and exercises to support team resource management in the aftermath of an attack. These exercises can be tailored to scenarios derived from previous incidents; this depends upon initiatives to exchange information about those attacks that have already occurred. At present, there is no forum for lessons of this nature. The final element of the roadmap proposes a new generation of tools that use lessons learned from previous attacks together with the insights from drills and exercises to assess the risks of future cyber attacks. For example, safety cases can be used to map the impact of a potential threat in terms of the arguments that are undermined by an attack (Johnson and Atencia Yepez 2011). Other techniques provide support for more formal reasoning about the safety consequences of malware and intrusions into critical infrastructures (Johnson 2011).

A series of site visits to European ANSPs informed and motivated this work. These revealed the need to provide engineering teams with a forum for sharing common concerns and proposed solutions to CyberSecurity threats. For example, many of the groups stressed the difficulty in distinguishing whether abnormal behaviours are due to a security breach or to everyday bugs. The visits also demonstrated the need for a more systematic overview of the vulnerabilities across member states; the European Commission should replicate the studies prepared by the US GAO and DoT.

We are now beginning to witness the first wave of successful attacks. Viruses are being detected on primary systems in safety-critical applications. There is, therefore, an urgent need to act without any further delay. We also need to think strategically and plan ahead for future threats. Several ANSPs have begun to consider ways in which their operations might exploit cloud-based infrastructures. This opens up powerful and cost-effective tools for operational and engineering staff; it also raises a host of security concerns about the threats to the next generation of safety-critical systems (Mather et al. 2009).

References

Abrams M, Weiss J (2008) Malicious control system cyber security attack case study – Maroochy Water Services, Australia. NIST/Mitre Corporation, NIST Industrial Control System Security Project. http://csrc.nist.gov/sec-cert/ics/index.html. Accessed 14 September 2011

Anderson R (2008) Security engineering: a guide to building dependable distributed systems. Wiley, Indianapolis, USA

DoT (2009) Report on review of web applications security and intrusion detection in air traffic control systems. FAA Report Number FI-2009-049. US Department of Transport, Washington DC, USA

EUROCONTROL (2004) European manual of personnel licensing - air traffic controllers. Edn 2.0. EUROCONTROL, Brussels, Belgium

GAO (1998) Air traffic control: weak computer security practices jeopardize flight safety. Letter Report, 05/18/98, GAO/AIMD-98-155. US General Accounting Office

Haley C, Laney R, Moffett J, Nuseibeh B (2008) Security requirements engineering: a framework for representation and analysis. IEEE Trans Softw Eng 34:133-153

Johnson CW (2011) Using assurance cases and Boolean logic driven Markov processes to formalise cyber security concerns for safety-critical interaction with global navigation satellite systems. In Bowen J, Reeves S (eds) Proc 4th Form Methods for Interact Syst Workshop, Limerick, Ireland

Johnson CW, Atencia Yepez A (2011) Mapping the impact of security threats on safety-critical global navigation satellite systems. In: Proc 29th Int Conf Syst Saf, Las Vegas, USA. International Systems Safety Society, Unionville, VA, USA

Johnson CW, Holloway CM (2011) A roadmap for safer systems engineering. IET Syst Saf Conf, The IET, London

Johnson CW, Shea C, Holloway CM (2008) The role of trust and interaction in GPS related accidents: a human factors safety assessment of the global positioning system (GPS). In: Simmons RJ, Mohan DJ, Mullane M (eds) Proc 26th Int Conf Syst Saf, Vancouver, Canada. International Systems Safety Society, Unionville, VA, USA

Maddalon JM, Miner PS (2003) An architectural concept for intrusion tolerance in air traffic networks. NASA Langley Technical Report, Integrated Communication Navigation and Surveillance (ICNS), Annapolis, Maryland

Mather T, Kumaraswamy S, Latif S (2009) Cloud security and privacy: an enterprise perspective on risks and compliance. O'Reilly Media, California, USA

Pederson P, Dudenhoeffer D, Hartley S, Permann M (2006) Critical infrastructure interdependency modelling: a survey of U.S. and international research. Technical Report INL/EXT-06-11464, Idaho National Laboratory, US Department of Energy

Theoharidoua M, Kokolakisb S, Karydaa M, Kiountouzisa E (2005) The insider threat to information systems and the effectiveness of ISO 17799. Comput & Secur 24:472-484

Including Electromagnetic Interference (EMI) in Functional Safety Risk Assessments

Keith Armstrong

Cherry Clough Consultants Ltd

Stafford, UK

Abstract EMI is a potential cause of malfunctions and failures in all electronic technologies. A safety-related system must therefore take EMI into account in its risk assessment. This paper discusses some of the major issues associated with including EMI in an IEC 61508 functional safety risk assessment.

1 Introduction

EMI is a potential cause of malfunctions and failures in all electronic technologies (Van Doorn 2007). A safety-related system must therefore take EMI into account in its risk assessment.

Applications where (for example) mission or financial risks are critical can be as demanding as safety-related applications, sometimes more so, and so this paper is also relevant for such non-safety-related applications.

Electromagnetic compatibility (EMC) is the scientific and engineering discipline of controlling EMI, and EMC engineers generally believe that their normal EMC tests do a good job of ensuring reliable operation, and indeed they do make it possible to meet normal availability (uptime) requirements in normal electromagnetic environments (EMEs). However, the levels of acceptable risk in safety-related applications require between one and four orders of magnitude greater design confidence.

Functional safety engineers usually leave all considerations of EMI to EMC engineers, or to EMC test laboratories. The result is that most major safety-related projects do little more to attempt to control functional safety risks caused by EMI, than check that the suppliers of the equipment claim compliance with the European EMC Directive (EC 2004). Because this directive has no safety requirements, and its listed EMC immunity tests are not safety tests, functional safety risks due to EMI are completely uncontrolled.

To comply with the basic standard on functional safety, IEC 61508 Edition 2 (IEC 2010a), or product and product family functional safety standards derived from it, it is necessary to demonstrate adequate confidence that safety-related systems will maintain their specified levels of safety risks in their operational EMEs over their lifecycles. This has always been a requirement of IEC 61508, but guidance on it was lacking until the 2010 edition that made compliance with IEC/TS 61000-1-2 Edition 2:2008 (IEC 2008) mandatory.

IEC/TS 61000-1-2 was specifically written to act as 61508's 'missing EMC annex', and requires the use of well-proven design, manufacturing, commissioning, maintenance, upgrade, refurbishment and repair techniques for EMC. It also requires the use of a wide variety of verification and validation techniques, including (but not limited to) EMC testing, to demonstrate the required levels of confidence in all of these issues.

As a necessary starting point for all these EMC activities, IEC/TS 61000-1-2 requires that all reasonably foreseeable EMI over the anticipated lifecycle be taken fully into account in the IEC 61508 risk assessment process. Unfortunately, it does not say how this should be done. Also unfortunately, the established risk assessment methods listed in IEC 61508 are unsuitable for direct application to errors, malfunctions and other types of failures caused by EMI.

Guidance on how to apply the established risk assessment methods to EMI is, however, provided by the IET's Guide on EMC for Functional Safety (IET 2008). This is a practical guide to applying IEC/TS 61000-1-2 and was the subject of a paper by this author (Armstrong 2010a). It goes beyond IEC/TS 61000-1-2 by describing how to take all reasonably foreseeable EMI over the anticipated lifecycle into account when performing a risk assessment for compliance with IEC 61508, or with any other functional safety standards – even those that are not derived from IEC 61508, such as ISO 14971 (ISO 2007).

This paper discusses some of the major issues associated with the topic of including EMI in a functional safety risk assessment under IEC 61508, and is based on the IET Guide and (Armstrong 2010b). The author has also presented papers on assessing lifetime electromagnetic, physical and climatic environments (Armstrong 2005), appropriate EMC design techniques (Armstrong 2006), and verification and validation methods (including testing) (Armstrong 2007a).

Prof. Shuichi Nitta says, 'The development of EMC technology taking account of systems safety is demanded to make social life stable.' (Nitta 2007). The author hopes this paper makes a start on the work needed to achieve this most desirable goal.

2 Cost-effective EMI risk assessments

100% freedom from risk is of course impossible, so instead we are required to ensure that risks are at least 'tolerable' (using the UK HSE's terminology) or 'acceptable' (using terminology typical of the USA). To achieve this we use the safety engineering technique 'Hazard Analysis and Risk Assessment' (sometimes called Hazard Identification and Risk Assessment), which takes the information on a safety-related system's environment, design and application and – in the case of IEC 61508 – creates the Safety Requirements Specification (SRS, or its equivalent in other standards).

Using hazard analysis and risk assessment helps avoid the usual project risks of over- or under-engineering the system.

The amount of effort and cost involved in the risk assessment should be proportional to the benefits required. These include: compliance with legal requirements, benefits to the users and third parties of lower risks (higher risk reductions) and benefits to the manufacturer of lower exposure to product liability claims and loss of market confidence.

Modern control systems can be very complex, and are increasingly 'systems of systems'. If they fail to operate as intended, the resulting poor yields or downtimes can be very costly indeed. Risk assessment – done properly – is a complex exercise performed by competent and experienced engineers.

Assessing the risks of a complex system is a large and costly undertaking, but not usually necessary because the usual approach (e.g. as used in IEC 61508) is to ensure the safety of the overall control system by using a much simpler and separate 'safety-related system', that can be risk-assessed quite easily. Safety-related systems often use 'fail-safe' design techniques – when an unsafe situation is detected, the control system is overridden and the equipment under control brought to a condition that prevents or mitigates the harms that it could cause.

For example, for many types of industrial machinery, the safe condition is one in which all mechanical movement is stopped and hazardous electrical supplies isolated. This safe condition might be triggered, for example, by an interlock with a guard that allows access to hazardous machinery.

This fail-safe approach can prove useless in life-support applications, or anywhere where continuing operation-as-usual is essential, such as 'fly-by-wire' aircraft or life support (e.g. diving rebreathers). However, even in situations where a guard interlock or similar fail-safe techniques cannot be used – and the control system is too complex for a practicable risk assessment – it is still generally possible to improve reliability by means of simple measures that can be cost-effectively risk-assessed.

A typical approach, for example, is to use multiple redundant (Wikipedia 2011a) control systems with a voting system so that the majority vote is used to control the system. Alternatively, control might be switched from a failing control system to another that is not failing (e.g. the Space Shuttle used a voting system based on five computers (IBM 2011)).

Unfortunately, many such legacy systems (for example the electronic throttle control systems still being used on some new models of automobiles) are designed on the assumption that all failures occur at random. Such risk-reduction approaches can be ineffective when dealing with systematic failures (such as software bugs) and/or common-cause failures such as those that can be caused by EMI or other environmental effects.

3 Quantifying EMI risk-reduction

Tables 1 and 2 show a number of safety-related parameters and how they relate to SILs, and were developed from Tables 2 and 3 of Part 1 of IEC 61508.

'Safety-critical' applications (and also applications known as 'high reliability' or 'mission-critical') might need to have a meantime to failure (MTTF) of more than 100,000 years, corresponding to Safety Integrity Level 4 (SIL4) in IEC 61508, see Tables 1 and 2.

Table 1. IEC 61508's SILs for 'on demand' safety functions

Safety Integrity Level (SIL)	Average probability of a dangerous failure of the safety function, on demand or in a year[1]	Equivalent mean time to dangerous failure, in years[1]	Equivalent confidence factor required for each demand on the safety function
4	$\geq 10^{-5}$ to $< 10^{-4}$	$> 10^4$ to $\leq 10^5$	99.99 to 99.999%
3	$\geq 10^{-4}$ to $< 10^{-3}$	$> 10^3$ to $\leq 10^4$	99.9 to 99.99%
2	$\geq 10^{-3}$ to $< 10^{-2}$	$> 10^2$ to $\leq 10^3$	99 to 99.9%
1	$\geq 10^{-2}$ to $< 10^{-1}$	> 10 to $\leq 10^2$	90 to 99%

Examples of safety functions that operate on-demand include the braking system of an automobile, and guard interlocks in industrial plant.

Table 2. IEC 61508'2 SILs for 'continuous' safety functions

Safety Integrity Level (SIL)	Average probability of a dangerous failure of the safety function per hour[1]	Equivalent mean time to dangerous failure, in hours[1]	Equivalent confidence factor required for every 10,000 hours of continuous operation
4	$\geq 10^{-9}$ to $< 10^{-8}$	$> 10^8$ to $\leq 10^9$	99.99 to 99.999%
3	$\geq 10^{-8}$ to $< 10^{-7}$	$> 10^7$ to $\leq 10^8$	99.9 to 99.99%
2	$\geq 10^{-7}$ to $< 10^{-6}$	$> 10^6$ to $\leq 10^7$	99 to 99.9%
1	$\geq 10^{-6}$ to $< 10^{-5}$	$> 10^5$ to $\leq 10^6$	90 to 99%

Examples of safety functions that operate continuously include the speed and/or torque control of automobile and other types of engines, and of the motors in some machines and robots.

Mass-produced safety-related products (e.g. automobiles, domestic appliances) also require very low levels of functional safety risk, because of the very large numbers of people using them on average at any one time.

It is usually very difficult to determine whether a given undesirable incident was caused by EMI, and the resulting lack of incidents officially attributed to EMI has led some people to feel that current EMI testing regimes must therefore be suf-

---

[1] Approximating 1 year = 10,000 hrs of continuous operation. 'Failure' includes any error, malfunction or fault that causes a hazard.

ficient for any application. Indeed, it is commonplace to read perfectly ridiculous words in suppliers' documentation such as '... passes all contractual and regulatory EMC tests and is therefore totally immune to all EMI'.

As Ron Brewer says, "... there is no way by testing to duplicate all the possible combinations of frequencies, amplitudes, modulation waveforms, spatial distributions, and relative timing of the many simultaneous interfering signals that an operating system may encounter. As a result, it's going to fail.' (Brewer 2007)

Prof. Nancy Leveson of MIT says, 'We no longer have the luxury of carefully testing systems and designs to understand all the potential behaviors and risks before commercial or scientific use." (Leveson 2004)

The IET states, 'Computer systems lack continuous behaviour so that, in general, a successful set of tests provides little or no information about how the system would behave in circumstances that differ, even slightly, from the test conditions.' (IET 2009)

Finally, Boyer says: 'Although electronic components must pass a set of EMC tests to (help) ensure safe operations, the evolution of EMC over time is not characterized and cannot be accurately forecast.' (Boyer et al. 2009) This is one of the many reasons why any EMC test plan that has an affordable cost and duration is unlikely to be able to demonstrate confidence in achieving an average probability of failure on demand of better than 90%. Other reasons for this have also been given (Brewer 2007, Armstrong 2004, 2008a, 2009, and section 0.7 of IET 2008).

An average probability of failure on demand of up to 90% (often unofficially called SIL0) is what IEC 61508 says can be achieved by the use of normal good engineering practices.

Because the confidence levels that are needed for functional safety compliance (for example) are a minimum of 90% for SIL1 in IEC 61508, 99% for SIL2, 99.9% for SIL3 and 99.99% for SIL4, it is clear that more work needs to be done to be able to demonstrate compliance with IEC 61508 and similar functional safety standards (e.g. ISO 14971, ISO 26262 (ISO 2009) and others such as IEC 61511 and IEC 62061), as regards the effects of EMI on risks.

As an example, life-supporting medical devices are generally manufactured by major corporations to achieve the equivalent of SIL3 (although of course they use ISO 14971, which does not use the SIL concept of IEC 61508).

So, if we assume that an electronic system has been designed and manufactured fully in accordance with good engineering practices, we can say that the risks caused by EMI over its lifecycle need to be reduced by 10 times for compliance with SIL1, by 10^2 for SIL2, 10^3 for SIL3 and 10^4 for SIL4, over and above the levels of safety risk achieved by passing all of the EMC immunity tests required by the European EMC Directive (EC 2004).

4 Declarations of conformity are not enough

It is tempting to brush over compliance with the European EMC Directive as being a mere starting point for the real work of ensuring that EMI cannot cause excessive safety risks given the SIL applied to the safety-related system in question.

But this would be a mistake akin to neglecting the construction of the foundations of a building, because it is much more interesting and challenging to design and construct the above-ground structures.

On many safety-related projects, all that is done as regards compliance with the European EMC Directive is to collect equipment suppliers' declarations of conformity to the EMC Directive and place them in a project file. But it is important to understand that manufacturers' declarations of conformity have no weight in UK law (Warwicks 2005). It seems likely that other countries' legal systems have reached similar conclusions concerning the likely veracity of suppliers' self-declarations.

That such cynicism is valid, is verified by official data on market surveillance actions performed by authorities in Sweden, Germany, Finland and the UK, which show that percentages of non-conforming products in these countries were 28.5%, 50%, 37.5% and 33% respectively (Hendrikx 2007). Some (but not all) independent third-party EMC assessment organizations provide services that can provide significant help in this vexed area.

Legal 'due diligence' therefore requires safety-related systems project managers and independent safety assessors to determine whether the actual items of equipment used to construct their projects really do comply with the European EMC Directive. This requires the creation of project documents that show that there is sufficient confidence, given the required SIL, that the supplied equipment would pass the immunity tests if tested in the manner in which they are installed.

It is important to be aware that the EMC immunity test standards listed under the European EMC Directive permit temporary errors or malfunctions for transient EMI (what they call 'Performance Criterion B and C'). The safety-related system must be designed to take this into account; alternatively supply could be limited to equipment proven to comply with Performance Criterion A (operation to specification) during the transient tests.

Because the European EMC Directive is not a safety Directive, and its listed EMC immunity test standards are not safety standards, we should perhaps not be unduly surprised to learn that – due to measurement uncertainty and economic considerations that ignore all safety issues – these tests only provide between 50% and 68% confidence that the tested items of equipment actually passed the tests (Armstrong 2009).

EMC test engineers and EMC testing standards committees are also well aware that the actual configuration of power signal, data and control cables can vary equipment immunity levels by ±10dB (i.e. down to 33% or up to 300%), sometimes ±20dB (i.e. down to 10% or up to 1000%) compared with the configuration used during testing. And the effects of component substitutions and hardware and software design modifications since the equipment was tested can also have significant effects on immunity to EMI (Vick and Habiger 1997).

So, it is perfectly clear that simply creating a file of supplier's declarations of conformity is totally inadequate for ensuring that good EMC engineering practices have been observed.

Remember, we are aiming to use good EMC engineering practices to achieve an average probability of failure on demand of 90% due to EMI, which further EMC work can build upon to achieve the SILs required by IEC 61508.

At the time of writing, a generic immunity testing standard on 'EMC for Functional Safety' for equipment used in safety-related systems in industrial applications is being developed by IEC MT15 (IEC 2010b), based upon IEC/TS 61000-1-2 (which is in turn based upon IEC 61508).

Where equipment actually does comply with this forthcoming standard, we should be able to be confident to have reached the 90% point at which further effort can then be applied to achieve SIL1, or above. Remember, ensuring that supplied equipment actually complies with its requirements involves much more than simply filing manufacturer's self-declarations.

The author is actively involved with computer simulation and testing initiatives that are hoped to be able to provide sufficient confidence for at least SIL1, such as the method described in (Grommes and Armstrong 2011).

5 EMI does not cover direct human health risks

Electromagnetic phenomena can affect human health directly, but this issue is not considered in this paper, or in IEC 61508, IEC/TS 61000-1-2 or the IET Guide, which are concerned solely with the effects of electromagnetic phenomena on electrical, electromechanical, electronic and programmable electronic safety-related systems.

6 Risk Assessment and EMI

EMI cannot cause functional safety hazards directly, but it can affect their probability of occurrence, which is why EMI must be taken into account when trying to achieve tolerable risk levels.

There is no requirement for a safety function to employ electronic technologies. In many situations mechanical protection such as bursting discs, blast walls, mechanical stops, etc. and management (such as not allowing people nearby during operation), etc., and combinations of them, can help achieve a safety function's SIL.

The most powerful EMC design technique for achieving a SIL is not to use any electronic or electromechanical technologies in the safety-related system!

7 Lack of evidence does not mean ignoring EMI

Many people, when faced with the information on hazards and risks above, say that because there is no evidence that EMI has contributed to safety incidents, this means that the EMC testing that is done at the moment must be sufficient for safety. However, anyone who uses this argument is either poorly educated in matters of risk and risk reduction, or is hoping that the education of their audience is lacking in that area (Armstrong 2008b).

The assumption that because there is no evidence of a problem, there is no problem, was shown to be logically incorrect in the 19th Century (Anderson 2008), and its use by NASA led directly to the Columbia space shuttle disaster (Petrowski 2006). Felix Redmill says, 'Lack of proof, or evidence, of risk should not be taken to imply the absence of risk.' (Redmill 2009)

EMI problems abound (Armstrong 1007b), but it is unlikely that incidents caused by EMI will be identified as being so caused, because:

- Errors and malfunctions caused by EMI often leave no trace of their occurrence after an incident.
- It is often impossible to recreate the EM disturbance(s) that caused the incident, because the EM environment is not continually measured and recorded.
- Software in modern technologies hides effects of EMI (e.g. EMI merely slows the data rate of Ethernet™, and blanks the picture on digital TV, whereas its effects are obvious in analogue telecommunications and TV broadcasting).
- Few first-responders or accident investigators know much about EMI, much less understand it, and as a result the investigations either overlook EMI possibilities or treat them too simplistically.
- Accident data is not recorded in a way that might indicate EMI as a possible cause.

If a thorough risk assessment shows EMI can cause functional safety hazards to occur, then functional safety hazards due to EMI will occur, whether they are identified as being caused by EMI or not. If the probability of the incidents caused by EMI is higher than tolerable risk levels, their rate should be reduced until they are at least tolerable, a process that IEC 61508 calls risk reduction.

8 Some common mistakes in risk assessment

These typical mistakes are not all directly related to EMI, but if they occur will significantly impair the effectiveness of the risk assessment as regards EMI.

8.1 Hazards can be caused by multiple independent failures

Some industries and some safety practitioners incorrectly assume that only single failures (and their direct consequences) need to be considered in a risk assessment. This is often called 'single-fault safety' and it is based on a faulty premise.

The number of independent malfunctions or failures that must be considered as happening simultaneously depends upon the tolerable level of safety risk (or the degree of risk reduction) and the probabilities of each independent failure occurring.

8.2 Systematic errors, malfunctions or failures are not random

Many errors, malfunctions and other faults in hardware and software are reliably caused by certain EMI, physical or climatic events, or user actions. For example:

- corrosion that degrades a ground bond or a shielding gasket after a time
- an over-voltage surge that sparks across traces on a printed circuit board when condensation is present
- an over-temperature that causes electronic components to fail in a predictable way
- an under-voltage power supply that causes electronic devices to operate outside of their specification
- a software bug that causes erroneous control outputs in response to combinations of perfectly correct inputs
- EMI that replaces, distorts or delays signals in electronic circuits or systems.

These are 'systematic' errors, malfunctions or other types of failure to operate as required. They are not random, and may be considered as being 'designed-in' and so guaranteed to occur whenever a particular situation arises. An example is shown in Figure 1.

Ariane V self-destructed on its first launch (Wikipedia 2011b), and this was found to be caused by a design error that made its explosion inevitable upon launch. The UK Health and Safety Executive found that over 60% of major industrial accidents in the UK were systematic, i.e. were 'designed-in' and so were bound to happen eventually (HSE 2003).

8.3 Errors, malfunctions, etc., can be intermittent or temporary

Many risk assessments assume that errors, malfunctions or other types of failure are permanent, but many can be intermittent or temporary, for example:

- intermittent electrical connections; a very common problem that can sometimes even create false signals that can be mistaken for real ones (e.g. Anderson 2007)
- transient interference (conducted, induced and/or radiated)
- 'sneak' conduction paths caused by condensation, conductive dust, tin whiskers, etc.

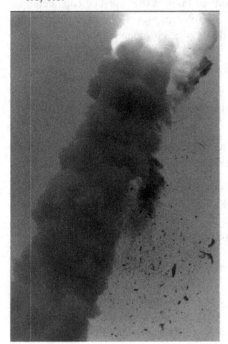

Ariane V

**Self-destructed
37 seconds into launch
June 4, 1996**

Cost $500 million

**A software module from Ariane IV
was re-used on Ariane V.**

**It contained a bug that had not
been a problem for Ariane IV's
higher latitude launch sites,
but triggered the self-destruct
when Ariane V was launched
from a more equatorial site**

Fig. 1. Example of a systematic failure

Sometimes an intermittent or temporary error, malfunction or other type of failure will enable a safety-related system to recover, reducing the risks that would be caused if it were permanent. But sometimes a safety-related system will respond in a worse way, to an intermittent or temporary error, malfunction or other failure. It is almost always the case that discovering why a safety incident has occurred and 'fixing it' is made much more difficult if the cause is intermittent or temporary.

The operation of error detection or correction techniques; microprocessor watchdogs and even manual power cycling can cause what would otherwise have been permanent failures in electronic systems to be merely temporary ones.

Accident analysis has traditionally assumed that the cause of an accident should be able to be found from evidence found during a sufficiently detailed analysis of all of the remains.

But now that safety functions are controlled by fleeting states of electrical activity, lasting perhaps for a microsecond or less, errors, malfunctions and failures leading to accidents may be caused by the perfectly correct (i.e. as designed) operation of electronics that have been momentarily disturbed by a transient EMI event, leaving no evidence in the wreckage.

All that we can do in such situations is a hazard analysis and risk assessment, and try to apportion the likelihood of the many potential causes of the accident, and reduce the risks of those found to greater than considered tolerable. 'Proof' that a given transient electronic event caused the accident will generally never be achievable where electronics are used in safety-related systems.

8.4 'Common-cause' errors, malfunctions and other failures

Two or more identical units exposed to the same conditions at the same time will suffer the same systematic errors, malfunctions, or other types of failure, which are then known as 'common-cause' failures. For example:

- under-temperature, or over-temperature
- under-voltage, or over-voltage electrical power supply
- EMI (conducted, induced, radiated, continuous, transient, etc.)
- condensation, shock, vibration, other ambient environmental conditions
- software bugs
- ageing and corrosion.

Redundancy (Wikipedia 2011a) is a very common method for improving reliability to random errors, malfunctions or other types of failures – but if identical units, hardware or software are used to create the redundant system, and if those multiple redundant 'channels' are exposed to the same environment (power supply, shock, vibration, EMI, etc.) they will suffer from common-cause failures and the redundancy will not reduce risks of systematic failures by as much as expected (possibly not at all).

8.5 Multiple techniques and appropriate expertise are needed

Because tolerable functional safety risk levels are generally quite low, it is usually the case that no one risk assessment technique (e.g. FMEA) will be able to give sufficient 'failure coverage', at least for SILs higher than 1. It is generally recommended by functional safety experts that at least three different types of methods should be applied to the design of a safety-related system:

- at least one 'inductive' or 'bottom-up' method, such as FMEA (IEC 2006a) or event-tree
- at least one 'deductive' or 'top-down' method, such as fault tree assessment (IEC 2006b) or HAZOP

- at least one 'brainstorming' method, such as DELPHI or SWIFT.

Doing risk assessment properly requires experience and expertise. It should never be a 'box ticking exercise' and should never be a job that is given to junior personnel, or personnel of any seniority who have insufficient expertise in the issues concerned, which in this case includes EMI.

It is important to use a modern, 'open' method to identify possible hazards, but a safety study should consider hazards identified by any means: previous incidents; checklists; design reviews; task analysis; etc. Whatever techniques are used, good hazard identification depends on experience and imagination. Unfortunately, many manufacturers apply hazard analysis and risk assessment methods in a 'rote' or mechanical way, just to put a tick in a management procedure box, a practice that functional safety experts warn against (Hollnagel 2008, Kelly 2008).

No risk assessment methods have yet been developed to cover EMI issues, so it is necessary to choose the methods to use and adapt them to deal with EMI. Successful adaptation will require competency, skills and expertise in both functional safety engineering and real-life EMI (not just EMC testing) – a combination that at the time of writing is in rather short supply (Armstrong 2011).

8.6 Electronic devices can suffer a range of simultaneous errors

EMI can cause one or more pins on a semiconductor device, such as an integrated circuit (IC), to take on erroneous signal states that lie anywhere within their normal range (possibly sometimes beyond it), simultaneously.

An extreme example is 'latch-up' – when all of the output pins of an IC simultaneously assume uncontrolled fixed states. This is caused by high temperatures, ionizing radiation and over-voltage or over-current on any pin of an IC. The presence of any one of the three causes increases an IC's susceptibility to latch-up due to the other two. Latch-up can only be recovered from by switching the IC's power off, waiting for it to cool down sufficiently, then switching it back on again. Modern ICs tend to be powered by power regulators that limit fault current and protect devices from actual thermal damage during latch-up, so once the power has been cycled no 'evidence' of the latch-up remains.

However, traditional risk assessment methods (e.g. FMEA) have often been applied very simplistically to electronics. For example the author has several examples of so-called risk assessments of safety-related engine control systems conducted by a major international manufacturer, that only used the FMEA technique, and simply went through all of the ICs one pin at a time and assessed whether a safety problem would be caused if each pin was permanently stuck high or low – an approach that fails to be comprehensive in several of the ways discussed in this paper.

8.7 Risk assessment must include reasonably foreseeable misuse

Operators will not always follow the Operator's Manual, and it should never be assumed that they will not do something that is considered 'too stupid'. Even very clever and well-educated people can be expected to make 'human errors'.

Assessing reasonably foreseeable use or misuse requires the use of 'brainstorming' techniques by experienced personnel, and can achieve better 'failure coverage' by including operators, maintenance technicians, field service engineers, etc., in the exercise.

As the author found during a recent brief stay in hospital, sometimes safety-related equipment is operated by people who are not its trained operators. So risk assessment should also take into account the possibilities for use/misuse by untrained personnel.

9 The two stages of risk assessment

When creating the SRS (or equivalent) the system has (of course) not yet been designed, so detailed risk assessment methods such as FMEA, FMECA, etc., cannot be applied. At this early stage only an 'initial risk assessment' is possible, but there are many suitable methods that can be used, and many of them are listed in section 3.7 of the IET Guide. Some of the risk management tools listed by (Wikipedia 2011c) may also be useful at this stage.

During the design, development, realization and verification phases of the project, detailed information becomes available on all of the mechanics, hardware and software. Appropriate risk assessment methods (such as FMEA and fault tree) are applied to this design information – as it becomes available – to guide the project in real-time, to achieve the overall goals of the initial risk assessment.

As the project progresses the initial risk assessment accumulates more depth of assessment, eventually – at the end of the project – producing the 'final risk assessment', a very important part of a project's safety documentation. But this can only be completed when the project has been fully completed, so its real engineering value lies in the process of developing it during the project, to achieve the acceptable risk levels (or risk reductions) whilst also saving cost and time (or at least not adding significantly to them).

10 Incorporating EMI in risk assessments

The reasonably foreseeable lifecycle EME is an important input to an EMI risk assessment process, because it directly affects the probability of a hazard occurring. Because exposure to other environmental effects like shock, vibration, humidity, temperature, salt spray, etc. can degrade the electromagnetic immunity characteristics of equipment, as can faults, user actions, wear and misuse, their reasonably foreseeable lifecycle assessments are also important inputs to an EMI risk assessment.

Many foreseeable environmental effects can occur simultaneously, for example:

- two or more strong radio-frequency (RF) fields (especially near two or more cellphones or walkie-talkies, or near a base-station or broadcast transmitter)
- one or more radiated RF fields plus distortion of the mains power supply waveform
- one or more radiated RF fields plus an ESD event
- a power supply over-voltage transient plus conductive condensation
- one or more strong RF fields plus corrosion or wear that degrades enclosure shielding effectiveness
- one or more strong RF fields plus a shielding panel left open by the user
- conducted RF on the power supply plus a high-impedance ground connection on the supply filter due to loosening of the fasteners that provide the bonding connection to the ground plane due to vibration, corrosion, etc.
- power supply RF or transients plus filter capacitors that have, over time, been open-circuited by over voltages, and/or storage or bulk decoupling capacitors that have lost much of their electrolyte due to time and temperature.

Hundreds more examples could easily be given, and all such reasonably foreseeable events and combinations of them must be considered by the risk assessment.

Intermittent contacts, open or short circuits, can cause spurious signals just like some kinds of EMI, and are significantly affected by the physical/climatic environment over the lifetime. One example of this kind of effect is contact resistance modulated by vibration. This effect is called 'vibration-induced EMI' by some.

EMI and intermittent contacts can – through direct interference, demodulation and/or intermodulation (Armstrong 2008a) – cause 'noise' to appear in any conductors that are inadequately protected against EMI (perhaps because of a dry joint in a filter capacitor). 'Noise' can consist of degraded, distorted, delayed or false signals or data, and/or damaging voltage or current waveforms.

When a 'top down' risk assessment method is used, it should take into account that significant levels of such noise can appear at any or all signal, control, data, power or ground ports of any or all electronic units – unless the ports are adequately protected against foreseeable EMI for the entire lifetime taking into account foreseeable faults, misuse, shock, vibration, wear, etc., etc. (For radiated EMI, the unit's enclosure is considered a port.)

The noises appearing at different ports and/or different units could be identical or different, and could occur simultaneously or in some time-relationship to one another.

When a 'bottom-up' risk assessment method is used, the same noise considerations as above apply but in this it can appear at any or all pins of any or all electronic devices on any or all printed circuit boards (PCBs) in any or all electronic units – unless the units are adequately protected against all EMI over the entire lifetime taking into account foreseeable faults, misuse, etc., as before.

Similarly, the noises appearing at different pins or different devices, PCBs or units could be identical or different, and could occur simultaneously or in some time relationship.

It is often quite tricky to deal with all possibilities for EMI, physical, climatic, intermittency, use, misuse, etc., which is why competent 'EMC-safety' expertise should always be engaged on risk assessments, to help ensure all reasonably foreseeable possibilities have been thoroughly investigated.

If the above sounds an impossibly large task, the good news is that one does not have to wade through all of the possible combinations of EMI and environmental effects, faults, misuse, etc. – there are design approaches that will deal with entire classes of EMI consequences – and risk assessment techniques are used to determine if they are (a) needed, and (b) effective.

For example, at one design extreme there is the 'EMI shelter' approach.

The electronic systems to be protected are placed inside one or more very sturdy shielded, filtered and surge-protected metal enclosures with dedicated uninterruptible power supplies and battery backup, often using fiber-optic datacommunications. The shelter is designed and verified as protecting whatever electronic equipment is placed within it from the EME for its entire life, up to and including a specified number of direct lightning strikes and nuclear electromagnetic pulses.

Such shelters can also be provided with protection against non-electromagnetic environmental effects, such as shock and vibration up to earthquake levels; humidity, condensation, rain, spray and flooding up to full immersion; and even the thermal and radiation effects of nearby nuclear explosions, if required. Several companies have manufactured such shelters for many years.

Nothing special needs to be done to the safety systems placed inside them. Of course, IEC 61508 (or whatever other functional safety standard applies) will have many requirements for the safety system, but EMI can be completely taken care of by an EMI shelter. Validation of the finished assembly could merely consist of checking that the shelter manufacturer's installation rules have been followed. Door interlocks connected to fail-safe trips, and periodic proof testing, can be used to ensure that the EMI shelter maintains the desired levels of protection for the required number of decades.

At the other design extreme is the 'signal integrity' approach.

It is possible to design digital hardware to use data with embedded protocols that detect any/all possible effects of EMI, however caused. When interference is detected, the error is either corrected or a fail-safe is triggered. Designing analogue hardware, sensors and transducers to detect any interference in their signals is not as immediately obvious as it is for digital data, but can usually be done.

Safety-related systems have been built that used this technique alone and ignored all immunity to EMI, but when installed they triggered their fail-safes so often that they could not be used. So, some immunity to EMI is necessary for adequate availability of whatever it is that the safety-related system is protecting.

Because passing the usual EMC immunity tests required by the European EMC Directive often seems to be sufficient for an acceptable uptime percentage, this may be all that needs to be done in addition to the signal integrity design.

11 Conclusions

Any practicable EMC testing regime can only take us part of the way towards achieving the reliability levels required by the SILs in IEC 61508 (or similar low levels of financial or mission risk).

Risk assessment is a vital technique for controlling and assessing EMC design engineering, but because no established risk assessment techniques have yet been written to take EMI into account, it is necessary for experienced and skilled engineers to adapt them for that purpose.

I hope that others will fully develop this new area of 'EMI risk assessment' in the coming years.

References

Anderson AF (2007) Reliability in electromagnetic systems: the role of electrical contact resistance in maintaining automobile speed control system integrity. IET Colloq Reliab Electromagn Syst, Paris

Anderson AF (2008) Presentation to the 20th Conference of the Society of Expert Witnesses, Alexander House, Wroughton, UK

Armstrong K (2004) Why EMC immunity testing is inadequate for functional safety. IEEE Int EMC Symp, Santa Clara

Armstrong K (2005) Specifying lifetime electromagnetic and physical environments – to help design and test for EMC for functional safety. IEEE Int EMC Symp, Chicago

Armstrong K (2006) Design and mitigation techniques for EMC for functional safety. IEEE Int EMC Symp, Portland

Armstrong K (2007a) Validation, verification and immunity testing techniques for EMC for functional safety. IEEE Int EMC Symp, Honolulu

Armstrong K (ed) (2007b) The First 500 Banana Skins. Nutwood UK. www.theemcjournal.com. Accessed 19 September 2011

Armstrong K (2008a) EMC for the functional safety of automobiles – why EMC testing is insufficient, and what is necessary. IEEE Int EMC Symp, Detroit

Armstrong K (2008b) Absence of proof is not proof of absence. The EMC Journal, Issue 78:16-19

Armstrong K (2009) Why increasing immunity test levels is not sufficient for high-reliability and critical equipment. IEEE Int EMC Symp, Austin, TX

Armstrong K (2010a) The new IET guide – how to do emc to help achieve functional safety. In: Dale C, Anderson T (eds) Making systems safer. Springer, London

Armstrong K (2010) Including EMC in risk assessments. IEEE Int EMC Symp, Fort Lauderdale, Florida

Armstrong K (2011) Opportunities in the risk management of EMC. IEEE Int Symp EMC, Long Beach, California

Boyer A, Ndoye AC, Ben Dhia S, Guillot L, Vrignon B (2009) Characterization of the evolution of IC emissions after accelerated aging. IEEE Trans EMC 51:892-900

Brewer R (2007) EMC failures happen. Evaluation Engineering magazine. http://www. evaluationengineering.com/index.php/solutions/emcesd/emc-failures-happen.html. Accessed 27 September 2011

EC (2004) The EU's Directive on electromagnetic compatibility. 2004/108/EC. http://eur-lex.europa.eu/LexUriServ/site/en/oj/2004/l_390/l_39020041231en00240037.pdf. Accessed 16 September 2011

Grommes W, Armstrong K (2011) Developing immunity testing to cover intermodulation. IEEE Int Symp EMC, Long Beach, California

Hendrikx I (2007) The future of market surveillance for technical products in Europe. Conformity magazine. http://www.conformity.com/artman/publish/printer_158.shtml. Accessed 16 September 2011

Hollnagel E (2008) The reality of risks. Safety Critical Systems Club Newsletter 17(2)20-22. http://www.scsc.org.uk/newsletter_17_2_h.htm?pid=103&pap=748&m1=Newsletters&m2= &sort=p1d. Accessed 19 September 2011

HSE (2003), Out of control – why control systems go wrong and how to prevent failure. UK Health and Safety Executive. www.hse.gov.uk/pubns/priced/hsg238.pdf. Accessed 19 September 2011

IBM (2011) IBM and the Space Shuttle. www-03.ibm.com/ibm/history/exhibits/space/space_ shuttle.html. Accessed 16 September 2011

IEC (2006a) Assessment techniques for system reliability – procedure for failure mode and effects assessment (FMEA). IEC 60812. International Electrotechnical Commission

IEC (2006b) Fault tree assessment (FTA). IEC 61025. International Electrotechnical Commission

IEC (2008) Electromagnetic Compatibility (EMC) – Part 1-2: General – Methodology for the achievement of the functional safety of electrical and electronic equipment with regard to electromagnetic phenomena. IEC/TS 61000-1-2 Ed.2.0

IEC (2010a) Functional safety of electrical/electronic/programmable electronic safety related systems. IEC 61508, edn 2.

IEC (2010b) Electromagnetic Compatibility (EMC) – Part 6-7: Generic standards – Immunity requirements for safety-related systems and equipment intended to perform functions in a safety-related system (functional safety) in industrial environments. IEC 61000-6-7 Committee Draft 77/389/CD, date of circulation 2010-11-19

IET (2008) EMC for Functional Safety, edn 1. www.theiet.org/factfiles/emc/emc-factfile.cfm. Accessed 16 September 2011

IET (2009) Computer based safety-critical systems. www.theiet.org/factfiles/it/computer-based-scs.cfm?type=pdf. Accessed 16 September 2011

ISO (2007) Medical devices – application of risk management to medical devices. ISO 14971 edn 2

ISO (2009) Road vehicles – Functional safety. ISO 26262 (draft)

Kelly T (2008) Are 'safety cases' working? Safety-Critical Systems Club Newsletter 17(2)31-33. http://www.scsc.org.uk/newsletter_17_2_l.htm?pid=103&pap=752&m1=Newsletters&m2=& sort=p1d. Accessed 19 September 2011

Leveson, N (2004) A new accident model for engineering safer systems. Saf Sci 42:237-270. http://sunnyday.mit.edu/accidents/safetyscience-single.pdf. Accessed 16 September 2011

Nitta S (2007) A proposal on future research subjects on EMC, from the viewpoint of systems design. IEEE EMC Society Newsletter, Issue 214:50-57.

Petrowski H (2006) When failure strikes. New Scientist. www.newscientist.com/channel/ opinion/mg19125625.600-the-success-that-allows-failure-to-strike.html. Accessed 16 September 2011

Redmill F (2009) Making ALARP decisions. Safety-Critical Systems Club Newsletter 19(1)14-21. http://www.scsc.org.uk/newsletter_19_1_d.htm?pid=110&pap=819&m1=Newsletter s&m2=&sort=p1d. Accessed 16 September 2011

Van Doorn M (2007) Towards an EMC technology roadmap. EMC Directory & Design Guide. Interference Technology. http://www.interferencetechnology.com/no_cache/technologies/testing/articles/features-single/article/towards-an-emc-technology-roadmap.html.   Accessed 16 September 2011

Vick R, Habiger E (1997) The dependence of the immunity of digital equipment on the hardware and software structure. Proc Int Symp EMC, Beijing

Warwicks (2005) Ensuring compliance with trading standards law. Warwickshire County Council. www.warwickshire.gov.uk/corporate/SmallBus.nsf/WebPrint/A0379B1341F8AD58 8025701300566FD2?opendocument. Accessed 16 September 2011. Geoffrey Garret v Boots Chemist Ltd (1980) is the most relevant case in the context of this paper.

Wikipedia (2011a) Redundancy (engineering). http://en.wikipedia.org/wiki/Redundancy_(engineering). Accessed 16 September 2011

Wikipedia (2011b) Ariane V. http://en.wikipedia.org/wiki/Ariane_5. Accessed 19 September 2011

Wikipedia (2011c) Risk management tools. http://en.wikipedia.org/wiki/Risk_management_tools Accessed 19 September 2011

Safety Engineering – a Perspective on Systems Engineering

Derek Fowler and Ronald Pierce

JDF Consultancy LLP

Chichester, UK

Abstract The thesis of the paper is that safety engineering should be not be considered to be 'special and different' but rather should be seen as a specific viewpoint on the more general practice of systems engineering, albeit with the appropriate degree of rigour applied to the processes involved. In recent correspondence with the authors, Dr Nancy Leveson of MIT expressed the opinion, based on her own experience, that:

> 'until recently, system safety was always part of the system engineering group. Over time and with ignorance, this interaction has faded.'

The paper uses empirical and analytical evidence to show that common practice – encouraged by process and regulatory standards in some industry sectors – has led to system safety assessments that are based on far too narrow a view that safety is fundamentally about system reliability. The paper shows that good systems engineering practice can help overcome the major deficiencies and provide a much better basis for safety engineering in the future.

1 Introduction

Safety is a viewpoint. By this is meant that safety is not in itself an attribute of a system but is a property that depends on other attributes *and* on the context in which the system is used. The question that the paper attempts to answer in some detail is *which* attributes of a system[1] determine whether it is safe or not, in its context of use.

The paper is derived from (Fowler and Pierce 2011); however, whereas the latter work was addressed to system engineers, this paper is intended to present a complementary perspective for safety engineers. It does not deal with the detail of

---

[1] Throughout the paper, the term system is used in the widest sense – i.e. it includes not just the technical elements (equipment) but also all other elements – e.g. the human operator and operational procedures – that necessarily make up the complete, end-to-end system.

safety cases or safety management systems, except to show how a simple requirements engineering model can also lead us to a sound safety argument, which drives the processes of *a priori* system safety assessment; the main focus of the paper is on the processes themselves, on which functional safety heavily depends.

The paper starts by addressing what seems to be a frequent misconception that safety is mainly dependent on reliability (and/or integrity, depending on one's definition of the terms); this leads to the conclusion that what is required is a broader view of system safety than is sometimes taken.

Then various safety standards and practices are reviewed to see the degree to which they help dispel, or in fact contribute to, the 'safety is reliability' myth.

Then, and for the most part, the paper explains how the broader approach to safety should work and shows that it is a part of (*not* 'special and different' from) systems engineering in general.

2 'Safety is reliability' – dispelling a myth

More than ten years ago, Dr Nancy Leveson, in a review of major software-related accidents and the implication for software reliability, presented compelling evidence that software reliability had never been the cause of such disasters – on the contrary, in every case investigated, the software had performed in exactly the manner that it was designed to (Leveson 2001). The problem was that the software was designed to do the wrong thing for the circumstances under which it 'failed' (or, as in the case of Ariane V, for example) was used for a purpose (i.e. in a context) different from that for which it was originally designed. Dr Leveson quite rightly, therefore, posed the question as to why, in most software safety standards, so much emphasis is placed on processes to improve software reliability whilst not ensuring also that the resulting systems actually perform the intended function – i.e. allowing them to be what one might call 'reliably unsafe'.

Of course that work is not suggesting that software reliability might not be a problem itself; rather that the empirical results are dominated by problems in what has been given little attention – i.e. functional correctness. We can illustrate the overall problem analytically by considering the simple, everyday example of a car airbag for which, for the sake of this discussion, we wish to make a safety case.

If we were to simply follow a *failure-based* process – i.e. focus on what could go wrong with the airbag – we would start (at the *wrong* point, as we will see shortly) by identifying the hazards presented by the airbag. Such hazards are those caused by the airbag's two main failure modes – i.e. failure to operate when required, and operating when not required. We would then use some method (for example a risk classification scheme) to derive safety requirements that specify the maximum frequency with which those failures could be allowed to occur and from that we would deduce more detailed safety requirements which limit the frequency with which the *causes* of the hazards could be allowed to occur.

However, even if the results were valid, they would lead us only to:

- an understanding of how reliable the airbag needs to be, so that it operates when required; this would *not* give any assurance that, when it did operate, the airbag would actually protect the front-seat occupants from death or serious injury in the event of a collision, and
- the totally *irrational* conclusion that putting an airbag in a car would only increase the risk of death or serious injury to the front-seat occupants, because of the finite (albeit small) possibility that it would operate when not intended to!

Thus by considering *only* the failure modes of the airbag, what we have missed is any evidence of the airbag's *positive* safety contribution – without which we would have no case for fitting one.

If instead we were to take a more *rational* view, we would start from the position that in the event of, say, a head-on collision *without* an airbag there is a very high risk of death or serious injury to the driver (and other front-seat occupant(s)) of a car. This risk – shown as R_U on the risk graph in Figure 1 – is called 'pre-existing' because, by definition, it is inherent in driving and has nothing whatsoever to do with the airbag – indeed it is to mitigate this risk that we are intending to fit the airbag in the first place.

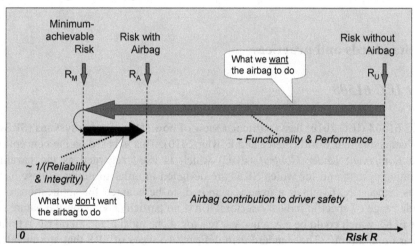

Fig. 1. Risk graph for a car airbag

On Figure 1, it can be seen that:

- R_M is defined as the theoretical minimum risk that would exist in the complete absence of failure or spurious operation of the airbag – it is *not* zero, because there are some accident scenarios for which an airbag might not provide mitigation (e.g. fire, or being hit from behind by a vehicle with high relative speed).
- Since R_M is the risk *in the absence of failure*, it is determined only by the *functionality and performance* of the airbag – i.e. what the airbag does, and how well it does it.

- The risk increase $R_A - R_M$ is *caused entirely by failure* or spurious operation of the airbag – thus it is called the *system-generated* risk and is determined primarily[2] by the *reliability and integrity* of the airbag.
- The safety case for the airbag depends on its making a significantly bigger positive contribution to safety when operating as intended (i.e. what we call the 'success case' as represented by the right-to-left arrow) than any negative contribution caused by its failure or incorrect/spurious operation (i.e. the 'failure case' as represented by the solid left-to-right arrow) – i.e. that $R_A \ll R_U$.

Thus, given the correct set of functional properties – e.g. shape, location, strength, compressibility, sensitivity to 'g' forces, speed of deployment – as well as adequate reliability and integrity, our safety case should show that the airbag would make a substantial, positive *net* contribution to the safety of the front occupants of the car in the event of, at least, a head-on, or near head-on, collision. This would be a much *more balanced, reasoned and rational conclusion* than what emerged above from considering only airbag failure.

The next section looks at a range of standards and practices to assess the degree and extent to which they support this broader, more rational, approach.

3 Standards and practices

3.1 IEC 61508

IEC 61508 (IEC 2010) has a particular view of how safety-related systems (SRSs) influence the real world (Pierce and Fowler 2010). This is based on the concept of the *Equipment Under Control* (EUC) which is itself regarded as the hazard-creating system and for which SRSs are designed in order to mitigate these hazards. Since IEC 61508 is a generic standard, to be adapted for application to a wide range of specific industry sectors, it has no particular view on the nature of the EUC, which could be e.g. a nuclear reactor, a chemical plant, an oil rig, a train, a car or an aircraft. The standard then defines two types of SRS that are intended to mitigate the hazards and risks associated with the EUC:

Control systems. These provide safety functions that are designed to maintain *continuously* a tolerable level of risk for the EUC (e.g. a railway signalling system).

Protection systems. These provide safety functions that are designed to intervene, *on demand*, when they detect a hazardous state developing within the EUC and/or

---

[2] The word 'primarily' is used here because (as is more generally the case) it is may be possible to provide additional functionality to mitigate some of the causes and/or consequences of system-generated hazards.

its control system(s), and put the EUC and/or its control system(s) into a safe, or at least safer, state (e.g. our car airbag).

The objectives of control and protection systems are *risk control* and *risk reduction* respectively and they are put in place to reduce the pre-existing risks (i.e. from the EUC) to an acceptable level. IEC 61508 refers to this as *Necessary Risk Reduction* – i.e. $R_U - R_T$ on Figure 1 – but does not actually stipulate what is 'acceptable', this being left to local or national considerations, including legal frameworks, for the applicable industry sector.

Safety integrity requirements on control systems are usually expressed as probability of failure per operating hour, whereas for protection systems they are usually expressed as probability of failure on demand. In either case, the target probability will (or *should*) depend on the level of the pre-existing risk and the effectiveness of the safety functions in reducing it.

In both cases, IEC 61508 is quite clear that the safety functional requirements (specifying functionality and performance of the safety functions) must be completely and correctly identified before the SRS can be designed. This requires hazard and risk analysis of the EUC *not* (initially) hazard and risk analysis of the SRS(s) themselves. Once the safety functional and performance requirements of the safety functions have been identified, the tolerable failure rates of the safety functions can *then* be identified, and the Safety Integrity Level (SIL) for each safety function is established. This is reinforced by the more generalised form of a Risk Graph, as shown in Figure 2.

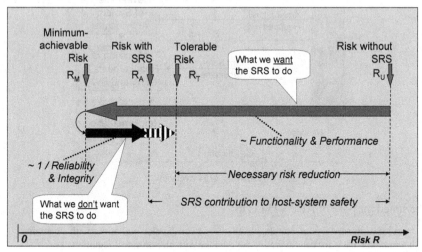

Fig. 2. Generalised risk graph

From Figure 2 it can be seen that if we introduce R_T, the maximum *tolerable* level of risk, and given that R_T is fixed (e.g. by a regulatory body), then the maximum tolerable failure rate of the airbag – i.e. a function of the length of the extended left-to-right arrow $(R_T - R_M)$ – depends on the length of the right-to-left arrow

$(R_U - R_M)$; in other words, the *tolerable failure* rate depends on how *successful* the SRS is in reducing the pre-existing risk in the first place[3].

Thus it is concluded that IEC 61508, with its concept of specifying safety functions for (pre-existing) risk control or reduction, fully supports the broader, more rational approach described in Section 2 above.

We next consider the extent to which this is reflected in the safety-assessment practices of international commercial aviation, European air traffic management and the UK railway industry.

3.2 Safety assessment in commercial aviation

In commercial aviation there is a well-established aircraft-certification procedure – ARP 4754 (SAE 1996a) – as outlined in Figure 3.

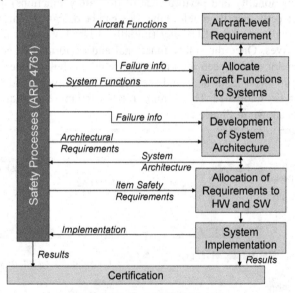

Fig. 3. ARP 4754 overview

The stated purpose of ARP 4754 is to:

'provide designers, manufacturers, installers, and certification authorities with a common international basis for demonstrating compliance with airworthiness requirements applicable to highly-integrated or complex systems.'

---

[3] Furthermore, although not strictly within the scope of this paper, it can be seen that in the limit R_M approaches R_T, so the integrity required of the SRS approaches infinity! This raises important questions regarding the origins and use of traditional risk-classification schemes, which are often based only on R_T and do not take any account of R_M in setting tolerable system failure rates!

The main aircraft systems-development process, outlined on the right-hand side of Figure 3, is very detailed and provides links to the supporting safety assessment process shown to the left. The detailed requirements for the safety assessment are expanded in a separate document – ARP 4761 (SAE 1996b) – and the results of applying both processes concurrently are included in the aircraft-certification application.

The key to the processes of both ARP 4754 and 4761 lies in the 'aircraft functions', which result from analysis of the needs of the aircraft as a whole and which include, for example, automatic flight control, engine control, collision avoidance, communications and navigation. ARP 4754 then follows a fairly typical system-development and implementation lifecycle, leading eventually into production.

The safety assessment process of ARP 4761 starts with the aircraft functions as its main input. It is concerned *not* with what the aircraft functions do, *nor* with whether they are adequate (both of these considerations are covered by ARP 4754 itself), but *only with the possible consequences and causes of failure* of those functions, and of the underlying systems which provide them.

This is followed by progressively more detailed levels of safety assessment linked to the corresponding stages of the ARP 4754 development lifecycle. At all stages in the system development, information about the functions/systems is fed into the safety assessment, for analysis of potential failures, and additional design requirements (i.e. safety requirements) are fed back for incorporation into the system development.

In the context of this paper, what is important about the ARP 4754 and 4761 standards is that between them they address both the success (what has to be achieved and how well) and failure (what can go wrong) of the aircraft functions.

Unfortunately, ARP 4754 and ARP 4761 apply to the aircraft as a vehicle but *not* to the flight crew operating it, the latter being the subject of a *separate*, subsequent operational approval. Herein lies a potential problem, as illustrated by an accident involving what are known generically as Airborne Collision Avoidance Systems (ACAS II).

In the early hours of 2 July 2002 two commercial aircraft, flying at an altitude of about 36,000 ft, collided near the town of Überlingen in southern Germany. Needless to say all on board – mainly children – died. If we focus on the period immediately prior to the collision, rather than on the precursors that led to the two aircraft being far too close to each other in the first place, then we find (BFS 2004) that the ACAS II equipment behaved as designed – i.e. it instructed the crew of one aircraft to climb and the other to descend. What finally led to the accident was 'dysfunctionality' within, and between, the *non*-equipment elements of the end-to-end system, which included the actions of the flight crew of the two aircraft, the air traffic controller, and their respective operational procedures and practices (both national and international) – briefly, the controller issued a contradictory instruction to the aircraft that had been advised by ACAS II to climb and the flight crew chose to comply with the former, rather than the latter, causing the two aircraft to descend into each other.

With the increasing complexity of aircraft, together with the planned much greater integration and interaction with the air traffic management system (see below), the continued separation of aircraft certification and operational-approval processes will become even less appropriate than is already the case for ACAS II.

3.3 Safety assessment in European air traffic management

The EUROCONTROL safety assessment methodology (SAM) was developed over a period of about 12 years from the late 1990s. From the outset, it was decided to base the SAM on well-established, aircraft safety procedure ARP 4761 (see above), albeit with adaptations to suit the perceived needs of ATM at the time. Unfortunately, in adapting ARP 4761 for ATM safety assessments, it would seem that the SAM developers either missed the point that there was no equivalent to the more general, systems-engineering aspects of ARP 4754 in ATM, or felt that such an equivalent was not necessary. Consequently, what was put in place for ATM was a safety assessment process, which:

- was largely restricted to technical systems that, in ATM, are not well-bounded because of the predominance of the 'human-in-the-loop', and
- was concerned only with failure of the system and not with what the system was required to do in the first place (i.e. its functionality and performance) since the latter was determined almost entirely by the capabilities of the human operators (the air traffic controller and flight crew).

The latter position would be understandable since *at that time* (late 1990s) the main 'functionality' of ATM was vested in the controller and had evolved in that way over many years. The problem is that this is no longer the case, leaving the failure-based, equipment-focused SAM incapable of meeting all of the current and future needs of ATM system safety assessment. The problem was compounded by the fact that the corresponding safety regulations were based on the SAM (see the document change history in EUROCONTROL 2001) and therefore suffered from the same deficiency.

As a result, the new Europe-wide, major ATM-development programme (known as SESAR) has recognised that a new regulatory approach (still awaited) will be required and has developed, in conjunction with EUROCONTROL, a broader (i.e. success and failure) approach to safety assessment.

3.4 Safety assessment in the UK rail industry

Guidance on safety management in the UK rail industry is contained in the 'Yellow Book' (RSSB 2007). At first sight, it appears that the standard deals only with negative contributions to safety – i.e. by seeking to limit what above we called *system-generated* risk. Indeed, Chapter 15 states:

> 'Your organisation must make a systematic and vigorous attempt to identify all possible hazards related to its activities and responsibilities…you should make sure that you understand how you might contribute to the hazard when carrying out your activities and responsibilities.'

This is borne out by the example hazards in Table D-3 in Section D.2.3 of Appendix D, all of which are system-generated (e.g. 'failure of level crossing to protect public from train' [4]). There is an allusion to pre-existing risk in Section 15.1.2 which states:

> 'Some things are done specifically to make the railway safer, that is to reduce overall railway risk, at least in the long run. You should still assess them in case they introduce other risks that need to be controlled.'

However, it seems from the wording that the motivation for addressing such issues still seems to be the same, i.e. to limit system-generated risk. So how are the safety functions of IEC 61508 identified in the railway network and how is pre-existing risk addressed? A clue lies in Section 15.2.1, as follows:

> 'The project guidance in this chapter is designed for a situation where risk cannot be controlled completely by applying standards. If the risk comes completely within accepted standards that define agreed ways of controlling it, then you may be able to control the risk and show that you have done so without carrying out all of the activities described in this chapter.'

So it seems that the success case, and where possible the failure case also, is normally demonstrated (implicitly at least) through the application of technical standards – indeed the following extract from the foreword to issue 4 of the Yellow Book reflects a trend towards the latter:

> 'we have also tried to serve better those railway professionals whose work affects safety but who control risk through the disciplined and skilful application of standards, procedures and assessments. This reflects in part a shift from absolute reliance on risk assessment to an increasing reliance on developing and using improved standards and procedures…'

Of course, where things are well proven and repeatable the use of technical standards makes complete sense. However, we leave this discussion with the rhetorical question as to how the railways deal with innovation from a safety perspective, and return to it in Section 6.1 below.

---

[4] Compare this with the example *pre-existing* hazard in section 6.1.2 below.

4 Requirements engineering – the key to safety assessment

Capturing, and then satisfying, a complete and correct set of safety requirements is as fundamental to any *a priori* safety assessment as requirements capture and satisfaction are to systems engineering in general, as explained below.

4.1 Requirements capture

Some crucial issues regarding requirements capture can be expressed through the simple, but rigorous, requirements-engineering model shown in Figure 4. This model has been adapted from (Jackson 1995), in the introduction to which Dr Jackson sums up the requirements-capture problem perfectly, as follows:

> 'We are concerned both with the world, *in which the machine serves a useful purpose,*
> and with the machine itself. The competing demands and attractions of these two concerns
> must be appropriately balanced. *Failure to balance them harms our work.*'

In this context, what has been said above about the lack of a success approach in safety assessments is an example of a preoccupation with the machine itself at the expense of considering its 'useful purpose' – i.e. to reduce pre-existing risk. Figure 4 may help clear our thinking as follows.

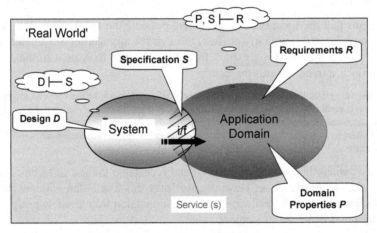

Fig. 4. General requirements-capture model

In the Jackson model, the system exists in the real world. The subset of the real world that influences the system, and into which the system provides a service through an interface (i/f), is known as the application domain. Requirements are what we want to make happen in the application domain and are defined in that domain – *not* in the system – and since the service users are in the application domain they are sometimes called *user* requirements.

A specification is what the system has to do across the interface in order that the requirements can be satisfied – i.e. a specification takes an external, or 'black-box', view of the system. Another way of thinking about a specification is that it contains all the shared properties between the service provider and the service user – therefore it might include things that the service user has to do, not just what the system has to do.

Design, on the other hand, describes what the system itself is actually like and includes all those characteristics that are not directly required by the users but are *implicitly* necessary in order for the system to fulfil its specification and *thereby* satisfy the user requirements. Design is essentially an internal, or 'white-box', view of the system.

The formal notation in the 'bubbles' in Figure 4 defines two relationships that must be shown to be true in requirements capture:

1. that the specification *S* satisfies the requirements *R*. However, this can be true *only* for a given set of properties *P* of the application domain; therefore, if any one of these three sets of parameters is changed then satisfaction demonstration is invalidated until one of the other sets is also changed.
2. that the design *D* satisfies the specification S.

The distinction, and relationship, between requirements, specifications, application-domain properties, and design are not merely academic niceties; rather, they provide the essential foundations for developing systems that do, and can be shown to do, everything required of them.

What has just been described applies, of course, to systems engineering in general. However, if the thesis of the paper is correct then it should be possible to apply the same principles to the safety perspective. By mapping the IEC 61508 principles on to Figure 4, as shown in Figure 5, we can see that there is indeed a direct equivalence for safety.

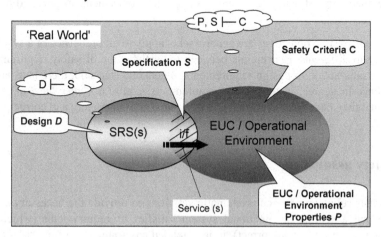

Fig. 5. Safety requirements-capture model

The main differences between Figures 4 and 5 are as follows:

- The application domain is now known as the EUC and its operational environment – merely a change in terminology.
- Requirements have become safety criteria – i.e. specifically the level of safety that has to be achieved for the EUC and its operational environment.
- The *pre-existing hazards* exist in the EUC and its operational environment – therefore, the 'useful purpose' of the SRS(s) is to reduce the associated pre-existing risks to a level below that defined by the safety criteria[5].

Otherwise, everything said above about requirements capture in general applies to safety and the Jackson model helps focus *initial* attention on the useful (safety) purpose of the machine, in line with the safety function concept of IEC 61508, and away from the machine itself.

4.2 Safety requirements satisfaction

Implementation of the design, in the built and integrated system, involves a *third* relationship that must also be shown to be true:

3. that the implementation *I* satisfies the design *D*.

The validity of this relationship requires two objectives to be satisfied:

- that the *required* properties (functionality, performance, reliability and integrity) of the built system satisfy the requirements established for the design, and
- that no *emergent* properties (e.g. common-cause failures) and unwanted functionality have been introduced inadvertently such that they could adversely affect the ability of the built system to satisfy the requirements established for the design.

Because these two objectives are generic – i.e. apply to all properties of a system – there is no difference in principle between the satisfaction of safety requirements and the satisfaction of design requirements in general. That said, there is usually a difference in degree, in that safety requirements require a *higher level of assurance* that they have been captured, and then satisfied, completely and correctly.

5 Safety assurance

Assurance relies on planned, systematic activities to provide the necessary confidence that a service or functional system satisfies its requirements (which are themselves complete and correct), in its intended environment. From a safety per-

---

[5] It has to be 'below' in order to allow for *system-generated* risk associated with the SRS(s).

spective, this would mean achieving an acceptable or tolerable level of safety. These assurance activities specify *how* the assurance objectives (i.e. *what* has to be demonstrated) are to be achieved, as indicated in Figure 6.

The assurance objectives that have to be achieved, and the rigour with which the activities are conducted, are often determined by assurance levels (ALs), which are based upon the potential risks or consequences of the anomalous behaviour of the system element concerned. The results (outputs) of the activities are then used to show that the assurance objectives have been achieved.

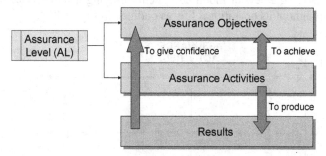

Fig. 6. Safety assurance – basic elements

In order to determine which assurance objectives and activities have to be done (or may be ignored) for a given AL, and to ensure that this would be appropriate for a particular application, we put safety assurance into the argument framework that would form the basis of the eventual safety case. Since it is the safety argument that determines ultimately what we need to demonstrate in a safety case, we can use it to drive the whole assurance process as shown in Figure 7.

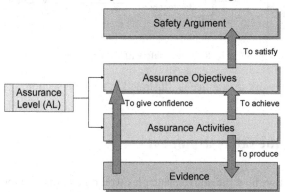

Fig. 7. Safety assurance within an argument framework

Thus the development lifecycle contains only those activities that are necessary and sufficient to support the argument.

In order to ensure that the safety argument itself is complete and rigorous, we derive it directly from the three formal requirements-capture and requirements-satisfaction relationships described in Section 4, as follows:

1. The system has been *specified* to be safe – i.e. meets the appropriate safety criteria for the EUC in the given operational environment.
2. The system *design* satisfies the specification.
3. The *implementation* satisfies the design.

Then, by adding two further arguments – about the transition from current system to the new (or modified) system and the monitoring of the achieved level of safety in service, respectively – we have a sufficient, high-level safety argument structure for developing a new or modified system, bringing it into service and maintaining it throughout its operational life, as outlined in Figure 8.

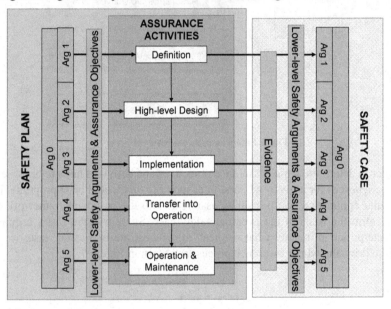

Fig. 8. Overall safety lifecycle process

How this would work in practice is illustrated in the next section.

6 Satisfying the safety argument

This section shows how the above principles would be applied to the development of a new system – focussing on the first three arguments or lifecycle phases[6]. The example used is from the railway sector but the processes described are those developed by the authors for the SESAR pan-European ATM programme.

---

[6] For the purposes of this paper we have assumed that the transition and operational phases of the lifecycle would be familiar to safety engineers and therefore need no further elaboration

6.1 Argument 1 – specification

In the definition phase, we need to show that the system has been *specified* to meet the appropriate safety criteria for the EUC in the given operational environment. We will use a new railway level-crossing control (and possibly protection) system for a planned new two-way suburban road in order to illustrate some of the points in the steps described in Sections 6.1.1 to 6.1.4 below; it should be noted that the analysis presented here is not intended to be exhaustive.

The proposed level-crossing control system is innovative in that it closes the crossing when an approaching train is at a certain time (rather than fixed distance) from the crossing, and has been chosen so that traditional railway technical standards for level crossings would not apply. The ultimate aim is to minimise the delay to road traffic whilst still maintaining an acceptable level of safety; note, however, that the 'useful purpose' of the system is the latter, whilst the former is merely a design constraint.

In order to satisfy Argument 1 we would need to demonstrate:

1. that the properties of the EUC (in this case, the crossing and its users) and its operational environment are properly described,
2. that the safety criteria are appropriate and correct for the operational environment, and
3. that the specification will satisfy the safety criteria, *given the properties of operational environment.*

These assurance objectives (or sub-arguments) are discussed as follows.

6.1.1 Operational environment

For the level-crossing, the operational environment properties need to include:

- users of the crossing – e.g. passenger and freight trains, road vehicles (of which 80% are cars or light vans and the rest are trucks up to 40 tonnes) and occasional pedestrians; exceptionally (say once every 1-2 months), large slow-moving vehicles carrying abnormally heavy loads will need to use the crossing
- average length of train – say, 120 m
- two-way rail traffic levels – say 150 passenger trains per day (mainly between 07:00 and 23:00) and 10 freight trains per day (mainly at night)
- road traffic levels – 3000 vehicles per day (mainly between 07:00 and 23:00)
- traffic performance – the current railway speed limit in the vicinity of the crossing is 140 kph for passenger trains and 60 kph for freight trains; the planned speed limit for the road is 100 kph for cars, 80 kph for vehicles over 2 tonnes and 65 kph for vehicles over 7.5 tonnes.
- details of the road and track layout – the geography of the area makes the construction of a bridge or tunnel prohibitively expensive; this might need to be justified on ALARP grounds.

- climate –generally temperate but vulnerable to periods of dense fog and occasional severe icing of the road during the winter months.

Some of the above items are to be used in the analysis under Argument 1 whereas others might be necessary to support design decisions later in the lifecycle.

6.1.2 Pre-existing hazards

The main pre-existing hazard is:

HAZ$_{PE}$#1. Any situation in which, on current intentions, a road user and a train would inadvertently occupy the crossing at the same time'[7].

The use of 'on current intentions' is crucial since it is describing a hazard not an actual accident. We could use mathematical modelling here to estimate, from the information given above, the frequency with which this hazard would occur for a completely uncontrolled crossing and hence estimate the *pre-existing* risk.

6.1.3 Safety criteria

A suitable quantitative criterion would be that the likelihood of an accident involving multiple fatalities shall not exceed one per 100 years, supported by a second, ALARP, criterion. Given a possible range of outcomes of the hazard in this case, it might be appropriate to make use of a suitable risk classification scheme in order also to set criteria for outcomes of lesser severity, though for the purposes of this illustration, we will assume that if a train travelling at normal speed collides with a road vehicle there would always be some fatalities in the road vehicle and/or on the train due to derailment.

6.1.4 The specification

We use the term 'Safety Objectives' to describe the requirements contained in the specification in order to remind us that, in accordance with the Jackson model of Section 4.1 above, what we are seeking to do here is describe, from the users' perspective, *what* the system must do, *not* to determine *how* the system will achieve that in its design.

First of all we need to consider the *success case* and assess how the pre-existing hazard is mitigated for all *normal* conditions in the operational environment – i.e. for all those conditions that our SRS is likely to encounter on a day-to day basis – constructing various operational scenarios (e.g. single and multiple trains) as necessary. Two examples of a Safety Objective for this are as follows:

---

[7] Compare this with the system-generated hazard quoted in Section 3.4 above.

SO#1. A road user shall not enter the area defined by the crossing until its exit from the crossing is clear.

SO#2. Road users shall not enter the crossing from [say] one minute prior to a single approaching train reaching the crossing until the train has cleared the crossing.

Next we need to assess how well the pre-existing hazard is mitigated for all *abnormal* conditions in the operational environment – i.e. all those adverse conditions that our SRS might *exceptionally* encounter – again, constructing various operational scenarios as necessary. An example of a Safety Objective for this is as follows:

SO#n. In the event that an abnormally large or heavy vehicle [to be defined] is required to use the crossing, all approaching trains shall be prevented from entering the section of track [say] one km prior to the crossing until the vehicle has completely cleared the crossing.

Since this situation is expected to occur infrequently, the system is allowed to operate in a different mode from the *normal* case – i.e. the train no longer has priority over the road vehicle. Again, some form of dynamic risk modelling could be used to determine a suitable exclusion distance for approaching trains.

Finally, we need to consider the potential failure modes of the system, at the service level. At this level/stage, we are *not* concerned with the causes of failure, only with the consequences of failure, for which we could use event-tree analysis for assessing multiple possible outcomes of a particular failure. The identification of possible failure modes must be as exhaustive as possible and a useful starting point taking each success-case safety objective in turn and asking what happens if it is not satisfied. This leads to the *system-generated* hazards, an example being:

HAZ$_{SG}$#1. Road vehicle enters a closed crossing[8] (failure to satisfy SO#2).

Using the operational data from Section 6.1.1 we can derive the following safety objective to limit the frequency of the hazard such that the appropriate portion of the tolerable-risk criterion (Section 6.1.3) is satisfied for this hazard:

SO#n+r. The probability of a road vehicle entering the crossing when it is closed shall not exceed 5×10^{-5} per operating hour.

This illustrative figure takes account of the total number of system-generated hazards (assumed to be four in this example), the frequency with which road and rail traffic uses the crossing, and the providential mitigation that even if a vehicle incorrectly enters the crossing there is a significant probability that it would not actually collide with a train. The hazard-occurrence rate is expressed as a frequency even though the SRS is not continuously operating because the demand rate on it is relatively high (i.e. up to 150 operations per day).

---

[8] *Closed* here is defined by SO#2 (i.e. from one minute before an approaching train reaches the crossing, until the crossing is clear) – it does not necessarily imply a physical closure.

Thus, by the end of the definition phase we should have a set of safety objectives sufficient to ensure that, if they are satisfied in the system design and implementation, the pre-existing risk is mitigated, *and* the system-generated risk is limited, such that the level crossing would satisfy the specified quantitative safety criteria – i.e. Argument 1 would be satisfied.

6.2 Argument 2 – high-level design

Having derived what is called a specification for the system (Jackson 1995), the system-development task becomes progressively less safety-specific and has more common with general system-engineering principles, except for one key feature – the higher level of assurance that is required in the results of safety assessment.

Design, as we have seen, is about the internal properties of the system but for Argument 2 we restrict the analysis to a logical design[9], in which safety requirements describe the main human tasks and machine-based functions that constitute the system, and the interactions between them. An illustration, based on our innovative level-crossing control system (LCCS), is given in Figure 9.

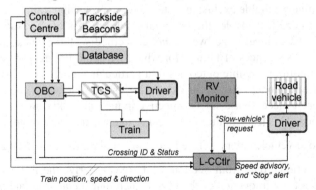

Fig. 9. Example of a logical model

A detailed description of this example and the way that the model works is beyond the scope of this paper – suffice it to say that the new system comprises a fully automated level-crossing controller and a road vehicle monitor that detects the presence of road vehicles within the crossing area. It is to be integrated into a regionally-based 'Moving Block' signalling system using communications based

---

[9] Whereas Figure 9 shows the actors and the way in which they interact quite clearly, the functionality that they provide is contained in the textural safety requirements, and the links between those functions are not easily seen. For this reason, on functionally-rich (and/or data-rich) systems we often use a functional model, showing an entirely abstract view of the system functions and data, as a bridge between the specification and the logical design, thus increasing the confidence of the completeness and correctness of the latter. This is entirely consistent with good systems-engineering practice.

train control – all the train control systems including ATP, but excluding the on-board computer, are subsumed into the TCS box[10].

The main points about the logical model are:

- It does *not* show elements of the physical design, such as hardware, software, procedures and training – nor does it separately represent human-machine interfaces, these being implicit in every link between a human and machine actor.
- Since the machine (e.g. onboard computer) and human (e.g. driver) elements are shown separately this implies that the degree of automation in the system has been decided, at least provisionally.
- It covers those elements of the end-to-end system that are in the train, in the road vehicle, and in the LCCS and those that are in external, interfacing systems. Elements that remain unchanged are shown with a striped background.

Safety requirements capture everything that each of these 'actors' needs to provide in terms of functionality, performance, reliability and integrity in order to satisfy the specified safety objectives.

However, making an argument for a logical design is not simply a matter of showing traceability of the individual safety requirements, for the logical design, back to the safety objectives of the specification. This would ignore three possibilities: that the design might be internally incoherent; that new failure properties could emerge at the design level that were not apparent at the higher, service level; or that the safety requirements are too demanding of technology and/or human performance. Thus it is necessary to demonstrate that the logical design:

1. has all of the functionality and performance attributes that are necessary to satisfy the safety objectives
2. will deliver this functionality and performance for all *normal* conditions of the operational environment that it is likely to encounter in *day-to-day* operations
3. is robust against (i.e. work through), or at least resilient to (i.e. recover easily from), any *abnormal* conditions that it may *exceptionally* encounter
4. has sufficient reliability and integrity to satisfy the safety objectives of the specification, and
5. is realistic in terms of the feasibility of a potential physical system to satisfy the safety requirements, *and* the ability of validation and verification methods to demonstrate, at the appropriate time and to the necessary level of confidence, that the safety requirements are eventually satisfied.

The activities needed to satisfy these five assurance objectives involve nothing more than classical systems-engineering techniques, including for example:

- requirements traceability
- use-case analysis and fast-time/real-time simulations – for the normal, abnormal and failure scenarios

---

[10] Although level crossing control would normally be integrated with the control centre, for the purposes of this illustration we assume a separate subsystem.

- Fault-tree Analysis (FTA) to assess the causes of failure, 'top down'
- Failure Modes Effects [& Criticality] Analysis to check the FTA, 'bottom up'.

Furthermore, since the human elements of the system have started to emerge, we can use standard human factors techniques such as cognitive task analysis and human reliability assessment to assess initially whether the task, performance and integrity demands that the safety requirements place on the human elements of the design are at least realistic.

By the end of the high-level design phase we should have a set of safety requirements – covering the success *and* failure cases – that are sufficient to ensure that, if they are satisfied in the implementation, would ensure that the safety objectives of the specification are met – i.e. Argument 2 would be satisfied.

6.3 Argument 3 – implementation

We have defined the implementation phase such that it comprises development of a physical design and the realisation of the physical design in the built system. In satisfying Argument 3, we need to show that:

1. The physical design satisfies the safety requirements for the logical design.
2. The causes or effects of any adverse, emergent safety properties (e.g. common-cause failures) or unwanted/non-safety functionality have been mitigated in the physical design such that they do not jeopardize the satisfaction of the safety requirements for the logical design.
3. The built system satisfies the safety requirements of the physical design (i.e. verification).
4. The built and integrated system is consistent with the original qualitative safety objectives (i.e. validation).

In the physical design, we take the safety requirements from the logical design and allocate them to the elements of the physical system, as follows:

- Human tasks map on to skills, knowledge, procedures and training.
- Machine-based functions map on to hardware and software design.
- Human-machine interactions map on to human-machine interface design.

These in turn lead to further design, safety requirements derivation, and implementation for each of these elements and then integration of the complete system, following, for example, the classical 'V-model' of system development. Again they involve mainly normal systems-engineering techniques for the hardware, software and human/procedural elements of the physical system, and should lead to sufficient evidence to satisfy Argument 3.

7 Conclusions

The misconception that adequate reliability and integrity are sufficient to ensure the safety of a system is dispelled in the specific context of software by the results of extensive research (Leveson 2001) and more generally herein by rational argument using the simple example of a car airbag.

Safety is as much dependent on correct functionality and performance of the system as it is on system reliability and integrity – the former set of attributes are necessary for the mitigation of *pre-existing* risk (inherent in the operational environment) and the latter for controlling *system-generated* risk (caused by system failure). This is entirely consistent with the principles underlying IEC 61508 but is not always evident in industry-specific safety standards.

By comparing the requirements-engineering principles advocated in (Jackson, 1995) with the principles of IEC 61508, we found direct equivalence between the derivation of the required safety properties of a system and the derivation of its non-safety properties, and showed how a safety argument (itself derived from the Jackson model) should drive all the processes of a safety assessment, through the lifecycle. Whilst recognising the importance of ensuring that the level of assurance is appropriate to the safety-criticality of the system, there is a high degree and extent of commonality between the safety and general system-development processes of a typical project lifecycle – i.e. safety is actually just a viewpoint (albeit a very important one) on systems engineering!

Finally, more than a decade after she first challenged the view that safety is mainly dependent on reliability, Nancy Leveson has written a new book (Leveson 2011) in which she reflects:

'For twenty years I watched engineers in industry struggling to apply old [safety engineering] techniques to new, software-intensive systems – expending much energy and having little success. The solution, I believe, lies in creating approaches to safety [that are] based on modern systems thinking and systems theory. While these approaches may seem new or paradigm-changing, they are rooted in ideas developed after World War II... originally to cope with the increasing complexity in aerospace systems...Many of these ideas have been lost over the years or have been displaced by the influence of more mainstream engineering practices, particularly reliability engineering.'

References

BFS (2004) Bundestelle fur flügunfallundersuchung investigation report AX001-1-2
EUROCONTROL (2001) Safety regulatory requirement ESARR4, risk assessment and mitigation in ATM, edn 1.0
Fowler D, Pierce RH (2011) A safety engineering perspective. In: Cogan B (ed) Systems engineering. InTech
IEC (2010) IEC 61508 – functional safety of electrical/electronic/programmable electronic safety related systems, V 2.0. International Electrotechnical Commission
Jackson M (1995) The world and the machine. Proc 17th Int Conf Softw Eng. IEEE
Leveson NG (2001) The role of software in recent aerospace accidents. 19th International System Safety Conference, Huntsville AL, USA

Leveson NG (2011) Engineering a safer world – systems thinking applied to safety. http://sunnyday.mit.edu/safer-world. Accessed 24 August 2011

Pierce R, Fowler D (2010) Applying IEC 61508 to air traffic management. In: Dale C, Anderson T (eds) Making systems safer. Springer

RSSB (2007) Engineering safety management (the Yellow Book), volumes 1 and 2 – fundamentals and guidance, issue 4. Rail Safety and Standards Board

SAE (1996a) ARP 4754 certification considerations for highly integrated or complex aircraft systems. SAE International

SAE (1996b) ARP 4761 guidelines and methods for conducting the safety assessment process on civil airborne systems and equipment. SAE International

Survey of Safety Architectural Patterns

Paul Hampton

Logica UK

London, UK

Abstract This paper presents the results of a survey to assess the extent of use of safety architectural patterns in Logica to solve commonly reoccurring problems in the safety domain. A number of Logica safety related projects, active during August 2011, were considered to establish which specific patterns had been used so a profile of pattern use could be established along with a view of their perceived effectiveness. The survey also presented the opportunity to determine if any new or novel approach or patterns were being used. The results and findings of the survey are documented in this paper.

1 Introduction

1.1 About Logica

Logica is a business and technology service company, employing 41,000 people. It provides business consulting, systems integration and outsourcing to clients around the world, including many of Europe's largest businesses. Logica creates value for clients by successfully integrating people, business and technology. It is committed to long term collaboration, applying insight to create innovative answers to clients' business needs (Logica 2011).

1.2 Origins of work

In systems engineering, we often come across similar or commonly reoccurring problems. For example, how do we design the system so it is scalable, available on demand, resilient to component failure and transient errors, is flexible to change, etc.?

Experience and the development of best practices have allowed us to develop and formalise collections of design approaches to solve these common problems. These design approaches lay out the concept and idea behind the solution rather than provide a prescriptive solution for the given context. In this sense we have a 'pattern' that can be reused in different contexts to solve similar types of problem.

While general architectural patterns are commonplace in our organisation, there was no centralised view of the use of patterns to solve the types of common problems we experience in the safety domain. This paper was therefore motivated from a desire to understand the extent of usage of safety architectural patterns on our projects, how effective these patterns are, and whether any new patterns or practices were emerging.

1.3 About the survey

In August 2011, a survey was conducted of the types of architectural and design patterns used on some of Logica's systems safety related projects. During this period Logica was operating about 70 safety related projects. A subset of these projects was then chosen to be analysed in more detail to determine the types of pattern used and to gain an insight into the perceived effectiveness of the pattern. Any new or novel approaches were also noted.

As well as higher level architectural patterns, the survey also took the opportunity to assess the extent of use of development techniques such as reduced code sets and static analysis, the results of which are also documented.

1.4 Patterns

The concept of a 'design' pattern is widely attributed to Christopher Alexander (Alexander et al. 1977) in the context of building design and has since moved into other disciplines such as computer software where it gathered pace after the publication of patterns for object oriented design (Gamma et al. 1995). This idea was later expanded to consider higher level patterns at the enterprise level (Fowler et al. 2002).

This paper will look at 'architectural patterns'; that is, patterns that influence the design or architecture of the entire system, and specifically those patterns that are used to address the architecture of systems used in safety critical and safety related environments.

Many of the patterns described are drawn from an excellent catalogue of patterns relevant to this analysis (Armoush 2010). Although the focus for that work was on safety critical embedded systems, the concepts will be broadened here to include safety related systems and those systems that don't necessarily have embedded aspects.

2 Safety Architectural Patterns

The following section describes the most significant safety architectural patterns that were identified during the survey. This section will give a brief overview of each pattern. More specific examples of the use of some of these patterns are discussed later in Section 3.

To provide a view of the effectiveness of the pattern, a rating of the relative value the pattern brings has been provided in the following areas:

Integrity. How well does this pattern assure the consistency and accuracy of the data and processing?

Reliability. How well does this pattern function in the light of failure; can it tolerate failure and continue or does processing have to stop or fail-safe when errors are detected?

Random. How well does this pattern handle random failures such as hardware component failures; can it detect them and carry on or does it cause the system to stop?

Systematic. How well does this pattern handle systematic failures, e.g. software faults that are reproducible given the same set of inputs and states?

For each of these, the pattern is rated between 1 and 5, with 1 being no or little protection/support to 5 being high protection/support.

2.1 Homogenous redundancy

Homogeneous redundancy is one of the more common patterns seen on our projects (see Figure 1). Our projects are typically implementing some form of distributed client/server architecture (predominantly 3 and n-tier) with client presentation layers physically separated from servers hosting application logic and servers hosting a datastore in the form of a proprietary relational database.

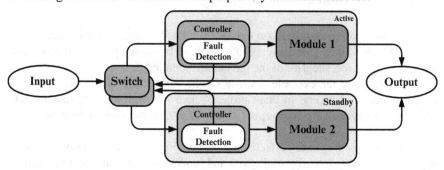

Fig. 1. Homogenous redundancy pattern

Redundancy is therefore often a natural design pattern to support scalability, resilience and high availability of the solution and not necessarily driven from specific safety requirements.

While it is important not to confuse high availability with safety assurance (Douglass 1998, Kalinsky 2005), there is often a serendipitous overlap especially in our decision support projects, where unavailability of the service would compromise the user's ability to make informed judgment in a safety related context.

In practice this pattern is commonly implemented on several layers:

Disk and disk controller redundancy. Individual disks are mirrored so that failure of a single disk will not entail loss of data; failed disks can then be hot-swapped without service interruption.

Data server clustering with multiple database nodes sharing the same data repository. Proprietary software ensures integrity of access between nodes.

Application server redundancy: multiple independent instances of identically provisioned servers. If a server fails, it is taken out of service and the remaining servers provide continuity of service.

Table 1 shows the pattern effectiveness evaluation.

Table 1. Homogenous redundancy pattern effectiveness evaluation

Integrity	Reliability	Random	Systematic
1	4	4	1

From a safety perspective, there are mixed reports of the effectiveness of this pattern to achieve the desired level of reliability. This is predominantly because of the increased complexity required to provide transparency of failover especially on transactional database server clustering. It is also often difficult to eliminate common mode failure amongst clustered nodes.

2.2 Protected Single Channel (PSC)

This is a common pattern used on our safety related projects. In this pattern (see Figure 2) there is only one channel but checks of inputs are performed at various stages to ensure the integrity of the data being supplied to downstream processes. Such checks may, for example, include Cyclic Redundancy Check (CRC) style checks or range checking. In these projects there is a well known fail-safe state such as '*stop processing and report to the user that the data cannot be relied upon*'.

Table 2 shows the pattern effectiveness evaluation. This pattern provides greater confidence in the integrity of the data and processing but being a single channel has little benefit in terms of improving availability. The additional checks increase the prospect of error detection but there is no additional resilience to these failures.

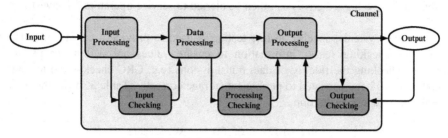

Fig. 2. Protected single channel pattern

Table 2. PSC pattern effectiveness evaluation

Integrity	Reliability	Random	Systematic
4	1	2	2

2.3 Built In Test (BIT)

There are several flavours of this pattern, which are generically referred to as 'Built In Test (BIT)'. These include, for example, Built In Test Equipment (BITE), Built In Self Test (BIST), and Power-On Self-Test (POST). There are two main types: BIT that runs only at start-up and continuous monitoring BIT that effectively runs all the time: both of these have been used on our projects.

A form of this pattern has widespread use in several of our safety projects, predominantly those in decision support systems. In this pattern, shown in Figure 3, additional checks are implemented to detect or predict specific failures so that they can be reported and addressed either through active management or preventative maintenance.

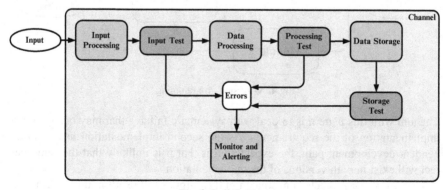

Fig. 3. Built In Test

For example, in many of our decision support systems, errors may be generated and handled as exceptions. Language features allow us to capture and log exceptions and these logged errors can then be alerted to service operators for investigation.

In other systems, specific in-line testing is used to provide a variety of tests, such as: checking sensor information to ensure values are within acceptable ranges, checking the fidelity of data transmissions (e.g. CRC checks) and testing that data has been persisted to permanent storage correctly. Table 3 shows the pattern effectiveness evaluation.

Table 3. BIT pattern effectiveness evaluation

Integrity	Reliability	Random	Systematic
4	2	2	2

This pattern has broadly similar benefits to the PSC pattern. Reliability may be slightly improved due to the ability of BIT designs to operate in degraded modes of operation.

2.4 N-Version Programming (NVP)

This pattern (illustrated in Figure 4) has been used on a number of our projects where it is essential that the system generates the correct output in accordance with a given set of functional requirements. Typically, the system's functional requirements are given to two independent teams to design and implement.

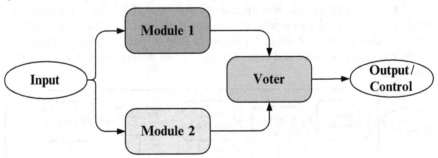

Fig.4. N-Version Programming

The aim with this pattern is to deal with systematic failures that may occur in one implementation of the requirements. As the second implementation has an independent development path, the expectation is that it is unlikely that the same defect will exist in both versions of the implementation.

In most of our projects, a mismatch in the outputs will result in the systems being placed into a fail-safe state.

Table 4 shows the pattern effectiveness evaluation.

Table 4. NVP pattern effectiveness evaluation

Integrity	Reliability	Random	Systematic
4	1	3	3

The effectiveness of this pattern in our experience is debatable, particularly when the implementation costs – which can be significant – are considered. While it may address systematic bugs in a particular version of the implementation it is difficult to secure complete design independence: often independent designers will still solve problems in similarly flawed ways. Furthermore, it is often the case that it is the *requirements* themselves that are flawed (Leveson 1995) and this pattern offers no protection from this type of issue.

2.5 N-Self Checking Programming (NSCP)

In a few projects we use the NSCP pattern (Figure 5), which is based on N-Version Programming but for four or more modules operating on separate hardware units. Components comprise two functionally equivalent versions that run in parallel and have a comparator to check that results are equivalent. If the comparator detects a difference, the next self-checking component is executed until a component produces a result that is equivalent. If all components fail to produce a result that passes the self-check, then the system fails-safe.

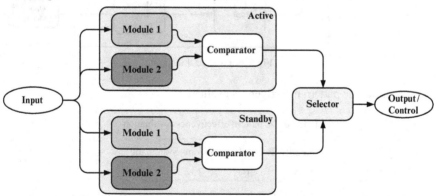

Fig. 5. N-Self Checking Programming

Table 5 shows the pattern effectiveness evaluation. This is one of the most effective patterns, dealing well with all of the aspects under evaluation. The pattern will however suffer from requirements related systematic failures as described for the NVP pattern and is also one of the most expensive patterns to implement – for example, each module needs to be independently developed and tested in addition to testing the final integrated system.

Table 5. NSCP pattern effectiveness evaluation

Integrity	Reliability	Random	Systematic
5	5	5	4

2.6 Sanity Check (SC)

A number of our projects implemented the sanity check form of monitor actuator pattern (Figure 6). In this pattern a second independent channel checks the output of actuators to ensure they are producing approximately correct results.

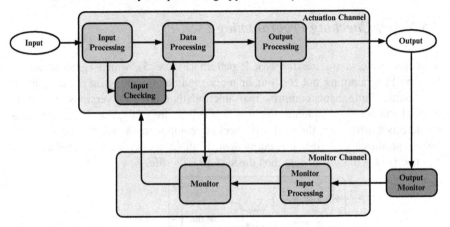

Fig.6. Sanity Checking

Table 6 shows the pattern effectiveness evaluation.

Table 6. SC pattern effectiveness evaluation

Integrity	Reliability	Random	Systematic
4	1	2	3

As the second channel has different functional requirements, this pattern benefits from requirement and implementation diversity, i.e. a defect in the requirement design of the control system will not necessarily be a problem in the sanity checking channel. Likewise, although both channels may be subject to systematic failures, diversity reduces the risk that the systems will fail in the same way at the same time.

2.7 Data Integrity Sampling (DIS)

A number of projects we have implemented involve large decision support systems that have millions or even billions of records, with high volumes of transactions. These systems are used to support safety related decisions made by an expert operator, for example clinical repositories of medical records. While the human makes the final decision and can use their experience and knowledge to detect data corruption and inconsistencies, there is still a risk that credible corruptions or record confusion could influence a decision in a way that contributes to the likelihood or frequency of harm.

This risk also has a tendency to increase over time because of what might be called the '*Safety Expectation Gap*' – a slow but increasing gap between the integrity of the safety data and the ambitions for its use; see Figure 7.

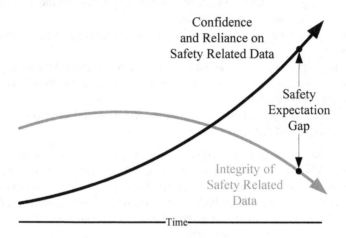

Fig.7. Safety Expectation Gap

When a system is first in operational use, it is likely that a high level of assurance and testing has been undertaken and so the integrity of the data is likely to be high and may increase as early operational wrinkles are ironed out. However, the integrity of the data may well subsequently decline over time due to a number of factors:

Divergence of the repository model from real world processes. Changes to political, business and social behaviours and processes in the real world may render the repository model less effective.

Difficulties in identifying and capturing real world changes. E.g. a record of *current medication* in a clinical repository will become inaccurate when the individual decides to stop taking the medication, an event that is unlikely to be notified at the time it occurs.

Ongoing changes to the system. It is unlikely that the entire system will be recertified for every change, some of which could be significant; regression testing will provide some confidence but there is still risk that issues are introduced.

Natural turnover of staff employed to provide on-going support. This will mean a gradual decline in the knowledge and experience of the system being supported.

In parallel with the change of profile in the integrity of the safety data we also see a change in the associated confidence and reliance users will have on this data. Initially, confidence may be low in the early days of operational use. This will naturally increase through the absence of issues and the realisation of the business benefits the system is bringing. However, other wider factors will also act as catalysts to increase the level of confidence and reliance:

- the increasing dependency on decision support systems and the commensurate decrease in required operator experience
- the social perception that data repositories are increasingly more reliable record keepers
- increasing expectations and dependency on the accuracy of data to support legislative actions, e.g. investigatory actions under the Regulation of Investigatory Powers Act (HMG 2000)
- unanticipated changes of use where the system is found to provide benefit in other safety related business areas.

As residual risk is still comparatively low it is not reasonably practicable to check such a high volume of records for consistency. However, we have employed a novel design pattern that helps mitigate the threat of the safety expectation gap. This is a new pattern, for which in this paper we will coin the term *Data Integrity Sampling (DIS) Architectural Pattern* (see Figure 8 and Table 7).

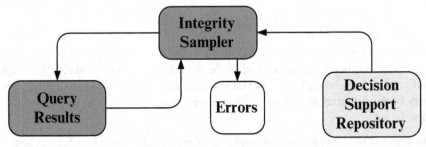

Fig.8. Data Integrity Sampling

Table 7. DIS pattern effectiveness evaluation

Integrity	Reliability	Random	Systematic
3	1	2	2

In this pattern a sample of records (chosen by random or using some selection policy) are periodically sampled and checked for consistency both in terms of compliance with the data relationship model (cardinalities, relationships, etc.) but also in semantic consistency. Results can also be captured in a separate repository so that equivalency of search results can be checked over time.

Sampling rates are typically dependent on resource costs and volume of data records being checked. For example, a full record set check of a particular feature may take hours or days to run so might only be practicable to be run quarterly. Other more lightweight checks might add less assurance value, but could be run more frequently such as hourly or daily. Further work is required to consider the optimal combination of resource costs versus check frequency versus associated assurance value.

Detected inconsistencies are then logged and alerted to the service provider for investigation and repair.

The pattern offers some improved assurance of integrity but this is not comprehensive due to the sampling nature of the pattern. The pattern has no additional benefit in terms of reliability. The pattern improves the detection of failure but has no automatic recovery from such failures.

3 Safety architectural patterns in practice

In this section we will look in more detail at some examples of safety architectural pattern use on projects that Logica has been involved in.

3.1 N-Self Checking Programming (NSCP)

3.1.1 Background

The European Geostationary Navigation Overlay Service (EGNOS) is a pan-European satellite navigation system used to augment existing GPS services to provide more precise horizontal and vertical positioning information (ESA 2009). In March 2011 (ESA 2011a) the system was officially declared suitable for use in a 'Safety of Life' context such as to guide aircraft into landing (ESA 2011b) and navigation of shipping through narrow channels.

EGNOS works by independently checking the accuracy of the GPS system. It then transmits corrections and information on signal integrity (the augmentation data) to users so a more accurate positioning picture can be built.

EGNOS works by capturing data from GPS satellites through a Europe-wide network of Ranging & Integrity Monitoring Stations (RIMS). Four Mission Control Centres (MCCs) process the data received from these RIMS to generate the augmentation data and integrity information for each satellite. The augmentation data is then transmitted by six Navigation Land Earth Stations (NLES) to the EGNOS geostationary satellites for onward broadcasting to users.

Logica played a key safety role in this programme by implementing a Check Set[1] to check the integrity of the information processing between the RIMS and the NLES. The checking ensures the EGNOS augmentation is sufficiently accurate to support the Safety of Life function. Where checks fall outside of safety margins, the users are alerted (within 6 seconds) that the system can no longer be used for safe navigation.

The Check Set followed Level B software development lifecycles to meet the objectives of the DO-178B (RTCA 1992) standard and the N-Self Checking Programming (NSCP) pattern was one of the patterns adopted.

3.1.2 The pattern in use

Figure 9 shows the pattern as used in the Check Set.

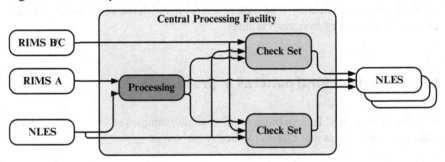

Fig.9. EGNOS Check Set Design

In this design, the Processing module takes input from a RIMS and a NLES and generates the augmentation data. The Check Set components run identical versions of the same software and take the results of the Processing module, the NLES and one or two independent RIMS systems to provide independent validation of data to be supplied to users. The Processing module and the Check Set modules were developed independently, using diverse software and hardware.

The Check Set modules perform checking functions, with one effectively checking the results of the other. If the results of the Check Set do not agree, then the Central Processing Facility (CPF) is deemed to have failed and another alternate CPF will be used until results match. If no other CPF provides matching results the system will be moved into a fail-safe state and users warned that the system cannot be relied upon for accurate positioning information.

---

[1] A 'Set' in this context is broadly equivalent to a small subsystem.

3.1.3 Pros and cons

This pattern is a variant on the generic NSCP pattern described earlier, in that the Check Set functions are not diverse implementations. However, this is justifiable as they are assuring the results of a function that has diverse implementation using input data generated from diversely implemented sources. Furthermore, in the light of widespread systematic failures, the system has a fail-safe state that it can reach within a short period of time.

This pattern provides a solution that offers higher levels of safety integrity assurance and this particular system contributes to a service that has now been certified for use in a 'Safety of Life' context. However, the pattern is one of the most expensive patterns to implement as not only is software and hardware duplicated within a CPF, but many CPFs are required to ensure availability and continuity of the service.

3.1.4 Effectiveness

The Service has only been live since March 2011 and will have only limited adoption so it is too early to draw any significant conclusions from a 'proven in use' form of argument. However, some useful insights have emerged during the development of this system:

- Where solutions of this nature are taking advantage of diverse input feeds, it is essential that during development, true independence of test data is achieved.
- Patterns in this form can be vulnerable to a systematic failure affecting all versions of the checking function so it is important that suitable mitigations are in place to counter this risk, e.g. through delivery of the implementation to an appropriate integrity assurance level.
- It is important to perform a common mode/common cause failure analysis.

3.2 Homogenous redundancy

3.2.1 Background

Following the Chernobyl reactor accident in 1986, RIMNET, the nuclear radiation monitoring and nuclear emergency response system, was installed in 1988 to monitor the consequences for the UK of nuclear incidents abroad. Radiation dose rate readings (gamma plus cosmic) from the 91 sites are collected every hour and checked by a Department of Energy and Climate Change (DECC) computer in London for any indication of abnormal increase. Any evidence of a nuclear incident of radiological significance for the UK would result in a national alert.

Logica designed, built and currently run the latest RIMNET system. The architecture makes extensive use of the homogeneous redundancy pattern. This is an example where high availability has a tangible role to play in providing safety mitigations. The system not only measures radiation levels across the country but also takes feeds of GIS information and forecasts from the Met Office to provide a predictive picture of the movement of radioactive particles entering the UK.

While during normal conditions, failure of the system will not bring any harm, this is not the case when a radiological incident is taking place. During an incident, it is feasible that the information produced will be used to determine the movement of large volumes of the population, or restrictions on what food is considered fit to eat. Unavailability of the service could have devastating implications for very large numbers of people. The system therefore needs high availability on demand.

Figure 10[2] shows the RIMNET monitoring sites in the UK.

Fig.10. RIMNET Monitoring Sites

---

[2] Diagram reproduced from DEFRA under the terms of the Open Government License.

3.2.2 The pattern in use

The solution uses standard COTS products to implement the pattern. These types of solution are well documented so not reproduced here. However, one aspect to highlight is that the redundancy at the hardware level also needs to be supported at many other levels to be effective and to avoid single points of failure. For example, amongst others, the following have to be considered and factored into the overall solution: desktops, terminal servers, application servers, database servers, sensors, firewalls, LANs/WANs and provisions for disaster recover.

3.2.3 Pros and cons

The primary benefit of this pattern is that it provides high availability of the solution, which can help support the safety objectives of a project. Although there are costs associated with duplicating hardware, there are no significant additional application development costs and the market is well provisioned with COTS solutions to provide high availability such as virtualisation, clustering and server farms. However, there are drawbacks with this pattern.

- It is often difficult to eliminate common failure modes across the homogenous components.
- COTS solutions introduce additional complexity and are rarely assured to the extent that all failure scenarios are anticipated and catered for.
- Hardware costs could be significant especially on the data tier, which are expensive to scale horizontally; costs can also escalate where technology refreshes are necessary and potentially bespoke migration activities are required – possibly incurring significant additional costs if there are requirements to keep the system continually available during upgrades.

3.2.4 Effectiveness

Experience of this pattern on a number of projects shows that high availability is possible but it is seldom realised 'out of the box'. A period of 'bedding in' is usually required to stabilise the system behaviour both in terms of the bespoke application and the COTS implementation. For example, in at least one case, a manual 'service protection' plan is required to detect and eliminate known issues that might threaten the service availability.

3.3 Data Integrity Sampling (DIS)

3.3.1 Background

A number of Logica systems are safety related Decision Support Systems (DSS). While failure of these systems will not lead to any immediate harm, the availability, accuracy and timeliness of the data is important from a safety perspective. For example, in clinical data repositories that contain medical records, credibly corrupted or missing information could lead a clinician into making an incorrect diagnosis or administering the wrong treatment.

Other examples are in the law enforcement sector where the national police database (NPIA 2010) will be used to build a picture of criminal activity across the country. Lack of a full intelligence picture has previously been *'putting unarmed officers into a dangerous situation'* so clearly it is important to ensure the intelligence picture held in the database is available and accurate.

In national DSSs, the volume of records held can rise into the billions, so a major challenge is to ensure that integrity of data is maintained throughout the life of the service. While the level of safety risk makes a record by record check not reasonably practicable, it is still important to establish a level of confidence in the quality, consistency and integrity of the data to counter the threat of the safety expectation gap.

To this end, the Data Integrity Sampling (DIS) architectural pattern has been adopted. In this pattern a periodic sampling of the data will be routinely run. This can take a number of forms, but will fall into the following categories:

- Is the collection of records that comprise an individual record semantically consistent?
- Do the query results performed when data is loaded still match the query results after several months?

As a DSS is subject to systematic failures, a data quality issue that is detected in one record is likely to occur in others. In this way, any detected issue can then be investigated further to determine the root cause, prevent further occurrences and to correct records that have already been compromised.

Note that it is recommended that a separate development team is used to implement these integrity checking functions – this ensures that implicit assumptions about data structures, semantics and usage do not contaminate the integrity checking design.

3.3.2 The pattern in use

Logica has been involved in a number of healthcare systems providing, sometimes national, clinical repositories. These repositories contain clinical information about patients that are built from a number of sources such as information entered directly by users, data migrated from legacy systems and data periodically updated from other clinical systems.

The repositories can, for example, contain information such as current medication, allergies, family history, previous procedures and operations, diagnoses and treatments. Other information can also be referenced in linked systems that may hold other information such as diagnostic imaging results.

These systems can be used by clinicians to directly inform their decisions on treatment. While failure of the system will not cause any immediate harm, and there is a human intermediary in the process, hazards around the credible corruption, loss or confusion of clinical data present significant cause for concern. Medication errors have been estimated to kill 7,000 patients in the US per annum (William 2007). This suggests that the human intermediary may not be as an entirely a reliable barrier as we might like to think.

Even when medication is correctly prescribed, knowledge of allergies and allergic reaction could have significant influence on outcomes. A study of 18,200 hospital admissions over a period of 6 months (Pirmohamed 2004) showed that 28 people died as a direct result of adverse drug reactions. We must therefore take steps to ensure that the decision support systems do not contribute additional risk to the clinical decision making processes by making sure *the right information is available to the right people at the right time.*

Use of this type of pattern has been employed on one of our national decision support systems. In this project an internal data consistency check is periodically performed on the demographic data held for patients. As a search on the demographic data is the first step in identifying the clinical record, it is essential that this search is robust, particularly as this is an area where data is changing frequently. To this end we implemented a self consistency check assuring the integrity of indexing information across contemporaneous record sets.

3.3.3 Pros and cons

Implementing this type of pattern allows us to increase our confidence level in the integrity and quality of the data and thus reducing the risk of harm that might otherwise have occurred due to (amongst others) incorrect, missing or corrupted data. As the pattern involves periodic sampling rather than full record by record integrity checking, the expectation is that the implementation costs will be low compared to the overall project implementation costs. This therefore will help support an 'As Low As Reasonably Practicable (ALARP)' claim for these types of system.

The pattern also supports extensibility so as new functions and features are introduced, the safety function can also be updated independently to provide assurance over the new implementation.

While this pattern might help support the safety case for this system, it is a 'weak' form of justification and so can only be reasonably justified on lower risk projects. This is because, by definition, it is a sampling pattern, so it will not guarantee to check every data record held in the system and will only be a point in time snapshot of the consistency of contemporaneous records.

3.3.4 Effectiveness

We have found this form of pattern to be relatively effective: in two major programmes where it is adopted, issues have been periodically detected allowing these to be assessed and resolved. For example, in one case the checking function detected an issue with the implementation of record merging functionality that had not previously manifested itself: merging of records is a complex area and automated merges need to be supported by many rules to resolve conflicts; it is therefore difficult, impracticable or simply impossible (Kaner 1997) to test all eventualities completely. Use of this pattern has therefore demonstrated that it has an important part to play in providing further safety assurance.

4 Overview of results

Tables 8 and 9 show the results of the survey. The 'Count' column shows the number of projects where the pattern or practice was used noting that one project may use several patterns. Pattern names are drawn largely from (Armoush et al 2010) and (Douglass 1998).

5 Conclusions

A subset of Logica's projects that have safety significance were analysed to see which safety architectural patterns were employed and what additional safety development practices were being used above the normal delivery quality assurance processes. Although not all explicitly mentioned the use of these patterns by name, they were being adopted on these projects as evidenced by the associated design documentation.

The following conclusions are therefore drawn from this analysis.

Conclusion 1: patterns tend to be used but are not always separately identified and promoted. Where patterns *are* used it seems reasonable that we should be more explicit about their use as this will:

- enhance the reviewability of a proposition to assure that the design approach will be commensurate with the risk
- enhance the reviewability of the safety justification
- help promote and disseminate best practice
- promote early thinking on testability and verifiability of the architecture.

Table 8. Logica survey results: architectural pattern use

Safety Pattern Name	Count
Homogenous Redundancy	3
Heterogeneous Redundancy	0
Triple Modular Redundancy	0
M out of N	0
Monitor Actuator	1
Sanity Check	4
Watchdog	1
Safety Executive	0
N-Version Programming	2
Recovery Block	0
Acceptance Voting	0
N-Self Checking Programming	2
Recovery Block with Backup Voting	0
Protected Single Channel	4
3-Level Safety Monitoring	0
Safe User Interface (Pap and Petri 2001)[3]	2
Grey Channel (Hansen and Gullesen 2002)	0
Fault Diagnosis, Isolation and Recovery	1
Built In Test Equipment	5
Data Integrity Sampling	6

Conclusion 2: patterns aren't the exclusive domain of the most safety critical projects. While the higher risk projects will most likely adopt a well known pattern, there is no reason why they cannot also be adopted on the lower risk projects.

Conclusion 3: use of patterns themselves do not make the safety case. While use of patterns may help articulate the safety justification, they are not justification in their own right. Indeed, we need to be careful that the use of many patterns may give a misleading impression that safety is being well managed on a given project.

Conclusion 4: use of patterns isn't always essential to sufficiently reduce safety risk. Safety development practices and sufficient rigour of quality assurance in software delivery methodologies can sometimes provide sufficient risk reduction depending on the nature of the project. For example, some of the low to medium safety significant projects in Logica still have compelling safety justifications without the explicit use of a safety architectural pattern.

---

[3] Pap and Petri define a specific pattern; we use the pattern name here in the broader sense of employing special design consideration to cater for human factors associated with the user interface.

Table 9. Logica survey results: development practices

Development Technique	Summary	Count
Restricted Codesets	Implementing coding standards that prohibit use of potentially unsafe language features	5
Static Analysis	Use of static analysis tools to inspect code for common bugs and ensure restricted codesets	7
Human Factors Analysis	Analysis and considerations of the safety implication of human factors	3
Data Independence	Use of test data provided from independent sources	4
Network Diversity	Use of network diversity	1
Redundancy (hardware/software)	Use of hardware/software or redundancy	3
Partitioning	Separation of safety critical and non-safety critical functions	5
COTS Wrapper	Wrapping COTS products to wrap and restrict functionality	4
Degraded Modes	Implementing a form of degraded service in the event of detected failures	2
Safety Function Tagging	Tagging a subset of functional requirements as 'safety requirements' to form the Safety Test suite	6

Conclusion 5: there is value in raising awareness and promoting the use of architectural patterns. As patterns are effectively good practice developed over time from real experience, it seems reasonable to promote their use not only to provide a *lingua franca* for architects but also to help educate and disseminate best practice to developing safety engineers.

6 Further work

A key benefit of patterns is to help describe and disseminate best practice for use in other projects. Building a detailed catalogue of patterns is therefore a logical next step. While this has largely been done for embedded safety critical systems (Armoush et al 2009, Armoush 2010), it seems reasonable to build on this work to include safety related systems and those that do not necessarily have an embedded component. This could be a global catalogue or an interesting possibility is the development of a company- or organization-wide catalogue that not only contains the theoretical benefits but also the track record of usage of the pattern. In this way a process of continual improvement typical of excellence models like CMMI (SEI 2011) can be developed where real field results can be used to validate the effectiveness of a pattern in order to inform future use of a given pattern.

Along with the idea of patterns, we also have the concept of anti-patterns (Koenig 1995). These are sometimes less formal descriptions of patterns of behaviour that, while appearing attractive in the first instance, experience shows that they inevitably affect the endeavour in a negative or counter-productive way.

While the body of anti-patterns have largely emerged from software engineering practices (and there will be some relevance to the delivery of safety significant projects), there is an opportunity to explicitly extend the concept to the safety context. By way of example, the following is offered as an example of an anti-pattern.

Anti-Pattern: 'Safety Design Preclusion'. While safety functions are ideally considered early in a project in parallel with the rest of the functional design of the system, in some cases the safety protections are added later, perhaps as a bolt-on wrapping system or independent checking system. In these latter cases there is risk that the original design of the system makes it very difficult to add such additional safety functions, so in a sense the original architecture *precludes* the addition of safety functions. Examples of preclusive design might be:

- use of binary storage format, making it difficult to verify and check outputs
- where results cannot be checked without interfering with the outcome, for example, performance would be too badly affected or timing aspects would mean different results would be generated.

Even if safety functions are going to be added later, it is nevertheless important to spend some time reviewing the system design and thinking about the feasibility of how these functions can be incorporated in the future.

Projects may fall into this pattern when delivery of the core requirements becomes paramount and the safety requirements may be considered a problem to address in a later release.

There are however many costly downsides to this pattern. For example, the safety functions may be much more expensive to implement or it may not be possible to add sufficient safety assurance without reengineering the original core design.

Raising the awareness and formality of anti-patterns should give greater empowerment to safety assurance functions. For example, a project seen to be adopting such a pattern could be stopped and realigned much earlier in the delivery process resulting in greater commercial success and safer systems.

References

Alexander C, Ishikawa S, Silverstein M et al (1977) A pattern language: towns, buildings, construction. Oxford University Press

Armoush A (2010) Design patterns for safety-critical embedded systems. Fakultät für Mathematik, Informatik und Naturwissenschaften der RWTH Aachen University

Armoush A, Salewski F, Kowalewski S (2009) Design pattern representation for safety-critical embedded systems. J Softw Eng Appl 2:1-12

Douglass BP (1998) Safety-critical systems design. http://citeseerx.ist.psu.edu/viewdoc/summary?doi=10.1.1.117.2814. Accessed August 2011

ESA (2009) EGNOS: European Geostationary Navigation Overlay Service. BR-284

ESA (2011a) What is EGNOS? http://www.esa.int/esaNA/GGG63950NDC_egnos_0.html. Accessed August 2011

ESA (2011b) Europe's first EGNOS airport to guide down giant Beluga aircraft. http://www.esa.int/esaNA/SEMTV1ASJMG_egnos_0.html. Accessed August 2011

Fowler M et al (2002) Patterns of enterprise application architecture. Addison-Wesley

Gamma E, Helm R, Johnson R, Vlissides J (1994) Design patterns: elements of reusable object-oriented software. Addison-Wesley

Hansen KT, Gullesen I (2002) Utilizing UML and patterns for safety critical systems. ABB Corporate Research Center, Norway

HMG (2000) Regulation of Investigatory Powers Act. http://www.legislation.gov.uk/ukpga/2000/23/contents. Accessed September 2011

Kalinsky D (2005) Architecture of safety-critical systems. http://www.eetimes.com/design/embedded/4006464/Architecture-of-safety-critical-systems. Accessed Aug 2011

Kaner C (1997) Impossibility of complete testing. www.kaner.com/pdfs/imposs.pdf. Accessed September 2011

Koenig A (1995) Patterns and anti-patterns. J Object Oriented Program 8:46-48

Leveson N (1995) Safeware: system safety and computers. Addison-Wesley

Logica (2011) http://www.logica.co.uk/we-are-logica/about-logica/. Accessed August 2011

NPIA (2010) The Police National Database: making a difference: a guide to getting the most from the PND.

Pap Z, Petri D (2001) A design pattern of the user interface of safety-critical systems. International PhD Students' Workshop Control & Information Technology

Pirmohamed M, James S et al (2004) Adverse drug reactions as cause of admission to hospital: prospective analysis of 18,820 patients. http://www.bmj.com/content/329/7456/15.long. Accessed August 2011

RTCA (1992) DO-178B: software considerations in airborne systems and equipment certification

SEI (2011) CMMI overview. http://www.sei.cmu.edu/cmmi/. Accessed September 2011

Williams DPJ (2007) Medication errors. J R Coll Physicians Edinb 37:343-346

The Application of Bayesian Belief Networks to Assurance Case Preparation

Chris Hobbs[1] and Martin Lloyd[2]

[1]QNX Software Systems, Ottawa, Canada

[2]Farside Technology Research, Reading, UK

Abstract Designers of dependable systems need to present assurance cases that support the claims made about the system's dependability. Building this assurance case, incorporating different types of evidence and reasoning, can be daunting. In this paper we argue that, thanks to their flexibility and expressive capabilities, Bayesian Belief Networks are particularly suitable for building such assurance cases. Drawing on our experience preparing and presenting an assurance case to certify a software product to IEC 61508 Safety Integrity Level 3, we describe how Bayesian Belief Networks can be used to simplify both the engineer's work in preparing the case, and the auditor's or customer's work in checking this case for coherence and completeness.

1 Terminology

The following terms are used with specific meanings in the remainder of this paper:

Assurance case. The term 'case' is used as in 'the case for the defence'. The assurance case is sometimes known as the 'dependability case', 'safety case' or 'compliance case'. Def Stan 00-56 (MoD 2007) defines a safety case as 'a structured argument, supported by a body of evidence that provides a compelling, comprehensible and valid case that a system is safe for a given application in a given operating environment'.

Auditor. Although there are several different readers of the assurance case, we use the term 'auditor' in what follows to represent all of them.

Safety manual. Some of the examples in the remainder of this paper are based on the quality of a 'safety manual'. This is the manual shipped with a product to define the constraints under which it should be used. The quality of the safety manual is a small part of an overall assurance case but, as it is easily understood and universally required, the safety manual is used as an example below.

2 Introduction

When implementing a safety- or mission-critical application, it is necessary to convince the authors, the management of the development company, potential customers and auditors that the system meets its safety, availability and reliability requirements. The argument presented to this audience can be captured in an *assurance case*.

Organising and presenting such a case in an unstructured, natural language presents difficulties both to the authors of the case, who have to struggle to maintain coherence as the case evolves, and to the auditors reviewing it, who have to extract the threads of the argument.

Bayesian Belief Networks (BBNs) have been proposed as a suitable tool to structure and quantify such an argument (e.g. Bouissoe et al. 1999, Fenton and Neil 2004, Fenton et al. 1998, Guo 2003, Littlewood et al. 1998) and this paper provides more detail from the authors' experience of how such a tool can be applied.

It is assumed that the reader of this paper is familiar with the basic structure and application of a BBN. If required, Krieg provides a thorough tutorial (Krieg 2001) and Fenton a useful summary (Fenton et al. 1998).

3 The assurance case

An assurance case lays out the argument as to why the implementer believes the application meets the claims that are made for it in the context of the appropriate standard (e.g. IEC 61508 for many safety-critical applications, IEC 62304 and ISO 14971 for medical devices, EN 5012x for railway applications) and also provides the supporting evidence. As Jackson states (Jackson et al. 2007):

'Because testing alone is usually insufficient to establish properties, the case will typically combine evidence from testing with evidence from analysis. In addition, the case will inevitably involve appeals to the process by which the software was developed – for example, to argue that the software deployed in the field is the same software that was subjected to analysis or testing.'

Jackson proposes a three-element approach to creating software for dependable systems:

1. explicit, precisely articulated claims about the dependability properties that the system must exhibit
2. evidence that substantiates the dependability claim
3. expertise and appropriate methods.

One characteristic of using a BBN to structure the assurance case to support the second of these is that it provides fewer opportunities for flaws in the argument or inappropriate reliance on untrustworthy evidence[1]. In an informally expressed assurance case, it is possible that such failings could inadvertently slip through review processes. As Fenton expresses it (Fenton et al. 1998): 'A major benefit of [the BBN] approach is that otherwise hidden assumptions used in an assessment become visible and auditable.'

In building an assurance case, evidence must be considered from different directions:

1. What claims are being made?
2. What evidence is provided to support the claims and how valid is that evidence?
3. Does the evidence support the claims?

An assurance case can be represented by a BBN where each leaf (i.e. node without incoming arrows) represents elementary evidence and the network's structure represents the argument. Thus the simple, example subnetwork in Figure 1 could lead to three types of question, corresponding to the axes above:

1. **What is being claimed?** This is represented by one or more nodes in the BBN, each containing a simple, declarative statement: in this example that 'the safety manual is adequate'.

Fig. 1. An example of definitional idiom

2. **What evidence justifies this claim?** In this (very simplified) example, three pieces of evidence: the competency of the user being defined, the inclusion of sufficient information and the review by a competent authority. Generally each such leaf would contain a link (url) to the actual evidence; to support the review evidence, this could be a link to the records of the review with the list of participants, their qualifications and their comments. This permits the auditor to deal separately with each piece of evidence and raise very focused concerns:

---

[1] Untrustworthy evidence may be valuable if its untrustworthiness is explicitly acknowledged and handled.

'Before I could accept that the review had been carried out, I would also need to see that the review participants agree that their concerns have been addressed.'

3. **Does the evidence support the claim?** This effectively poses the question to the auditor: 'Do you agree that if the three subsidiary items in this subtree were demonstrated, then the conclusion that the 'safety manual is adequate' would also be demonstrated?' By sharing the structure of the BBN with the auditor even before it is quantified, weaknesses in the argument can exposed early: 'No, that would not convince me, I would also require evidence that the safety manual contains all the necessary constraints on the developer using the product.'

The level at which evidence is supplied must, to some extent, be subjective. In Figure 1, for example, the evidence that the 'safety manual has been reviewed by a competent authority' could have been broken down further as illustrated in Figure 2. The necessary level of breakdown depends, of course, on the level of rigour demanded by the audit criteria.

4 Using a BBN to present evidence

The advantages of using a BBN to present an argument of the type described in Section 3 include its ability to quantify risk and uncertainty, to combine subjective and objective data, to reason from cause to effect and *vice versa* and to arrive at decisions based on incomplete data (Fenton and Neil 2004).

From the point of view of the person reading and assessing the assurance case, the graphical structure of the BBN represents the structure of the argument, the nodes represent the evidence. This makes it easy to understand not only what evidence is being presented but also how the argument is constructed.

The evidence represented by the leaves of the BBN typically:

- includes both hard and soft evidence. Hard evidence is normally quantitative, e.g. '15 problems were detected and reported during final system test.' Soft evidence tends to be qualitative, e.g. 'The development team is highly skilled.' Even when evidence appears to be quantitative, it is often necessary to convert it to qualitative form: is 15 a 'very low', 'low', 'normal', 'high' or 'very high' number of problems to find during system test?
- has an associated level of confidence. The analyst may be 100% confident in the evidence that exactly 15 problems were detected during system test but the confidence that a particular supplier delivers high quality product may be lower.
- includes both *a priori* and *a posteriori* evidence. *A priori* evidence can be thought of as evidence arguing from cause to effect, e.g. 'The development team is highly skilled, therefore the software is of higher quality than would be expected from an average team.' *A posteriori* evidence is that argued from ef-

fect to cause, e.g. 'The software is of higher quality than would be expected from an average team and so we can conclude that the development team must have been highly skilled.' (Polya 1990) is the classic text describing *a posteriori* reasoning in an exact field.

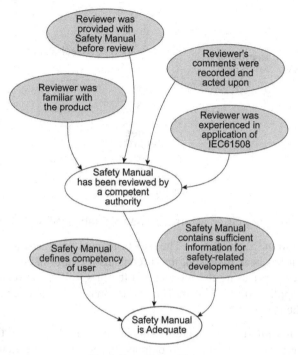

Fig. 2. Extending evidence

5 BBN idioms

Krieg explicitly defines a BBN as '...a specific type of causal belief network' (Krieg 2001) but, in practice, the arrows on a BBN often represent relationships more subtle than causality.

The emphasis on causality may arise from the extensive use of BBNs in medical diagnosis applications. However, consider Figure 3 which is a tiny part of a BBN presented in a medical paper (Watt and Bui 2008). This sub-model encompasses causality (osteoarthritis presumably can cause back-pain) but also other associations: a history of knee pain does not cause knee osteoarthritis; on the contrary, knee osteoarthritis causes a history of knee pain.

Fenton relaxes 'causality' to 'strengthens my belief in' (Fenton et al. 1998) and this is much closer to the meaning used in an assurance case. In Figure 3, for example, a history of knee pain would 'strengthen the [doctor's] belief in' the existence of knee osteoarthritis.

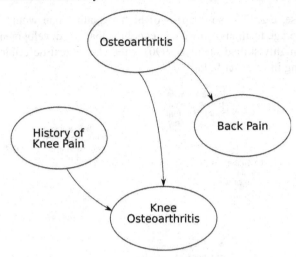

Fig. 3. Part of a medical BBN

The general idioms used in an assurance case preparation (SERENE 1999) are:

Definitional idiom. See Figure 1. The 'safety manual being adequate' is *defined* to mean that it has been reviewed, that it contains the information needed by the application developer using the product and that it specifies the required competency of the application developer. The auditor may, of course, consider such a definition to be inadequate.

Process-product idiom. See Figure 4. This idiom is used to model the argument where a process transforms inputs to outputs. In the case of the example in Figure 4, the quality of the processes that the programming team is following affects the quality of the resulting code. Note that this idiom could be redrawn as a causal tree by connecting each of the leaf nodes to the result, e.g. 'clear requirements are one of the factors that cause higher quality code.'

Measurement idiom. See Figure 5. This idiom is used, for example, to express the argument that, as the product has already been used satisfactorily in applications certified to various standards (medical, nuclear, aviation, etc.), this increases confidence in its suitability for certification to IEC 61508.

There are many safety-related standards of varying relevance. A naive BBN would list them all and identify which are known to have been applied to applications of the product in question. The *measurement* idiom can be used to present the number of possibly applicable standards *and* a quantitative estimate of the worth of the standards actually employed. For example, certification to a general standard such as IEC 61508 might count for more than certification to a pre-IEC 61508 gas detector standard. Similarly it can be assumed that a law of diminishing returns applies: the difference between 1 and 2 standards being more important than the difference between 100 and 101.

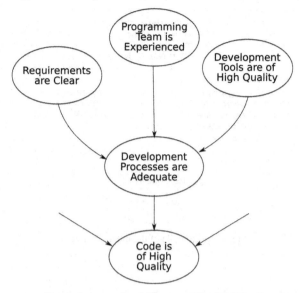

Fig. 4. An example of the process-product idiom

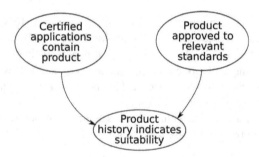

Fig. 5. An example of the measurement idiom

Induction idiom. See Figure 6. This idiom is used to argue from historical data (e.g. the confidence-in-use figures for release $N - 1$ of the product) to a confidence in release N. If it can also be argued that there has been no statistically significant change in failure rate and no change in processes between release $N - 1$ and release N, this provides a level of confidence in release N.

It might be thought difficult to combine sub-models built using different idioms but, in practice, this is not so – each sub-model presents a level of support for *its* claim and these claims are combined using an appropriate idiom for the common node. Figure 4, for example, uses the process-product idiom to justify the claim that the code is of high quality. This could, for example, be combined with other evidence using a definitional idiom: 'implementation is adequate' being true *by definition* if the code is of high quality and various other claims are true.

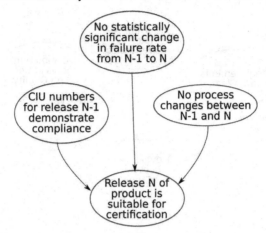

Fig. 6. An example of the induction idiom

6 Quantifying the assurance case

There are many ways to associate a value with a node in a BBN, including enumerating states (e.g. 'True, False' or 'High, Medium, Low'), or specifying continuous or integer ranges of values. In general, it is perhaps best to try to maintain the strategy of making each node a simple declarative statement with a fuzzy Boolean value (True or False to some extent). This is sometimes inappropriate and integer or continuous ranges have to be used.

Once the range of possible values is chosen for each node, there are several steps to quantifying the safety case as described below.

6.1 Defining node dependencies

This step defines computationally how the value of a node depends on the value of its parents (the nodes from which it receives incoming arrows). With Boolean nodes, it is tempting simply to use the logical AND and OR operators. For example, in Figure 7, we say that the Conclusion is untrustworthy if Evidence1 OR Evidence2 is untrustworthy.

If our confidence in the trustworthiness of each piece of evidence is as given in Figure 7, the resulting confidence that we can place in the Conclusion is $0.63158 \times 0.61364 = 0.38756$. In using logical AND or OR we are, however, making two implicit assumptions:

1. that Evidence1 and Evidence2 are both equally important in determining the truth of Conclusion

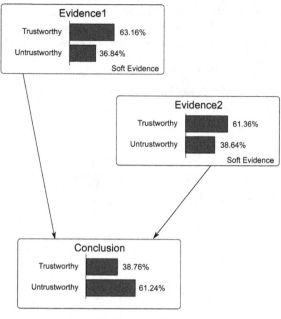

Fig. 7. Logical OR

2. that Evidence1 and Evidence2 between themselves constitute *all* the evidence required for Conclusion.

A more realistic operator for reasoning within an assurance case is the Noisy-OR function (see Appendix A.1 and, e.g. Cozman 2004).

The Noisy-OR function takes a 'link probability' associated with each incoming arrow in the network. This value is defined formally in Equation 1 of Appendix A.1; it can be thought of informally as the confidence we place in the conclusion given that the particular piece of evidence is true, but that all other pieces of evidence are false. A further parameter, called 'leakage', k, represents the level of confidence that the given pieces of evidence represent all the evidence required to support the conclusion. k is the measure to which the conclusion may be true even if *all* the given evidence is false.

Figure 8, for example, illustrates the condition where a Conclusion is supported by Evidence1 and Evidence2. Of these, Evidence1 is the more significant: even if Evidence2 were false, Evidence1 alone would provide a 60% level of confidence in the Conclusion. Evidence2 is less significant: its link probability is 40%. In addition, the leakage has been set to 10%: even if Evidence1 and Evidence2 are both false, there is believed to be a 10% chance that the Conclusion is nevertheless true.

In Figure 8, the condition has been set where Evidence1 and Evidence2 are both considered 100% false. The Conclusion can therefore be considered 10% true: the leakage value. Table 1 summarises the level of trust that can be put in the Conclusion given the various states of Evidence1 and Evidence2. Again it can be seen that, if both pieces of evidence are known to be absolutely false, then there is still a probability of 10% that the Conclusion is true. Notice also from Table 1 that if Evidence1 were known to be 100% true and Evidence2 completely false, then the truth of Conclusion would be 64%: 60% plus an element of the leakage.

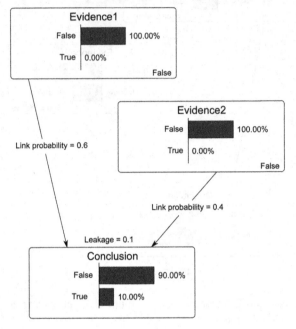

Fig. 8. Noisy-OR

Table 1. Example Noisy-OR truth table

If...		Conclusion	
Evidence1 is...	Evidence2 is...	False	True
False	False	0.90	0.10
False	True	0.54	0.46
True	False	0.36	0.64
True	True	0.216	0.784

Noisy-OR is accompanied by a Noisy-AND. Analogously to Noisy-OR, Noisy-AND expresses the concept that 'both Evidence1 AND Evidence2 are needed to draw the Conclusion but, even if both are true, there is still a k% chance that the Conclusion is false (because other pieces of evidence have been missed)'. In practice, Noisy-AND is much more useful than Noisy-OR in an assurance case because evidence tends to be cumulative: the Conclusion is based on Evidence1 and Evidence2. Noisy-AND, as used in an assurance case, is defined in Appendix A.2.

Figure 9 presents a slightly more realistic use of the Noisy-OR function: the two pieces of evidence have been weighted as 0.6 (Evidence1) to 0.4 (Evidence2) and, from consideration of those pieces of evidence, we have 80% confidence in the truth of Evidence1 and 70% confidence in Evidence2. Together we believe that these two pieces of evidence cover 90% of the evidence required to support the Conclusion fully (i.e. the leakage factor is 0.1).

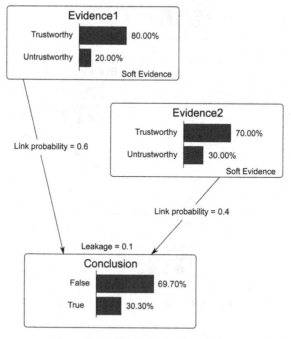

Fig. 9. Noisy-OR: strength of conviction

The flexibility of the Noisy-OR and Noisy-AND parameters permit a model to be created that reflects the views of subject-matter experts on the relative weights of the pieces of evidence *and* the completeness of the evidence. This provides the structure of the argument. Independently, the experts' assessments of the veracity of the evidence can be entered and the result calculated. Zagorecki describes a charming experiment to determine the accuracy of human experts in presenting inferences through Noisy-OR parameters (Zagorecki and Markov 2004).

Using Noisy-OR and Noisy-AND eliminates the assumptions implicit in Boolean OR and AND (see above) but brings their own implicit assumption: that the parents of the conclusion are independent of each other. The link probabilities reflect the dependence of the conclusion on one piece of evidence, assuming all the other pieces of evidence to be false.

The strength of a Bayesian network can be seen in its ability to argue from effect to cause and Figure 10 illustrates this. In that scenario it is assumed that we can be totally confident that the Conclusion is true. The Bayesian calculation allows us then to place a confidence on each of the pieces of evidence.

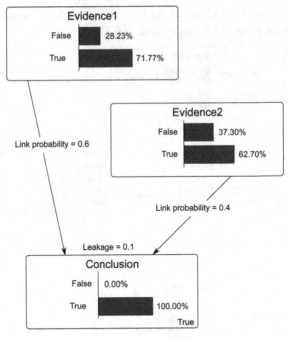

Fig. 10. Reasoning from effect to cause

6.2 Assigning prior probabilities

Prior (or marginal) probabilities may be assigned to all nodes (whether with or without incoming arcs) and these are the probabilities which, without any information to the contrary for the specific scenario being considered, should be assumed. In the absence of explicit values, most tools will assign equal probabilities to all states. If, in the absence of other evidence, the probability of a member of the public having osteoarthritis (Figure 3) is 0.05, then that would be assigned to the value 'True' in the appropriate node within the BBN.

In the particular instance of an assurance case, subject-matter experts would normally estimate the prior probabilities. Considering one of the pieces of evidence in Figure 11, for example, the prior probability for the node 'SM [safety manual] defines system safe state' might be based on the expert's assessment of how often the design safe state is included in the safety manuals she has reviewed. If this is a topic that is often omitted then the prior probability would be low; if normally present then it would be high.

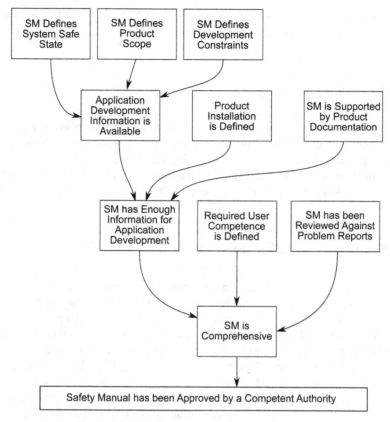

Fig. 11. Subnetwork for completeness of safety manual

6.3 Adding observed evidence

Performing the Bayesian calculation on the assurance case, with just the prior probabilities defined, effectively asks, 'In the absence of evidence regarding this particular product, how strong is the argument that a generic product meets its dependability requirements?' In this manner the model could be deployed as a standard template for use by anyone presenting an assurance case, such a template perhaps being an area of possible standardisation.

For a particular product, observations can be added to some or all of the nodes (not just leaf nodes). Taking the example of the inclusion of a description of the design safe state referred to in Section 6.2, the person preparing the assurance case would inspect the safety manual and look for that description. The observation could then be added to the network. Note in the same figure that the observation 'SM defines product scope' may only be assessed as being 85% true: perhaps there are some areas that need additional work.

Where observations are placed against other than leaf nodes, the Bayesian algorithm will backtrack as illustrated in Figure 10.

6.4 Performing the computation

Once the quantification is complete, Bayes' theorem can be applied to the resulting network and the probabilities thereby propagated to all nodes. Drawing and evaluating a BBN is obviously best done using a software tool capable of handling hierarchical subnetworks. The quantified diagrams in this paper were prepared using the AgenaRisk (Agena 2004) and Netica API (Norsys 2010) tools.

6.5 Performing sensitivity analysis

When the Bayesian calculation is first performed, it is probable that the final result will not be to the liking of the analyst: the level of assurance may be too low. In this case a sensitivity calculation may be performed to find where the 'biggest bang can be achieved for the buck'. It would be uneconomic to invest significant effort into improving an area which had little impact on the final result.

To continue the example from Sections 6.2 and 6.3, it might be found that, if the level of confidence in 'SM defines product scope' could be increased, then this would have a significant effect on the result. Effort could then be focused on increasing the clarity of the product definition, allowing the associated observed value to be increased.

7 Simplified example

Figure 11 is a simplified version of one subtree of a possible assurance case. This subtree addresses the argument for the safety manual being adequate.

Note that, in Figure 11, 'SM [safety manual] has been approved by a competent authority' is seen as an implication of the statement that the network is trying to justify: 'SM is comprehensive'. In principle, the relationship between these two concepts could be modelled in either direction:

1. Part of the evidence that 'strengthens the belief that' the safety manual should be considered comprehensive is that it has been approved by a competent authority. In this case the arrow would appear in the opposite direction to the way it appears in Figure 11 and the argument would form part of the *definitional* idiom.

2. The comprehensiveness of the safety manual 'strengthens the belief that' it would be approved by a competent authority. This is the way it is drawn in Figure 11 and the argument uses the *process-product* idiom.

If it is assumed that the prior probabilities based on the analyst's experience are as listed in Table 2[2], then, with reasonable assumptions about the node dependencies, it can be calculated that the strength of the argument 'SM is comprehensive' is 25%. One example of the possible node dependencies (using Noisy-AND) is illustrated in Table 3 where it can be seen that the requirement that the 'safety manual defines the system safe state' dominates: this reflects the fact that a clear definition of the system's safe state is essential to any developer integrating the system into a larger product. Even if the other conditions are completely true, if the system safe state is not well defined then the result can be at most 20% true.

Table 2. Example prior and post strengths for Figure 11

Node	Prior probability	Strength assessed during audit
SM has been reviewed against problem reports	0.5	0.8
Required user competence is defined	0.5	0.8
SM has been approved by competent authority	0.1	1.0
SM is supported by product documentation	0.4	0.9
Product installation is defined	0.7	0.4
SM defines development constraints	0.6	0.8
SM defines system safe state	0.5	1.0
SM defines product scope	0.4	0.8

When the results of the audit have been entered (the right-most column of Table 2) and the calculation performed again, then the strength of the argument that the 'safety manual is comprehensive' is now 92%. This value would then be fed into the larger calculation of the strength of the overall assurance case.

8 Presenting the case

As mentioned above, it is useful to engage the auditor to whom the assurance case will eventually be presented early in the development of the BBN. This allows the question '*If we were to present evidence as indicated by this BBN, then would this structure of argument convince you of our case?*' to be posed before work is carried out on quantification.

Of course, if an authoritative body were to define and publish standard BBNs for particular applications or industries, this first step would not be required. Until

---

[2] Table 2 can be read as follows: 'without any evidence about a particular product, the experience of the analyst is that the product installation process is defined in 70% of safety manuals.'

that occurs, some (mutual) education might be needed if the auditor has not met this format before, but we have found that auditors quickly realise that a BBN will reduce the auditing workload (by removing the need to extract the argument manually from a loosely structured natural language document) while allowing the audit to be deeper and more focused. In particular, clearly separating the questions 'is the structure of the argument convincing?', 'is this evidence convincing?' and 'does this evidence support the argument?' makes the job of auditing much easier.

Table 3. Example Noisy-AND truth table

If...			Application development information available is...	
'SM defines development constraints' is...	'SM defines product scope' is...	'SM defines system safe state' is...	False	True
False	False	False	0.952	0.048
False	False	True	0.76	0.24
False	True	False	0.92	0.08
False	True	True	0.60	0.40
True	False	False	0.88	0.12
True	False	True	0.40	0.60
True	True	False	0.80	0.20
True	True	True	0.00	1.00

9 Summary

Preparing an assurance case for a complex system, particularly one containing sophisticated software, by means of a BBN allows activities to be separated cleanly: 'how should we argue about the evidence?' and 'what evidence should we present?'. It prevents unstructured 'dumping' of material into a document by forcing the role of each piece of material to be considered individually. We have found that auditors to whom we have presented these cases have welcomed the structured argument.

In summary, applying a BBN to represent an assurance case, when backed by a suitable computation tool, appears to be a flexible and powerful technique.

Appendix: Noisy Booleans

This paper describes the use of Noisy-OR and Noisy-AND. There are other noisy operators such as Noisy-MAX and Noisy-SUM (Norsys 2008).

A.1 Noisy-OR

Given a variable X (a child node in a Bayesian network) that depends on N variables Y_1, Y_2, ..., Y_N (its parent nodes), then N link probabilities are defined, one associated with each Y_i by:

$$p_i = p\left(X \mid Y_i, \{\overline{Y}_j\}_{j=1, j \neq i}^N\right).$$
(1)

The distribution of X conditional on the Y_i can then be defined as

$$p(X \mid Y_1, \ldots, Y_N) = 1 - \prod_{i:Y_i} (1 - p_i).$$
(2)

Effectively, with Noisy-OR, p_M says: 'if node M were true but all other inputs to a node were false then p_M is the strength of belief that we could attribute to the node.'

This does not take into account leakage: the level at which the Y_i are the only variables on which X depends. This can be incorporated by defining k to be the level of confidence in X when all the Y_i are false:

$$k = p\left(\overline{Y}_1, \overline{Y}_2, \ldots \overline{Y}_N\right).$$
(3)

Equation 2 can then be rewritten as

$$p(X \mid Y_1, \ldots, Y_N) = 1 - (1 - k) \prod_{i:Y_i} (1 - p_i)$$
(4)

A.2 Noisy-AND

Noisy-AND is less well defined in the literature than Noisy-OR but can be constructed from Noisy-OR by using a form of de Morgan's laws. Noisy-AND *is* supported in many of the Bayesian network tools.

$$X_1 \otimes X_2 \otimes \ldots \otimes X_N \equiv \overline{X}_1 \oplus \overline{X}_2 \oplus \ldots \oplus \overline{X}_N$$
(5)

where $\oplus$ is Noisy-OR and $\otimes$ is Noisy-AND. With a leakage defined of $0.0 \leq k \leq 1.0$, Equation 5 represents the situation where 'all of the X_i are needed to support the conclusion but, even if all are true, there is still a chance of k that the conclusion is false'. This can then be rewritten as

$$p(X \mid Y_1, \ldots, Y_N) = (1 - k) \prod_{i:Y_i} p_i .$$
(6)

Effectively, with Noisy-AND, p_M says: 'if node M were false but all other inputs to a node were true then $1 - p_M$ is the strength of belief that we could attribute to the node.'

References

Agena (2004) Agena's Bayesian network technology. Whitepaper

Bouissoe M, Martin F, Ourghanlian A (1999) Assessment of a safety-critical system including software: a Bayesian belief network for evidence sources. In: Proc Annu Reliab Maintainab Symp

Fenton NE, Neil M (2004) Combining evidence in risk analysis using Bayesian networks. Safety-Critical Systems Club Newsletter 14(1)8-13

Fenton N, Littlewood B, Neil M, Strigini L, Sutcliffe A, Wright D (1998) Assessing dependability of safety critical systems using diverse evidence. IEE Proc Softw Eng 145:35-39

Cozman FG (2004) Axiomatizing Noisy-OR. Proc 16th Eur Conf Artif Intell (ECAI-04)

Guo B (2003) Knowledge representation and uncertainty management: applying Bayesian belief networks to a safety assessment expert system. Proc Int Conf Nat Lang Process Knowl Eng

Jackson D, Thomas M, Millett L (eds) (2007) Software for dependable systems: sufficient evidence? The National Academies Press

Krieg ML (2001) A tutorial on Bayesian belief networks. Tech. Rep. DSTO-TN-0403. Defence Science and Technology Organisation (Australia)

Littlewood B, Strigini L, Wright D, Courtois P-J (1998) Examination of Bayesian belief network for safety assessment of nuclear computer-based systems. DeVa TR70

MoD (2007) Safety management requirements for defence systems. Defence Standard 00-56. Ministry of Defence

Norsys (2008) Noisy-OR, -And, -Max and -Sum nodes in Netica. Norsys Net Library

Norsys (2010) Netica API: programmer's library, reference manual

Pólya G (1990) Mathematics and plausible reasoning, volume 1: induction and analogy in mathematics. 3rd edn. Princeton University Press

SERENE (1999) Safety and risk evaluation using Bayesian nets: SERENE. Tech. Rep. SERENE/5.3/CSR/3053/R/1. The Serene Partners

Watt EW, Bui AA (2008) Evaluation of a dynamic Bayesian belief network to predict osteoarthritic knee pain using data from the osteoarthritis initiative. AMIA Annu Symp Proc

Zagorecki A, Druzdzel MJ (2004) An empirical study of probability elicitation under noisy-or assumption. In: Barr V, Markov Z (eds) FLAIRS conference. AAAI Press

Accident Investigation – are we reaching the Systemic Causes of Accidents?

Graham Braithwaite

Safety and Accident Investigation Centre, School of Engineering, Cranfield University

Bedford, UK

Abstract Large scale transport accidents are rare, yet carry the potential for significant loss of life and property. Investigations into the causes of such events are likely to come from many different, and sometimes competing, interest groups. Whilst the concept of multiple causality is well understood, are accident investigations able to beat the multiple competing interests, biases and influences that face them to reach the systemic causes of accidents? The paper considers fundamental challenges in accident investigations that go way beyond the initial technical challenge into practical, political and philosophical differences. As investigation capability increases, care must be taken to ensure that the increased threat of criminal litigation does not destroy the opportunities for learning created through good accident investigation.

1 Introduction

The investigation of accidents is a vital component of safety management, driven not just by legal obligations and the need to identify remedial actions to prevent recurrence, but also a strong moral obligation to explain why the tragedy occurred. The responsibility to conduct an investigation often lies with multiple organisations, each with their own priorities. This creates one of many major hurdles for investigations which are discussed below.

2 Competing interests

The initial response to any accident is, rightly, focused on the preservation of life and property. However, the emphasis soon shifts to the investigation of the causes and circumstances behind the event and at this stage, multiple and often competing interests start to appear. Whilst some are focused on the allocation of responsibility or blame, others are more focused on the prevention of recurrence. With a diverse range of interests and timescales, how effectively are the real causes of accidents being identified? To answer this question needs a review of the various interested parties.

2.1 The technical audience

Following a large accident, the technical audience – those who have a particular interest in the design or operational lessons that may be learned – may be wide and varied. In the aviation industry, for example, the standards and recommended practices of ICAO Annex 13 (which refers to aircraft accident investigation) detail the parties who are entitled to participate in an investigation (ICAO 2010). When a serious incident or accident occurs, the state of occurrence is responsible for instituting a not-for-blame investigation. In addition, the state of the registry of the aircraft, the state of the operator, state of design and state of manufacture are all entitled to appoint 'accredited representatives' to the investigation. On top of this, the state conducting the investigation is entitled to appoint one or more technical advisers to assist with the investigation. This can quickly lead to a large investigation team from multiple countries with different and, at times, competing interests.

On 1 June 2009, Air France flight 447 crashed into the Atlantic Ocean with the loss of all on board. As the accident occurred in international waters, the state of registry (France) commenced the technical investigation through the BEA (Bureau d'Enquêtes et d'Analyses pour la sécurité de l'aviation civile). Accredited representatives were appointed from the technical investigation agencies of Brazil, Germany, UK and USA and, through them, technical advisers from manufacturers such as Airbus, CFM and Thales. States which had citizens on board were also afforded observer status and hence introduced representatives from China, Croatia, Hungary, Ireland, Italy, Lebanon, Morocco, Norway, South Korea, Russia, South Africa and Switzerland. Immediately, the geographic spread of the larger investigation team can be seen and this is before an investigation starts to work with states which may have experienced similar events (e.g. the Australian Transport Safety Bureau, which had previously investigated an in-flight upset involving a similar Airbus A330 aircraft).

The State leading the investigation needs to be mindful of the independence of the investigation to ensure that evidence is not tampered with, findings are not leaked inappropriately and so on. This is a difficult 'ringmaster' role, particularly if the occurrence is in a smaller or less affluent state that needs to rely on the input of a larger state. For example, Egypt handed over its investigation of Egyptian flight 990 (which crashed into the Atlantic Ocean with the loss of all on board) in 1999 to the USA. When the National Transportation Safety Board (NTSB) investigation focused on a deliberate act on the part of the relief first officer, the Egyptian authorities tried to take back control and ended up running a parallel investigation that drew different conclusions to the state of manufacture (USA).

2.2 The affected parties

Those affected by a major catastrophe may include those injured by, or who witnessed, the event, as well as the friends and families of victims. It could also include colleagues of those killed or injured and staff who feel that their actions may have had some influence. For a major industrial accident or transport accident, the number of affected parties may run into the hundreds or even thousands and can be spread across the world. The needs of this audience have not always been well recognised or provided for. Problems encountered following a number of high profile aircraft accidents in the late 1980s and 1990s led the US Government to establish the Aviation Disaster Family Assistance Act of 1996. The Act, amongst other things, places a responsibility on the NSTB to work closely with victims and their families throughout an investigation, providing regular briefings (NTSB 2005), but not making them part of the investigation as such. The latter distinction is important as families are often frustrated by the speed of an investigation or its non-punitive nature and would create problems for the scientific, investigative process.

This is not to say that victims and their families are not important – quite the opposite in fact. They have a need for an accurate and timely investigation in the same way that the technical audience does. However, they are likely to be unfamiliar with the process, traumatised by what has occurred and in many cases wanting some sort of restitution, which may well be in conflict with the no-blame aspect of the technical investigation.

2.3 The general public

The public interest following an accident can be substantial, especially if there are significant third-party losses (to life or property) or the event causes real or perceived anxiety in the local community about the particular activity. For example, some residents became genuinely more concerned about third party risk following the crash landing of a Boeing 777 short of the runway at Heathrow in January 2008. However, there were also those who saw an opportunity to use the event as a reason to object to the proposed third runway.

The public's interest is also represented through a variety of legal and quasi-legal processes, which may run consecutively or concurrently with each other depending on the circumstances or jurisdiction. For example, in England, Wales and Northern Ireland, an accidental death must be reported to the relevant coroner who will chair an inquiry into the circumstances. This inquiry will often be suspended until the technical investigation is complete as factual information will be required from it. Where multiple deaths occur, a public inquiry may be called, either immediately or after a period of time. Such inquiries are *ad hoc* and infrequent. The last public inquiry into an aircraft accident in the UK followed the loss of a British

European Airways Trident in 1972 whereas more recent inquiries followed the capsize of the Herald of Free Enterprise (1987); the Piper Alpha production platform explosion (1988); and the Ladbroke Grove and Southall rail accidents (1999). Many accidents receive multiple calls for public inquiries without one ever being convened, such as following the Potters Bar and Grayrigg rail accidents (2002 and 2007).

In the Thames Safety Inquiry (2000), Lord Justice Clarke remarked, 'The public interest is not of course the same as the interest of the public. The public may be interested in many things which it would not be in the public interest to investigate publicly.' In many endeavours, processes exist whereby thorough investigation can take place without the time and cost of a public inquiry, which arguably has common objectives (at least with transport accident investigation) '...namely ascertaining the facts and learning lessons for the future' (Clarke 2000). This notwithstanding, public inquiries have led to substantial changes in the way that safety is managed and events investigated. The UK Marine Accident Investigation Branch was founded partly in response to the Sheen Inquiry and the Rail Accident Investigation Branch following the Ladbroke Grove Inquiry.

Both public inquiries and coronial hearings are inquisitorial in nature rather than adversarial. Whilst these processes may involve the need to criticise organisations or individuals, they cannot determine questions of civil or criminal liability (Cullen 2007).

2.4 The legal process

A more concerning trend is towards the criminalisation of accident investigation. In 2006, the Flight Safety Foundation (FSF), the Civil Air Navigation Services Organisation (CANSO), the Royal Aeronautical Society (RAeS) and the Academie Nationale de L'Air et de L'Espace (ANAE) issued a joint resolution '...decrying the increasing tendency of law enforcement and judicial authorities to attempt to criminalize aviation accidents, to the detriment of aviation safety'. This followed a range of high profile accidents in France, Greece, Brazil, Italy, USA and Switzerland where criminal investigations had been instigated against crew, air traffic controllers, maintainers and senior staff. This statement was reissued in 2010 with further signatures from the International Federation of Air Traffic Controller's Associations (IFATCA), International Society of Air Safety Investigators (ISASI), European Regions Airline Association and Professional Aviation Maintenance Association (PAMA).

Whilst criminal investigations are right and proper where a criminal act is suspected, the threat of such investigations can have a negative impact on the effectiveness of a safety investigation. Where witnesses believe that their testimony could be used against them later, there is little incentive to cooperate. Where states fail to provide protections against not-for-blame investigation reports being used as evidence for criminal proceedings, the quality of safety investigations will suffer.

Acknowledging this as a potential problem, the Crown Prosecution Service (CPS) of England and Wales and the air, marine and rail accident investigation branches (AAIB, MAIB and RAIB) agreed a memorandum of understanding (CPS 2008) setting out the principles for liaison following an accident. One of the basic principles is:

> The public interest requires that safety considerations are of paramount importance, the consequence of which may mean that the interests of an AIB investigation have to take precedence over the criminal investigation.

However, this does not mean that parallel investigation will not take place or that certain elements of evidence collected by the not-for-blame investigation process cannot be used by the CPS. A second principle of co-operation identifies that:

> All evidence and factual information, except where there are specific legislative bars, can be disclosed between the AIBs and the CPS. The AIBs will not share their own opinions or analysis.

Striking the right balance is hard, particularly if the investigation process is overly protective of evidence sources such as data recorders. The legal investigation can argue that, without evidence, it is not possible to deliver justice, whereas misuse of evidence (such as witness interviews or voice recordings) may lead to an unwillingness for people to assist. As Quinn notes, '...when considering the chilling impact the threat of prosecution can and does have on safety investigations, it becomes clear that the future of aviation safety depends on unhindered communication between investigators, witnesses and those involved in accidents' (Quinn 2007). The fear that evidence collected for not-for-blame purposes may subsequently be used for criminal litigation is of great significance. As Michaelides-Mateou and Mateou observe, 'This view undoubtedly results in the fear of prosecution which impedes safety and casts doubts upon the integrity of the technical investigation' (Michaelides-Mateou and Mateou 2010).

3 Speed of investigation

In addition to the multiple interests detailed above, the speed of investigation differs greatly. Public expectations can be unrealistic, no doubt influenced by news media clichés such as 'Twenty-four hours on and investigators still don't know the cause of yesterday's accident...' when in reality an accident investigation may barely have begun.

Accident investigation is often complex, requiring detailed forensic analysis of evidence and careful cross checking. Whilst the International Civil Aviation Organisation (ICAO) places a target of one year to complete an aircraft accident investigation, many take much longer, e.g.:

- The investigation into the loss of Swissair *flight 111* near Peggy's Cove, Nova Scotia took five years, involved over 350 investigators and cost approximately US$48.5 million to complete.
- The investigation by NTSB into the explosion of TWA *flight 800* off Long Island took four years and was the mostly costly aircraft accident investigation in US history.
- The NTSB investigation into the loss of US Airways *flight 427* near Pittsburg took four and a half years to complete.
- The NTSB investigation into the loss of United Airlines *flight 585* near Colorado Springs took 3,677 days to complete.
- The investigation following the loss of Air France *flight 447* took 23 months before it was able to locate and recover the flight data recorders, and is ongoing (as of October 2011).

Investigators face the difficult trade-off between the need for an industry to continue to operate, versus the need to pursue systemic causes that may well be very deep. The resourcing available will make some difference to the ability of the investigation team to do its job, but so too does the available evidence and the willingness of the agency to keep 'digging'. This was clearly demonstrated following the loss of Air New Zealand flight 901 at Mount Erebus, Antarctica in November 1979. The official technical report was released in June 1980 and focused on the actions of the flight crew, who descended below the minimum safe altitude limit and continued at that height despite being unsure of their position. However, in response to public demand, a Royal Commission of Inquiry was formed under Justice Peter Mahon and in 1981 reported its findings (Mahon 1981). The Commission concentrated on deeper, systemic issues within the airline and regulator as well as a tragic combination of factors which had induced at least some of the crew's errors. The findings were controversial and the final report was not tabled in Parliament until 1999.

In transport accidents where a particular vehicle type may come under question, there is a critical need to assess whether it is suitable to continue in service. Similarly where a common fault may affect different vehicles, there may be a drop in confidence in components, technologies or even infrastructure. For example, following the crash landing of British Airways flight 38 at Heathrow in 2008, operators of both the Boeing 777 aircraft (around 60 airlines) and Rolls-Royce Trent 800 engines (Boeing and Airbus) were understandably concerned, as were those using fuel supplied at Beijing airport, the origin of the flight. The potential effect was dramatic if aircraft type, engine or fuel were found to be at fault, especially if grounding was an option. Finding the right answer is critical, not just to the credibility of the investigation, but also to the financial health of many companies and even the global economy. Imagine the effect of grounding the entire fleet of Boeing 777 aircraft which in 2011 stood at nearly 1,000 aircraft.

4 The quality of the investigation

Accident investigation is a multidisciplinary pursuit that draws upon a wide range of technical skills and personal traits. Whilst investigators are frequently recruited based on their technical specialism, it is their methodical, analytical approach that is most valuable, and in particular, how they deal with the collection, preservation and interpretation of evidence.

First responders to accidents are generally motivated by the principle of preserving life. This is not necessarily the first priority of the safety investigator who is concerned with securing evidence. This is not to say that the two types of responder are incompatible. Indeed investigators may well provide useful guidance on an accident site regarding hazards or advice for mounting rescue attempts. Once survivors are rescued and fires extinguished, the investigator must ensure that the site is safe for them to conduct their work. This involves striking a balance between the hazards on site and mitigations that destroy the least amount of evidence.

The crucial point is that from the moment an accident occurs, the investigation will be faced with challenges and compromises. Evidence will be changed, occasionally with intent, but more often due to other priorities such as access to wreckage by rescue workers. Evidence is often perishable (such as ground marks, volatile memory, witness testimony), vulnerable or may never be available to the investigation at all. Any accident investigation is only as good as the quality of evidence it is able to draw upon and in some cases, there is just not sufficient evidence to draw a satisfactory level of proof. As former Australian Transport Safety Bureau (ATSB) Executive Director, Kym Bills notes, 'Investigative bodies find the analysis aspect of their work among the most difficult tasks, with complex crash scenarios likely to involve missing, obscure or even deceptive data' (Rosenkrans 2008).

The quality of the investigators is also a major influence on the outcome of an investigation. This can be affected by wilful factors (such as politics and corruption) or natural biases and heuristics. ISASI has a code of ethics for its investigators to try and overcome such factors through principles of integrity, objectivity and logic. These are explained as follows:

4.1 Integrity

Members should not make any misrepresentations of fact to obtain information that would otherwise be denied to them.

An investigator may cause irreparable damage to the established safety culture if they use unethical means to get hold of information. However frustrating it may be, or however convinced an investigator may be that someone is not telling the truth, they must not lie or use deception to illicit further information. If a witness is assured that their testimony will not be used against them, the investigator must be confident that this is true and not just being used as a technique to encourage cooperation.

> Members should avoid actions or comments which might be reasonably perceived during the fact-finding phase of the investigation as favouring one party or another.

Objectivity is a fundamental quality of any investigator or researcher. The facts will indeed speak for themselves and by favouring one side, the investigator may fall foul of confirmation bias – i.e. seeing what they expect to see, or of inducing bias on the part of witnesses. Without evidence, an investigator becomes just another person with an opinion.

> Remain open-minded to the introduction of new evidence or opinions as to interpretation of facts as determined through analysis, and be willing to revise one's own findings.

Over time, safety professionals get to see the same things happen over and over again. It is often said that there are no accidents; only people with short memories. This may well be true in the majority of cases, but for any given investigation, this may well be the first time something has occurred, or indeed, something completely different from what is first thought. An individual seeking to prove a particular theory may do so by ignoring the evidence to the contrary. A group of people may even become susceptible to group-think whereby suggestions that contradict the group's view will be actively discouraged.

4.2 Objectivity

> Ensure that all items presented as facts reflect honest perceptions or physical evidence that have been checked insofar as practicable for accuracy.

One way to conclusively prove something is to try and disprove it. Evidence may well appear to mean one thing, but could it actually mean something else? If something seems to be too good to be true, then maybe it is? Objectivity is paramount if an investigation's findings are to be truly valuable.

> Follow all avenues of fact determination which appear to have practical value towards achieving accident prevention action.

Accidents are never caused by a single factor. Indeed, an investigation that finds only one contributory factor is likely to be deficient. Therefore, whilst there may be a quick and apparently easy answer, there are likely to be other avenues that need exploration. The key is to know how much depth an investigation requires and which avenues to explore. Except perhaps for major, multiple-fatality disasters, resources for an investigation are likely to be limited and the investigator must decide how wide a net to cast.

> Avoid speculation except in the sense of presenting a hypothesis for testing during the fact-finding and analysis process.

Speculation is the right of the news media and not the investigator as it can introduce bias into any investigation. However, hypothesising is part of the investigative process and to be encouraged. As with all forms of research, hypotheses are to be tested and not just proved, i.e. consider all evidence that supports and refutes the hypothesis before drawing a conclusion based upon both sides of the argument.

> Handle with discretion any information reflecting adversely on persons or organisations and, when the information is reasonably established, notify such persons or organisations of potential criticism before it becomes a matter of public record.

Accident investigations always reveal deficiencies in the way people do their jobs. No one is perfect and it should be remembered that the aim of a safety investigation is to prevent recurrence rather than to shame or blame those who may have been involved. Careless talk will create a culture of distrust for the investigative process and reduce the willingness of people to cooperate in future.

4.3 Logic

> Begin sufficiently upstream in each sequence of events so as to ascertain practicable accident prevention information.

A good investigator will do well to remember what it was like to be five years old when any explanation usually led to the next question 'why?' (The use of five year olds in accident investigation is not to be recommended, but the principle is a worthwhile one.) It is important to question why something happened and not be tempted to just focus on who was the last person to do something wrong. Individuals do make errors and commit violations, but was there a reason for it? The higher level the causes are found, the easier it may be to effect a change that benefits a larger number of people.

> Ensure that all safety-meaningful facts, however small, are related to all sequences of events.

Investigations uncover things that are wrong – that is very much one of the objectives of investigation. However, it is important to limit coverage to the matter that is being investigated. Investigators who are also safety managers may well make a mental note of problems they discover along the way for future reference, but an investigation report should be clear and focused and only include information relating to the event – otherwise they will dilute their message and, in turn, their effectiveness.

> Be alert to value judgements based upon personal experiences which may influence the analysis; and where suspect, turn to colleagues for independent assessment of the facts.

Investigators are often recruited to the role as a consequence of their operational knowledge. However, it is vital that previous experience does not cloud judgment during an investigation. What may be blindingly obvious to someone who has done the job may not be to others and sometimes an expert may be too close to an issue to see something that is obvious to someone else. Investigators are human and accepting another viewpoint is not a weakness.

> Prepare illustrative material and select photographs so as not to present misleading
> significance of the data or facts thus portrayed.

The use of images or diagrams can be very powerful, sometimes to the point of biasing the reader. Do photographs assist the reader in understanding something or could they be misinterpreted? For example, are the weather conditions or light in the photographs similar to those when the event occurred? Is the photographer in the same position as the individual whose view they are attempting to portray? This point is becoming increasingly relevant where animations of accident sequences are used, particularly in litigation. Moving pictures are even more compelling and, if not used appropriately, utterly misleading.

Along with insufficient or misleading evidence, biases such as hindsight are probably the greatest threat to successful accident investigation. Dekker warns '...that the bias of hindsight is one of the human factors investigator's worst enemies' (Dekker 2002). If understanding the vagaries of human performance and their influence on accident causation was not enough, investigators must also acknowledge their own human performance weaknesses in trying to solve complex, multifaceted problems.

5 Getting to the 'right' answer

Accident investigations, quasi-legal (such as coronial or fatal accident inquiries) and legal proceedings may ultimately be looking for different answers. Whilst they are effectively investigating the same contributory events and factors, their purpose is likely to be satisfied by different levels of answer. For example, the aim of safety investigations is to develop recommendations to prevent recurrence; the coronial process is aiming to establish the cause and circumstances of death; and legal proceedings are concerned with allocating responsibility liability.

Commensurate with this, different investigations often work to different levels of proof. This can be problematic and cause conflict, such as following the ATSB's investigation into the aircraft accident which occurred near Lockhard River in Queensland in 2005 where the regulator (CASA) took exception to the Bureau's analysis model and standard of proof. This in turn led the investigation agency to re-examine its approach. As Walker and Bills note, 'Despite its importance, complexity, and reliance on investigators' judgements, analysis has been a neglected area in terms of standards, guidance and training of investigators in most organisations that conduct safety investigations' (Walker and Bills 2008).

There is an industry-wide acceptance of the need for investigations to consider not just what Reason describes as active failures (Reason 1990, 1997), but also the latent conditions that may lie deep within an organisation or system (or indeed in designs or decisions made months or years prior to an accident). This is evidenced through endorsement by the ICAO and the International Maritime Organisation (IMO) and through the successful application in a range of high profile investigations (e.g. see investigation into the overrun of Boeing 747 VH-OJH at Bangkok, Thailand in September 1999 (ATSB 2001)). Such focus on the systemic causes of accidents rather than the immediate actions or technical failures lies at the heart of not-for-blame safety investigations. However, application across the global transport sector is far from universal for a variety of reasons including:

- the competition for evidence between agencies
- different views regarding primacy in the investigation
- fundamental differences in philosophy regarding the accident causation
- standards of training for investigators
- resources available for the conduct of the investigation
- the level of independence of the investigation agency
- the political will to go deeper into systemic factors such as regulation
- reporting deadlines
- concerns about the use of not-for-blame investigation reports in litigation.

So many competing interests will inevitably lead to either real or perceived compromises. If the push towards a deeper, systemic understanding of causation is thwarted by fear, then high reliability organisations lose great, and often expensive, opportunities to learn from the mistakes of others. It is with this in mind that FSF, RAeS, ANAE, CANSO, ERA, IFATCA, PAMA and ISASI, through their joint resolution (FSF et al. 2010) regarding criminalization of aviation accidents,

'...urge national aviation and accident investigating authorities to:

1. assert strong control over accident investigations, free from undue interference from law enforcement authorities
2. invite international cooperation in the accident investigation under Annex 13
3. conduct professional investigations to identify probable cause and contributing factors and develop recommendations in a deliberative manner, avoiding any 'rush to judgment'
4. ensure the free and voluntary flow of essential safety information
5. provide victims' loved ones and their families with full, accurate, and precise information at the earliest possible time
6. address swiftly any acts or omissions in violation of aviation standards.'

6 Conclusion

Faced with practical, political and philosophical challenges as detailed in this paper, it may seem remarkable that accident investigation within the transport sectors has achieved as much as it has. Starting immediately after an occurrence, the rush to start an investigation and collect what may be vulnerable, perishable, in-complete or inaccurate evidence comes at the same time that multiple agencies compete for primacy and access. Faced with multiple pressures from the technical audience, such as manufactures, regulators and operators, as well as from those who may have been directly affected, such as through the loss of loved ones, in-vestigators need to find the right balance of timeliness and accuracy. Doing so re-quires strict professional ethics and a disciplined approach towards the analysis of evidence. The value of success is enormous. However, the loss of trust or damage to safety culture that can be sustained through failure is similarly far reaching.

References

ATSB (2001) Investigation report 199904538 Boeing 747-438, VH-OJH Bangkok, Thailand, 23 September 1999. Department of Transport and Regional Services, Canberra

Clarke, Lord Justice (2000) Thames safety inquiry final report. Presented to Parliament by the Secretary of State for the Environment, Transport and the Regions by command of Her Majesty

CPS (2008) Memorandum of understanding between the Crown Prosecution Service and the Air Accidents Investigation Branch, Marine Accident Investigation Branch and the Rail Accident Investigation Branch. Crown Prosecution Service

Cullen, Right Honorable Lord (2007) Public inquiries and the advancement of safety. Proc 5th Int Semin Fire Explos Hazards, Edinburgh, UK

Dekker S (2002) The field guide to human error investigations. Ashgate, Aldershot

FSF, RAeS, ANAE, CANSO, ERA, IFATCA, PAMA, ISASI (2010) Joint resolution regarding criminalization of aviation accidents. http://flightsafety.org/files/resolution_01-12-10.pdf. Accessed 15 October 2011

ICAO (2010) Annex 13 to the Chicago convention on international civil aviation – aircraft accident and incident investigation. Tenth Edition. ICAO, Montreal

Mahon, Justice PT (1981) Report of the Royal Commission to inquire into the crash on Mount Erebus, Antarctica of a DC10 aircraft operated by Air New Zealand Limited. New Zealand Government

Michaelides-Mateou S, Mateou A (2010) Flying in the face of criminalization: the safety implications of prosecuting aviation professionals for accidents. Ashgate, Aldershot

NTSB (2005) Information for friends and family – major accident investigations. Leaflet SPC0501. National Transportation Safety Board. http://www.beta.ntsb.gov/publictn/2005/SPC0501.pdf. Accessed 18 September 2011

Quinn KP (2007) Battling accident criminalization. Aerosafety World. J Flight Saf Found, Arlington, Virginia

Reason J (1990) Human error. Cambridge University Press, Cambridge

Reason J (1997) Managing the risks of organizational accidents. Ashgate, Aldershot

Rosenkrans W (2008) Defensible analysis. Aerosafety World. J Flight Saf Found, Arlington, Virginia

Walker MB, Bills KM (2008) Analysis, causality and proof in safety investigations. ATSB Transport Safety Report, Aviation Research and Analysis Report AR-2007-053

The Fukushima Accident

Peter Ladkin

University of Bielefeld CITEC and Causalis Limited

Bielefeld, Germany

Abstract I recount the accident to the Fukushima Daiichi nuclear plant starting on 11 March 2011 and continuing. I highlight some system-safety aspects, and compare with an idealised 8-step process for assessing and ensuring engineered-system safety to see where it went wrong. Nuclear accidents such as this have political and social consequences in a way in which even the worst commercial aircraft accident does not. I suggest some questions about engineered-system safety which the polity must answer somehow.

1 Introduction

On 11 March 2011 an unusually strong earthquake, now called the Tohoku earthquake, occurred off the north-eastern coast of Japan's main island, Honshu. While the earthquake caused some destruction, the ensuing tsunami about three quarters of an hour later largely destroyed numbers of towns and devastated cities such as Sendai (USGS 2011, Wikipedia 2011a).

While there is some evidence to think that the earthquake itself caused some damage to critical systems at the Fukushima Daiichi ('Fukushima Number One') nuclear plant, located at the edge of the ocean in Fukushima province, some few hundred kilometres north of Tokyo, and indeed cut the supply of outside electricity, the tsunami flooded the plant, including the basements in which the back-up power generators were situated. There are videos of this happening posted on the World Wide Web (WWW). The generators ceased operating after they were flooded. This event, losing primary as well as backup power generation, is known in the US as a 'station blackout' (Lochbaum 2011). There are batteries which supply power for a few hours in the event of a station blackout.

2 What's the problem?

There are six reactors at Fukushima Daiichi. At the time of the earthquake, Reactors 1-3 were operating, Reactor 4 was defueled – its fuel was stored in the spent fuel pool inside the reactor building along with spent fuel from previous operation – and Reactors 5 and 6 were in 'cold shutdown' (see below for terms). Reactors 1-3 shut down automatically immediately upon detecting the strong earthquake.

The reactors here are a GE design, known as a Boiling Water Reactor (BWR) with Mark I containment in Reactors 1-5 and Mark II containment in Reactor 6. In a shut-down of this kind of reactor, the chain reaction which sustains the usual power generation is halted by the insertion of 'control rods', made from neutron-absorbing material such as boron or cadmium, directly into the reactor core. The rods are inserted automatically from below. However, current reactor designs require continued and continual cooling as the radioactivity in the core remains. Although it decreases in the usual exponential manner over time, a matter of days for the by-product iodine-131 but many months for the other major by-product caesium-137, the reactor must be actively cooled for years until the radioactivity in the core decreases to a point at which passive cooling (that is, just letting it siphon off its heat through static, passive heat sinks) suffices.

The core, plus the cooling/heat transfer water in a BWR, is contained first in a Reactor Pressure Vessel (RPV) and associated piping taking the superheated steam into turbines, as shown in Figure 1. (This figure is also used on page 12 of the UK Office of Nuclear Regulation interim report (ONR 2011).) The primary prophylaxis against a release of radioactive substances into the environment in case of a physical failure is physical containment. The RPV is thus enclosed in a Primary Containment Vessel (PCV); the reactor building itself is designed to be the secondary containment structure.

The water in the RPV is (super)heated by the heat of the core chain reaction, and converts to steam, which is led to pass through the turbines, which generate electricity. After passing through the turbines, the steam is condensed and passed, cooler, back into the RPV. The RPV and some cooling/generation system piping is contained within the concrete and steel Primary Containment Vessel (PCV), itself enclosed in the reactor building (secondary containment), which also contains the Spent Fuel Pool (see below), as shown in Figure 2 (the same diagram appears as Figure 4 on page 14 of the ONR interim report (ONR 2011)). The turbine building is a separate structure, but the system of RPV, generation/cooling circuit, and turbines is part of one enclosed pressure system in the form of a loop. For more technical details of BWR systems and their various cooling systems, see the US Nuclear Regulatory Commission's Reactor Concepts Manual (NRC undated).

The phenomenon of persistent active cooling is basic to contemporary reactor design. From being on-line, after a shutdown, the reactor *must* – and this is a 'must' without exceptions – be actively cooled for years. This is and has been well known for half a century. The first reactor at Fukushima Daiichi went on-line forty years before the accident, in 1971, was operating at the time of the tsunami, and had been recently granted a licence to continue operating until 2021 (Wikipedia 2011b).

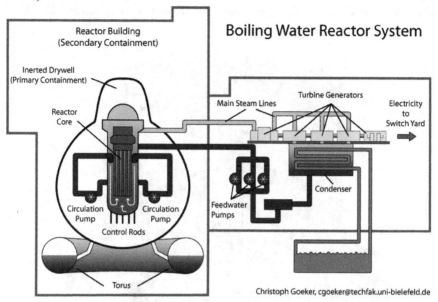

Fig. 1. A schematic diagram of a BWR with Mark I containment[1]

The reactor itself is not the only installation in a BWR with Mark I containment which requires cooling. The Spent Fuel Pool (SFP) is located in the upper stories of the reactor building, as shown in Figure 2, under the orange and yellow crane used for transferring fuel rods out of the top of the reactor into the pool, and vice versa if refuelling. Spent fuel must be actively cooled until the residual radioactivity is low enough that passive cooling – i.e. allowing the heat to distribute itself through the immediate surroundings, which then transfer the heat to the atmosphere – suffices. This process takes years. The fuel is cooled in the SFP by being submerged in sufficient quantities of actively-cooled water. The SFP at Reactor 4 was also being used to store the current fuel; the reactor had been defueled. The fuel in the SFPs requires significant active cooling; more so of course when the current fuel is sitting there as well.

A reactor is said to be in 'cold shutdown' when the temperature of the cooling matter is below its atmospheric boiling point, in the case of water 100°C. In cold shutdown, the water in the core cooling is no longer superheated and the cooling system may be opened to the atmosphere, say for some maintenance tasks, without a high-pressure release of suddenly-generated steam. In normal operations, the cooling water is only lightly contaminated, but in the case of, say, a meltdown (see below) it might well be highly contaminated, as indeed it is in some of the units at Fukushima. Reaching cold shutdown normally takes days after shutdown, but the

---

[1] Graphics: Christopher Goeker

reactor must still be actively cooled, indeed for years after shutdown. The Fukushima Daiichi Reactors 1-3 may achieve cold shutdown by the end of 2011, that is, somewhat over nine months since shutdown (Dow Jones Deutschland 2011).

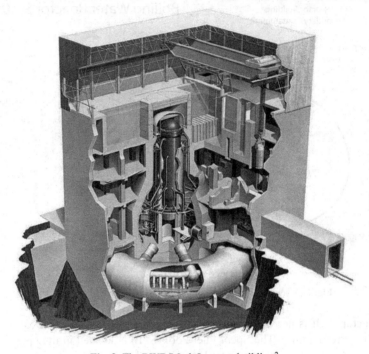

Fig. 2. The BWR/Mark I reactor building[2]

All the active systems, not only for active cooling, but also for the control of semi-passive cooling systems such as those driven by steam turbines operating from residual core heat, require a supply of electricity to operate. When there is no local power (the reactors are shut down), no external power (the grid is not supplying), no backup power (the generators are out of commission), one is reliant solely upon the electricity stored in the batteries, which lasts at most hours, whereas cooling must continue for years.

'It is assumed' that a station blackout can be somehow 'fixed' within the few hours which the batteries last. This one obviously wasn't and couldn't be.

The result of all this is that the reactor cores in the then-operating Reactors 1-3 have melted down (so far as is known six months after the accident – nobody and nothing is able to get close enough to see). That is, the heat from the continuing radioactivity was enough to convert the cores into liquid, which becomes even hotter because the same amount of radioactivity is now concentrated in a smaller volume, and likely melts – has melted – partially or completely through the concrete-and-steel floor of the RPV and maybe the PCV.

---

[2] With kind permission of GE

3 Measuring bad and worse

It used to be assumed by nuclear engineers as well as Hollywood that a 'meltdown' was the ultimate catastrophe with nuclear-reactor operations. It was assumed that if a meltdown occurred, *all* the radioactive substance in the core would somehow make it into the environment, rather rapidly. Although we cannot yet say how much will make it into the environment, it is clear the release has not been as rapid as Hollywood imagined and the nuclear engineering industry feared. The country operating the reactor is required by treaty to tell the International Atomic Energy Agency (IAEA) how much it thinks *has already* made it into the environment. The Japanese regulator NISA said one month after the accident: about a tenth as much as Chernobyl. The estimate has subsequently been doubled, and we are not yet done counting, as recent ocean research by Woods Hole Oceanographic Institute has shown (Jolly 2011).

In fact, the official estimate of radioactivity released on 12 April 2011 was largely based upon atmospheric releases, due in part to three oxyhydrogen explosions, two of which were captured on video posted on news WWW sites and WWW video sites within hours. There appears to be no such record of the third, in the defueled Reactor 4, with which the main concern was keeping the SFP, containing also the core fuel of the defueled reactor, cooled. Atmospheric release occurred also in escaping steam, still a problem at the time of writing, as well as release into quantities of water which are open to the atmosphere, such as that which accumulated in the turbine and reactor buildings of various units, and in trenches surrounding some of those buildings, and which the operator has been attempting to pump into containment and processing structures. Some of this, according to Woods Hole, must still be escaping, because the concentration of radioactivity they have measured in specific areas of ocean water, about 10,000 Becquerels per cubic metre (a Becquerel, Bq, is a count of the number of decay events occurring per second) remained constant from May to July, whereas if leaks had ceased, dispersal would have caused this to reduce considerably over this time. (In April, the count was 100,000 Bq per cubic metre. 'Background', from natural causes as well as the result of atmospheric nuclear bomb tests, is about 1.5 Bq per cubic metre as measured in 2010). Rather than overt releases of water from accumulations, it could be that this radioactivity is being carried through groundwater and thereby into the ocean, say from the melted cores.

The IAEA has a scale, called the INES, which measures accidents on a scale of 0 to 7. The handbook is quite detailed, at over 200 pages (IAEA 2011). However, roughly speaking the types of accident severity can be classified into loss of redundancy (called 'defence in depth' in traditional nuclear power thinking) which alone may take one only up to INES Level 2; serious mechanical engineering failure, which may take one up to INES Level 5; and significant environmental release of radiation, which is solely responsible for Levels 6 and 7.

The IAEA says that the responsible government determines the INES Level. The Japanese government, after the oxyhydrogen explosions in Reactor Buildings

1, 3 and 4, and the suspected events in Reactor 2, initially classified each of Reactors 1-4 as INES Level 5, and Reactors 5 and 6 as Level 0. The French disagreed, saying it was at least Level 6. But the protocol is not open to debate: if the Japanese said Level 5, then Level 5 it was.

Presumably, until the estimate of environmentally-released radioactivity was completed (in April), the main proof of accident consisted in the physically-destroyed plant, and this in four cases (Units 1-4) was given the most severe INES classification for such events, which is Level 5. After the estimate was publically issued, the events in Units 1-3 were jointly classified as a single Level 7 event (presumably since contamination was supposed to have issued from all three), Unit 4 remained a Level 5 event and Units 5 and 6 Level 0.

In fact, there is clear evidence of loss of redundancy in cooling Units 5 and 6. The data clearly show alternating cooling and heating of RPVs and SFPs, which means that of the four required cooling systems, fewer than four were working (indeed, in early days only one) up until about 15 September: an obvious loss of defence in depth. This observation and analysis by Bernd Sieker was presented at the Eleventh Bieleschweig Workshop (Bielefeld 2011); Sieker's data plots are also available (Sieker 2011).

This all shows that the protocol used for classification is not ideal. The French were right: indeed, they were optimistic. As was the Japanese organisation that disagreed with NISA's estimates on the original Level 7 classification move. Sieker is right. The people performing the classification and reporting it to the IAEA were wrong as they did so; sometimes one suspects deliberately wrong (Units 5 and 6) and sometimes just making mistakes in judgement where others knew better. Whatever the purpose of classification, objectivity is better: being right is even better. The classification should surely aim first to be right, and that entails serious engagement with dissenting technical views, for which there is no place in the current classification protocol.

4 Just bad? Or worse? What went right?

It has been claimed by industry insiders as well as knowledgeable observers for some time that a meltdown was not necessarily the worst consequence of a lack of cooling. Meltdown allows radioactivity to contaminate ground and groundwater, which is relatively immobile compared with, say, air. A SFP which overheated, boiled away its cooling water, exposing fuel rods directly to the air, would release radioactivity directly into the air, where it would be transported much more quickly, and less predictably, allowing far less time to evacuate people in its path, and in principle contaminating far greater areas of the planet. Even worse, active fuel, as was stored in the SFP of Reactor 4 (SFP 4), if it is somehow uncovered and uncooled, could actually restart a chain reaction, in which case most of the material – the entire contents of a core – would burn into the atmosphere very quickly – a completely uncontained and uncontrolled reaction of rather greater intensity than the reactor itself when operating. Not good.

This hasn't happened. Due to emergency measures, namely shipping Putzmeister mobile concrete pumps with 62-metre arms, some even bigger, and 20+ wheels each, from Germany and the US (Putzmeister 2011), and pumping 100 tonnes of water (about equal to 100,000 litres) per day into SFP 4 in the first few months, any releases from SFP 4 have been kept to what most observers agree is a minimum.

So this accident is a catastrophe. But it is by no means worst-case.

The Putzmeister process for cooling the SFPs was by any measure a success. Another success was the emergency cooling of the reactors by seawater.

The salts in seawater, when used to cool the RPV of a BWR, are extremely corrosive and can coagulate in and slowly destroy the piping. So this is an emergency measure of limited temporal effectiveness. Not only that, but if indeed subsystem failure is induced through using seawater, there is no apparent way to get in immediately and fix it: the internals of the cooling system are open to the core; the cooling water is highly radioactive if the core has been compromised; and when a leak ensues through mechanical failure of some sort – which becomes almost inevitable if you were to use seawater for too long and the reactor has not reached 'cold shutdown' at which it is cooled to below the atmospheric boiling point of the coolant – all that substance converts into steam and is uncontained, and so contaminated that no human can get anywhere near it to fix it. Cold shutdown takes some days to occur in normal operation, and may be attainable only with considerable difficulty, if at all, in the case of a meltdown (as we are seeing at the time of writing with Reactors 1-3). This is all well known. During the first few days of the accident, the manager of the plant decided on seawater cooling of the RPVs, and reports say he refused to stop doing so even when commanded by senior authorities (the government, deriving, some say, from the Prime Minister himself) to do so.

Had the seawater cooling ceased within the first days of the accident, there is little doubt that the meltdown would have been far worse than it is, maybe even reaching Hollywood standards. Seawater cooling was finally substituted with freshwater cooling, and nothing had catastrophically broken. By all measures, a success.

5 Should we have known? Should we have guessed? Did we blow it? Or is it bad luck?

The design basis at Fukushima Daiichi for flood resistance is reported to have been a little under a 6-metre wave. The bluff on which the plant stands used to be higher, but was reduced to make construction and cooling water management easier (Yoshida and Fukada 2011).

Was the design basis appropriate? Obviously not. Was it reviewed? Yes, as far as we can tell. But when and how and what the conclusions were, the 'safety case' if you like, has not been made public, despite the very public consequences of this mistake.

'Mistake', I say? Was it? This was initially reported as a '1,000 year tsunami', with recent geological research having uncovered evidence of a similar event 1,100 years ago or so. So let's see: a thousand years is 10^7 operating hours (op-hours); that means based on this reasoning that the expectation of flooding at this plant is 1 in 10^7 ophours. And what is the expectation that flooding leads to a severe accident? Here is industrial and organisational sociologist Charles Perrow in his book The Next Catastrophe (Perrow 2007):

> [p134] 'Emergency power at nuclear plants is provided by diesel generators (which have a long history of failing to start and other problems). Clearly visible in some places, these generators could be taken out with grenades. Or, a hurricane could do the work of the terrorists' dynamite and take out the power, and the storm could easily render the emergency generators inoperative as well.'

He then recounts an occasion, in 1996 at Nine Mile Point, when power and emergency power were out for twenty minutes. And again,

> [p173] '[Nuclear power plants] are vulnerable to natural disasters. There have been emergency shutdowns in the face of hurricanes, for example, though no storms or floods have as yet disabled a plant's external power supply and its backup power generators.'

These plants were known to be vulnerable to flooding taking out backup power. US nuclear power plants, except for Diablo Canyon and San Onofre in California, are not located on the ocean, so the word 'tsunami' is not to be expected here, but 'hurricane' is, along with 'tornado' or 'torrential rain'. Such events would occur to Perrow's readers. (Lee Clarke has noted that such US plants as Salem and Oyster Creek might also be vulnerable to flooding from oceanic events.) Indeed, the nuclear engineer, trainer, and failure analyst David Lochbaum, the leader of the Nuclear Project at the Union of Concerned Scientists, has written of station blackouts caused by flooding, and the risks, in his weekly 'Fission Stories' series (UCS undated). I understand Lochbaum first drew attention to the inadequacy of station-blackout provisions in 1992.

There is a good engineering case to be made, indeed I would say it is pretty clear, that a '1,000-year tsunami' of this magnitude is almost certainly going to cause a station blackout for longer than the batteries will hold, in other words the chances of an severe accident due to loss of cooling are better than even, and in any case certainly way more than one in ten. The conclusion follows that the hazard that a '1,000-year tsunami' event occurs and causes an accident has a likelihood of the order of magnitude of 1 in 10^7 per ophour.

Observe that this is two orders of magnitude less than what is acceptable for certifying a commercial airliner (certification guideline says it is acceptable that a 'catastrophic' event from a single cause be shown to occur not more frequently than 1 in 10^9 ophours. A 'catastrophic' event is one that *prevent[s] the continued safe flight and landing of the aircraft'* (Lloyd and Tye 1982, p37). That is two orders of magnitude less probable.

And what about severity? For a commercial aeroplane, loss of everyone on board plus the aeroplane plus maybe some people on the ground (usually few, even in the case of the aeroplane landing in a city, e.g. AA587 in Queens in November 2001, although, as we saw, up to about 3,000 if it flies directly into a very large skyscraper, as on 11 September 2001, which is unlikely unless deliberate). In contrast, estimates of deaths due to the Chernobyl accident range from a few hundred (comparable with a commercial aircraft accident) to tens of thousands and more (see below), to which we could apply discount factors, as economists and epidemiologists do, for not being immediate.

So it looks as if, even with the 1,000-year event, the risk known to have been taken with this power plant is two orders of magnitude more likely that that known to be taken with a commercial airliner. What in safety-engineering reasoning accounts for this enormous difference in conventionally 'acceptable' risk?

But in fact a '1,000-year' tsunami was not needed to cause this accident in this way. See Figure 6, p22 of the Interim Report of 19 May 2011 of the UK Office for Nuclear Regulation on the implications for the UK nuclear industry (ONR 2011). There are four tsunamis in the last 120 years on the east coast of Japan whose magnitude exceeded the design basis for Fukushima Daiichi, and two of those waves were over 20 metres.

Indeed, the tsunami data was well known. The Washington Post reported an astonishing instance of seismologist Yukinobu Okimura being put down by a TEPCO official for raising the issue of tsunamis at a meeting at the industry regulator in 2009 (Nakamura and Harlan 2011). At the Eleventh Bieleschweig Workshop, Robin Bloomfield presented some evidence that the tsunami threat was being taken seriously by the operator and regulators, and old assumptions and behaviour revised (Bloomfield 2011).

So, I judge, yes, 'we' should have known, and indeed were on our way. Should we have 'guessed'? Most certainly, and that back in 1971 at the latest. Did 'we' blow it? I would say obviously, yes. Or was it just bad luck? Well, one could say it was 'luck', indeed of the bad sort, that led the tsunami to occur when it did, rather than, say X years in the future after we had potentially sorted out the tsunami risk, starting first with the acknowledgement of its possibility. On the other hand, random-seeming events are like that: they just occur at some point. Engineers of safety-critical systems are supposed to take such phenomena into account, and it looks very much, also from newspaper reports, as though this was not adequately done (see, for example, the translation of an article in the Süddeutsche Zeitung on p43 of my Fukushima diary (Ladkin 2011a)). So, no, it wasn't just bad luck. There was some amount of not paying attention.

So what does 'paying attention' consist in here?

6 How one engineers safety-critical systems

The first step is common to all engineered systems, indeed to many human artefacts.

Step 1. Say what the system is supposed to do, along with maybe some amount of how you think it is going to do it.

A nuclear power plant is intended to generate electricity through using the heat of an atomic chain reaction to move fluids or gases through a turbine, the energy of whose subsequent motion is converted into electricity.

One designates a system as *safety-critical* if one thinks that the system is capable, either in normal operation or in failure behaviour, of some behaviour which causes harm (harming people or distressing the environment). *Safety* is in some sense the absence of harm; ensuring safety is ensuring the absence of harm. Let us assume there is a general social mandate to ensure safety as far as reasonably possible (this assumption can be justified, but this lies beyond the scope of this note).

Functional safety concerns those aspects of safety that are associated with the intended function, or associated failure behaviour, of the system. For example, the strip of metal which fell off an airliner on take-off in Paris, lay on the runway, and according to the investigators punctured the tyre of a Concorde on take-off on 25 July 2000 is a matter of functional safety: the strip had a function, was attached so as to perform this function, and the attachment failed. However, if a part is coated with a substance whose application could harm the workers applying it, this is not a matter of functional safety concerning the part as a subsystem of the finished artefact. It nevertheless might well be a functional safety concern for the factory which applies this coating, for applying the coating is a function of the coating factory. Functional safety concerns the operation of a system in its context, and it is this aspect which I am addressing here.

Step 2. Decide whether the system is capable of harmful behaviour.

This may seem obvious. However, the constant recall of children's toys should suggest to us that it is not always obvious if an artefact is capable of harmful behaviour. It is clear that a nuclear power plant is capable of harmful behaviour.

Step 3. Since the system is capable of some harmful behaviour, or capable of inducing, or even not hindering some harmful behaviour, list all the harmful behaviour of which you believe the system to be capable/to be capable of inducing/not to hinder, taking into account the behaviour of its environment which enables this harmful behaviour.

The trick here is to be complete.

In the case of nuclear power, one can well believe the list to be more or less complete. Harm consists of:

1. the usual kinds of local physical harm connected with the malfunction of large industrial plant which operates under extremes of temperature and pressure,

and subject to chemical reactions amongst the substances used. We know about these mostly from long experience with all kinds of plant.

2. the harm associated with release of radioactive substances into the environment.

(Notice that I have already applied here an intellectual grouping. Instead of listing all the things that can go physically wrong with plant, I use the phrase I wrote in (1). And instead of listing all the things that can go wrong when the environment contains substantial quantities of radioactive substances, I designate rather the initiating event in (2). It is possible to give a complete listing by using such grouping, but it should also be clear that completeness attained in this conceptual manner contrasts with the detail and precision needed for engineering concrete avoidance and mitigation measures. Indeed, I hold this to be one of the great challenges of safety engineering: to attain completeness while enabling the necessary detail and precision.)

As we have seen, the INES from the IAEA recognises (2) as the major factor in severity, the other factors (loss of 'defence in depth' and physical malfunction or destruction of plant) come under (1). So it seems as if Step 3 is pretty well covered also in the case of nuclear power plants. The influence of the environment is taken into account in so far as the distribution of any released radioactive material over the earth and into the atmosphere is taken into account.

Step 4. Associate with the harmful behaviour from Step 3 all the consequences of that harmful behaviour.

We have harm from Step 2, and we have harmful behaviour, from Step 3. This step associates the specific harm with the specific harmful behaviour.

For nuclear power at this level of generality, the harm resulting from (1) is harm to workers, which involves not only the usual industrial trauma but also potential exposure to radiation. This is traditionally controlled through the use of crude measurement devices (dosimeters) and limits on the maximum exposure to which workers may be subjected over a given period of time. These limits are apparently flexible, as the Fukushima accident showed: they were raised by the regulator for continuing workers at the plant to the level previously reserved for once-only exposure in an emergency situation. It should be clear that they are controversial, as indeed is the harm generated by (2). 'Plausible' estimates of deaths due to the Chernobyl accident differ by orders of magnitude. The United Nations Scientific Committee on the Effects of Atomic Radiation (UNSCEAR) reported in 2005 57 direct deaths in the accident and 4,000 additional cancer deaths among the 600,000 people regarded as significantly exposed (Wikipedia 2011c, with links to archived original documentation). However, Greenpeace reported in 2006 an estimate of 250,000 cancer cases, of which 100,000 would be fatal (Greenpeace 2006). This does not take into account other human health effects, which people believe have been seen as far away as Berlin (see articles by Watts, Pflugbeil and Sperling, as well as effects on other living organisms by Achazi (Metz et al.

2010)). There are serious estimates of harm even higher than this (Yablokov et al. 2009).

With an order of magnitude difference in serious estimates of deaths, let alone other illnesses and environmental damage, we may conclude that a consensus on Step 4 is lacking for nuclear accidents. It's not like an aeroplane or train accident, or apparently even an oil spill.

Step 5. (Hazard Analysis, HazAn): For all the behaviour you have identified in Step 3, identify precursor behaviour, or states of the system + environment, at which point there is still room for intervention before the harmful behaviour inevitably ensues.

If there is a severe thunderstorm in the flight path of your aircraft, you can deviate. Severe thunderstorms often contain weather sufficient to induce loss of control in any aircraft. Once you're in it, luck (mostly) lets you out. But you want to identify the hazard and deviate before that. When the pressure is rising in your pressure vessel, you want to try to contain that rise before it rises to the point at which the vessel ruptures. So uncontrolled undesired rising pressure is a hazard. If two commercial high-performance aircraft come within a few hundred feet of each other, they may not reliably be able to avoid collision, so coming that close, an 'airprox', is a hazard. Since a BWR must be continually cooled, even after shutdown, at a known rate, in order to prevent core meltdown, overpressure in heat-transfer mechanisms and breach of containment, station blackout is a hazard.

Step 6. For each hazard, designate the consequences (namely the harmful behaviour of which the hazard behaviour, or entry into the hazard state, is a precursor).

This makes clear that HazAn is a technical grouping, for the purposes of mitigation and avoidance, of the harmful behaviour identified in Step 3. With a hazard is associated a *severity*, which is variously the harm which may result from the hazard.

There is some controversy about how to assess severity. Traditionally, engineering takes the worst-case outcome. Loss of power on all engines in a commercial airliner has 'catastrophic' severity, even though British Airways Flight 9 in 1982 landed safely at Jakarta after having had the engines flame out due to a volcanic ash encounter; British Airways Flight 038 crashed at London Heathrow airport in January 2008 after losing significant engine power on short final, with one broken leg and two other minor injuries, but a very broken aircraft; and Air Transat Flight 236 glided to a successful emergency landing in the Azores islands after losing engine power through fuel exhaustion. The classification is appropriate: many or all the people on board might well have died in any of these cases, and their survival has little to do with the event which caused the emergency. But there are also situations in which worst-case classification might not be quite as appropriate. If I fall off a mountain bike on a hill trail, the worst case is that I am run over by the off-road vehicle following right behind. But this is so unlikely, and so easily mitigated (let him by!), that mountain bikers, with reason, usually do not think this way.

Step 7. Design into the system avoidance mechanisms for that behaviour. If you can't find any, then design in some mechanisms which mitigate the consequences identified in Step 4.

Step 8. Demonstrate that the mechanisms you have devised in Step 7 are adequate, to some measure of 'adequate'.

Step 7 is self-explanatory. Step 8 is usually undertaken by judging 'risk', usually taken as some combination of the likelihood of a hazard associated with its (modified) severity, further combined over all hazards. The original definition of risk, and that still used in finance, is due to Abraham de Moivre, in his paper De Mensura Sortis in the Proceedings of the Royal Society in 1711 (Hald et al. 1984): the expected value of loss. However, engineering definitions differ from this (Ladkin 2001, 1998).

This is an idealised process. In fact, all of these steps are iterated many times during the life of a complex project. Steps 2 through 8 are applied recursively to subsystems as they are designed.

7 Problems with this process

For a complex system, the eight steps of this idealised process must be performed by a variegated human organisation, indeed a collection of partly cooperating, partly competing formal organisations, which within themselves are rarely if ever perfect. Very often, parts of these organisations will want to keep certain relevant matters secret, or at least undisclosed to certain other groups, for a variety of reasons.

One could imagine a regulatory regime for certain safety-critical systems defining specific documentary products to be generated for each step of this idealised process, which products would enable a rational reconstruction of an argument that a system is adequately safe (whatever 'adequately' is taken to mean).

A question then arises as to who shall see and analyse the rational reconstruction, and who shall assess that it is correct. Generally speaking, *quis custodiet ipsos custodes?*

8 Application to Fukushima

Although there is considerable ongoing discussion about what we have seen during the unfolding of the Fukushima accident, there are some general, generally agreed, conclusions one can draw.

First, quite apart from the builder in (originally) 1971, it seems that the operator TEPCO did not accurately estimate the risk from tsunamis to its Fukushima Daiichi plant and the regulator, NISA, did not correct this misestimate, for whatever reason. That seems to be a failure of Steps 6, 7 and 8: the consequences (station blackout and thereby loss of cooling after batteries were exhausted) do not seem to have been appropriately assessed (Step 6); the avoidance (a seawall capable of withstanding a tsunami of, I understand, less than 6 metres, less than some which have occurred on the Japanese east coast in the last 120 years) was obviously inadequate; and the oversight (discussion of the reasoning behind any claim that the tsunami risk had been adequately considered) also inadequate.

There was and is clear room for engineering improvement.

The first question, then, is whether other crucial safety aspects of the design and operation of these plants are in a similar condition of having been inadequately assessed, handled and shown to be so.

The second question is whether a different form of human organisation around nuclear power will circumvent these inadequacies. This is in general the *quis custodiet* problem.

And the third question is whether such a human organisation, if it exists, is implementable by the polity.

9 General application

This isn't just about Japan. These three questions arise for all societies and political cultures.

Japan is one of the most advanced societies in the world in terms of engineering and its applied benefits to society, including arguably the best-functioning public transport systems in the world as well as some of the most sophisticated city living (which depends heavily on engineering). And, until recently, one of the apparently best-functioning nuclear power supply systems for electricity.

Some engineers and politicians have been able to argue, after Chernobyl, that 'something like that couldn't happen here' because of the obvious lack of control, both intellectual and physical, over the artificial situation induced by the reactor operators. There is no such question arising with Fukushima. Robin Bloomfield suggested a more appropriate general stance in his presentation at the 11th Bieleschweig Workshop: 'We don't have tsunamis like that, but what is it that *we* have missed in *our* operations?' (Bloomfield 2011). The main lesson to be learned by many from the Fukushima accident is that 'something similar could happen here!'

In the aftermath of the accident, I argued that a public safety case for all safety-critical engineered systems would be a positive step (equivalent in the terms of this note to making Step 8 public) (Ladkin 2011b). Martyn Thomas and Nancy Leveson pointed out privately that there are significant issues around retention of intellectual property by the companies involved: a full safety case involves details of the design, and these designs are how companies succeed in being better than others and they – legitimately – are reluctant to reveal them. Besides, arguments can be blocked socially or by the polity for other reasons, as I have considered

(Ladkin 2011c). As I said there, I don't know how to ensure that such arguments cannot be blocked in general.

The safety case for other safety-critical systems is not generally publically-available, for example for commercial aircraft or for oil drilling operations. Why should it be for nuclear power? The answer, for me, is that total costs of nuclear power accidents are an order of magnitude more expensive than the total costs of accidents in these other sectors (see Slide 10 of my Bieleschweig talk (Ladkin 2011d) for some crude estimates), even without taking into account the current externalities (Slide 11 of (Ladkin 2011d)). The severity of significant nuclear accidents is greater than in most if not all other engineering endeavours. (Here one might think of the Bhopal accident, and comparisons may be instructive. More people were killed directly than in either the Chernobyl or Fukushima accidents. It seems also that dangerous substances involved are persisting in the environment (Wikipedia 2011d). But there are likely different factors at play here than purely technical ones. My thanks here to Martyn Thomas for the reference.)

Also, certain fundamental issues with nuclear power plants have been solved by no society yet: what to do with the waste. There are ways to handle existing waste: the question is whether they, given the vagaries of human operation, suffice. Germany may be thought to have a relatively good regime, but even here there have been questionable practices and decisions concerning some repositories, such as at Asse (Süddeutsche Zeitung 2008). The question here is whether anything can reasonably be left to sit for 10,000 years if there are ongoing maintenance problems on a time scale of decades, three orders of magnitude smaller. The US has publically suffered a lack of what is termed a 'long-term solution'. But even the German regime only works (if one believes it does work) because the amount of waste is limited: the issue is 'solved' only because of Germany's planned exit from nuclear power generation. The 'solutions' issue is in many societies overtly political, and seems likely to remain so. The issue of waste disposal needs to be part of the public discussion, and a public 'safety case' would be one way of ensuring it is so.

The *quis custodiet* question of the adequacy of the safety assessment and reasoning must somehow be resolved. It seems to me likely, given the aftermath of significant nuclear accidents, that, as with the issue of nuclear waste products, the polity will somehow be involved. How? How does technical engineering and the polity interact to form policy? A fundamental political problem here is that safety involves the *absence* of something, namely harm. In a politically relevant sense, everything was somehow OK with Japanese nuclear power production up until 10 March 2011, and then it suddenly, on 11 March and subsequently, was not. The polity does not seem to me to cope with such point-in-time phenomena in the way in which safety engineers might wish it would.

For another example of point phenomena and how society deals with them, consider driving behaviour and severe road traffic accidents. A deadly road traffic accident might be and is often socially localised to those involved and their friends and relations, whose lives have been irreversibly changed. An accident such as Fukushima has such consequences for proportionately very many more people.

The social phenomenon associated with road accidents, many small groups of victims and associated sufferers, each group largely socially isolated from each other group, offers no guide to dealing with a point-of-time event with potentially hundreds to thousands to tens of thousands of victims and associated sufferers.

(For a similar phenomenon in social sensitivity, consider STEC (Shiga-like Toxin-producing Escherichia Coli) illnesses, deriving from some strains of the common animal gut bacterium E. coli. Individual occurrences happen all the time, in their low thousands in the EU and a hundred thousand in the US each year, and we hear little of them. However, a collection of cases which appear to be causally related to each other engender a very different set of social reactions. See my note (Ladkin 2011e) for a little more detail and references.)

Finally, and maybe most importantly, who believes that Fukushima is the last significant nuclear accident that the world will ever see? After 4,000 years of engineering, ships still sink. After 170 years of engineering, trains still crash into each other. After 100 years of engineering, commercial aeroplanes still crash into land and sea and, after 75 years of air traffic control, occasionally into each other. So where is the next big one going to happen? How? How many people, how many even of us, would have been that interested had I asked this question on 10 March 2011?

10 Coda

Charles Perrow pointed out that there are some significant issues not addressed above. Indeed not. Here are some.

- There appears to be some evidence that at least one cooling system lost its integrity as a direct consequence of the quake, before the tsunami hit (e.g. McNeill and Adelstein 2011). I am not aware of any reliable assessment of the anticipated severity of the accident even if the flooding had not taken out secondary power.
- Perrow has drawn attention to 'normal accidents', accidents that happen to tightly-coupled, interactively complex systems during normal operations, and has developed significant theory about them (Perrow 1984, 1999). Perrow observes '[t]his failure ... was not a 'normal accident', [in Perrow's sense] the unexpected interaction of multiple failures; it was a design accident, the failure to design in safeguards for extreme events that are rare but possible' (Perrow 2011). Issues of normal accidents in nuclear power plants are very important, and I haven't addressed any of them here – as Perrow says, Fukushima was not one.
- I haven't discussed claims that nuclear power is 'clean', and how to adjust those claims to account for the accidents, which tend to be 'dirty'. But unless one believes there will never be another nuclear accident, ever, such claims must be adjusted.

- I haven't discussed the trope of *'We're OK, we do nuclear power properly, but those people over the border, they don't pay so much attention, they don't do it right, they are the ones to watch.'* This trope is moderately pervasive. If normal accident theory is true, as it may well be, it is disingenuous to use this trope to deflect attention from one's own safety efforts, for no one is immune from accidents if normal accident theory is true.
- I have argued that an appropriate engagement of the polity with engineered-system safety involves a certain transparency – of information, about safety measures, their strengths, weaknesses, their failings; as well as of intent and planning. Transparency is also an issue in the response to accidents and emergency planning for their mitigation. It has been questioned by some as to whether the necessary transparency was evident in the operator's and regulator's response to the Fukushima accident. This particular issue, while important, I take to be outside the scope of this note.

Acknowledgments I acknowledge the substantial contribution of the presenters at the 11th Bieleschweig Workshop on the Fukushima accident, in particular Robin Bloomfield, Lee Clarke, John Downer, John Knight, Nancy Leveson, Charles Perrow, Martyn Thomas, Axel Schneider and Bernd Sieker, and the distinguished discussants, to the views discussed here. The workshop arose through the ProcEng mailing list we set up in Bielefeld for discussion of this accident; thanks to Jan Sanders for installation and maintenance. I have benefitted from insightful comments of Martyn Thomas, Charles Perrow, Bernd Sieker, Lee Clarke and Jan Sanders on previous versions of this note.

References

Bielefeld (2011) Eleventh Bieleschweig workshop: the Fukushima accident and systems prone to EUE. University of Bielefeld RVS Group. http://www.rvs.uni-bielefeld.de/Bieleschweig/eleventh/. Accessed 6 October 2011

Bloomfield R (2011) Fukushima: some observations. Presentation at the Eleventh Bieleschweig Workshop (Bielefeld 2011). http://www.rvs.uni-bielefeld.de/Bieleschweig/eleventh/BloomfieldB11Slidesv01a.pdf. Accessed 6 October 2011

Dow Jones Deutschland (2011) Japan trade min: possible to achieve 'cold shutdown' of Fukushima Daiichi by year-end. http://www.dowjones.de/site/2011/09/japan-trade-min-possible-to-achieve-cold-shutdown-of-fukushima-daiichi-by-year-end.html. Accessed 6 October 2011

Greenpeace (2006) The Chernobyl disaster – consequences on human health. http://www.greenpeace.org/international/en/publications/reports/chernobylhealthreport/. Accessed 6 October 2011

Hald A, de Moivre A, McClintock B (1984) A de Moivre: 'de mensura sortis' or 'on the measurement of chance'. Reprinted version of 1711, with an introduction and commentary. International Statistical Revue 52(3), December 1984

IAEA (2011) The international nuclear and radiological event scale. 5 April 2011 update. International Atomic Energy Agency. http://www-ns.iaea.org/tech-areas/emergency/ines.asp. Accessed 6 October 2011

Jolly D (2011) Fukushima's contamination produces some surprises at sea. New York Times. http://green.blogs.nytimes.com/2011/09/28/fukushimas-contamination-produces-some-surprises-at-sea/. Accessed 6 October 2011

Ladkin PB (1998) Hazards, risk and incoherence. Report RVS-Occ-98-01. University of Bielefeld RVS Group. http://www.rvs.uni-bielefeld.de/publications/Reports/risk.html. Accessed 6 October 2011

Ladkin PB (2001) Problems calculating risk via hazard. Chapter 5 of Causal System Analysis. University of Bielefeld RVS Group. http://www.rvs.uni-bielefeld.de/publications/books/CausalSystemAnalysis/Chapter_5_Problems_calculating_risk_via_hazard.pdf. Accessed 7 October 2011

Ladkin PB (2011a) A Fukushima diary, 13 July 2011. http://www.rvs.uni-bielefeld.de/Bieleschweig/eleventh/LadkinFukushimaDiary.pdf. Accessed 6 October 2011

Ladkin PB (2011b) Fukushima, the tsunami hazard, and engineering practice. Weblog article. http://www.abnormaldistribution.org/2011/03/27/fukushima-the-tsunami-hazard-and-engineering-practice/. Accessed 6 October 2011

Ladkin PB (2011c) The epidemiology of memes and its effect upon safety. Weblog article. http://www.abnormaldistribution.org/2011/04/14/the-epidemiology-of-memes-and-its-effect-upon-safety/. Accessed 6 October 2011

Ladkin PB (2011d) The Fukushima Daiichi accident: some themes. Presentation at the Eleventh Bieleschweig Workshop (Bielefeld 2011). http://www.rvs.uni-bielefeld.de/Bieleschweig/eleventh/Ladkin11Bieleschweig.pdf. Accessed 6 October 2011

Ladkin PB (2011e) Food safety. Note to the University of York safety-critical systems mailing list. http://www.cs.york.ac.uk/hise/safety-critical-archive/2011/0631.html. Accessed 6 October 2011

Lloyd E, Tye W (1982) Systematic safety. CAA Publications, UK

Lochbaum D (2011) Nuclear 'station blackout'. MRZine journal 24 March 2011. http://mrzine.monthlyreview.org/2011/lochbaum240311.html. Accessed 6 October 2011

McNeill D, Adelstein J (2011) The explosive truth behind Fukushima's meltdown. The Independent newspaper. http://www.independent.co.uk/news/world/asia/the-explosive-truth-behind-fukushimas-meltdown-2338819.html. Accessed 6 October 2011

Metz L, Gerhold L, de Haan G (eds) (2010) Atomkraft als risiko. Peter Lang Verlag

Nakamura D, Harlan C (2011) Japanese nuclear plant's safety analysts brushed off risk of tsunami. Washington Post. http://www.washingtonpost.com/world/japanese-nuclear-plants-evaluators-cast-aside-threat-of-tsunami/2011/03/22/AB7Rf2KB_story.html. Accessed 6 October 2011

NRC (undated) Reactor concepts manual, boiling water reactor (BWR) systems. U.S. Nuclear Regulatory Commission Technical Training Center. http://www.nrc.gov/reading-rm/basic-ref/teachers/03.pdf. Accessed 6 October 2011

ONR (2011) Japanese earthquake and tsunami: implications for the UK nuclear industry. Interim report. UK Office for Nuclear Regulation. http://www.hse.gov.uk/nuclear/fukushima/interim-report.pdf. Accessed 6 October 2011

Perrow CB (1984) Normal accidents. Basic Books

Perrow CB (1999) Normal accidents. Reprinted and extended edition. Princeton University Press

Perrow (2007) The next catastrophe. Princeton University Press

Perrow CB (2011) private communication, 14 March

Putzmeister (2011) Press Information Number 1628. _http://www.pmw.de/cps/rde/xchg/pm_online/hs.xsl/9419_ENU_HTML.htm. Accessed 6 October 2011

Sieker B (2011) Graphical plots of the fundamental parameter values over time at the Fukushima Daiichi reactors. http://nuxi.homeunix.org/Fukushima/Fukushima-Plots.pdf. Accessed 6 October 2011

Süddeutsche Zeitung (2008) Schwere Vorwürfe: 'Es gab nie ein sicheres Endlager Asse'. http://www.sueddeutsche.de/politik/schwere-vorwuerfe-es-gab-nie-ein-sicheres-endlager-asse-1.691321. Accessed 6 October 2011

UCS (undated) All things nuclear weblog. Union of Concerned Scientists. http://allthingsnuclear. org/. Accessed 6 October 2011

USGS (2011), Poster of the great Tohoku earthquake (northeast Honshu, Japan) of March 11, 2011 – Magnitude 9.0. US Geological Survey. http://earthquake.usgs.gov/earthquakes/ eqarchives/poster/2011/20110311.php. Accessed 6 October 2011

Wikipedia (2011a) 2011 Tohoku earthquake and tsunami. http://en.wikipedia.org/wiki/2011_ Tōhoku_earthquake_and_tsunami. Accessed 6 October 2011

Wikipedia (2011b) Fukushima Daiichi nuclear power plant. http://en.wikipedia.org/wiki/ Fukushima_Daiichi_Nuclear_Power_Plant. Accessed 6 October 2011

Wikipedia (2011c) Chernobyl disaster, assessing the disaster's effects on human health. http://en.wikipedia.org/wiki/Chernobyl_disaster#Assessing_the_disaster.27s_effects_on_hum an_health. Accessed 6 October 2011

Wikipedia (2011d) Bhopal disaster: ongoing contamination. https://secure.wikimedia.org/ wikipedia/en/wiki/Bhopal_disaster#Ongoing_contamination. Accessed 6 October 2011

Yablokov AV, Nesterenko VB, Nesterenko AV (2009) Chernobyl: consequences of the catastrophe for people and the environment. Annals of the New York Academy of Sciences. Wiley-Blackwell

Yoshida R, Fukada T (2011) Fukushima plant site was originally a hill safe from tsunami. Japan Times Online. http://search.japantimes.co.jp/cgi-bin/nn20110712x2.html. Accessed 6 October 2011

A Risk-based Approach towards Assessment of Potential Safety Deficiencies

Jens Braband

Siemens AG

Braunschweig, Germany

Abstract On August 1, 2009, a standard DIN V VDE V 0831-100 was published, which deals with the risk assessment of potential safety deficiencies (PSD). This paper presents the assessment process and a specific procedure complying with the requirements of this standard and ensuring that decision-making in the case of potential safety deficiencies is both traceable and transparent. The so-called PSD risk priority number (PSD-RPN) procedure has been proven by many years of practical application in different variants. It has been designed in accordance with sound engineering principles and produces dependable decisions if used correctly. It makes a major contribution to both increasing the cost-effectiveness of railway operations and improving quality, in particular in the field of complaint management. The procedure is explained and illustrated by a real-world example.

1 Introduction

In the case of potential or existing safety deficiencies, a suspected or real deviation from the specified normal behavior, i.e. a potentially hazardous operational situation, exists. The risk of the in-service (re)occurrence of a potential safety deficiency (PSD) must be assessed quickly and it must be decided which (immediate) measures might be necessary for ensuring at least the same level of safety until removal of the PSD. While common risk analyses focus on assessing the risk of a number of hazards which have usually not yet occurred, i.e. on making a proactive evaluation of a (mostly) hypothetical case, the problem is encountered exactly the other way round in the case of a PSD.

If a PSD in a railway system becomes known, all stakeholders (e.g. supplier, operator, assessor and safety authority) are directly faced with a dual dilemma in view of the advanced highly available and highly centralized technical systems:

1. It is known that operation in degraded modes (e.g. after switching off a technical system because of a PSD) is less safe than technically protected normal operation.
2. If the PSD requires taking risk-reducing measures (RM), several possible measures will usually be available which have to be assessed quickly as regards their efficiency and economic reasonability.

Let us illustrate this using a real-world example (UUS 2008): on 16 October 2007, a train derailed in the entrance of the Lötschberg Base Tunnel in Switzerland. A software failure in the radio block centre (RBC) of the European Train Control System (ETCS), which had been installed on the line, was soon established as one of the causes of the accident, which fortunately resulted only in limited damage, but major operational disturbances. So, as a first reaction, the operator took immediate precautionary and risk-reducing measures, e.g. taking the system out of service. But as part of the causal analysis it was soon found out that this software failure can only result in a hazard under very particular operational and technical circumstances. Thus the operator was able to put the system into service again by implementing measures that should prevent the reoccurrence of these circumstances. But how can the effectiveness of the measures be evaluated? How does the operator know whether the risk is sufficiently reduced? How can different measures be compared in order to choose the most cost-effective ones?

In such a case, support can be offered by a risk-based approach:

1. It provides an objective aid for deciding to what extent and with which urgency measures must be taken for the purpose of maintaining the safety of operations.
2. It provides an objective aid for deciding how long a PSD can possibly be tolerated (potentially with RM).
3. It allows comparable measures to be derived for similarly critical PSDs.

It must be ensured that the decisions made on the basis of such an approach, on the one hand, are reliable and, on the other hand, can be taken shortly after occurrence of the PSD. Therefore, in particular risk priority numbers (RPN) or other variants of semi-quantitative procedures are natural candidates.

2 Normative background

The RPN is a very popular tool which is standardized as part of the FMECA standard IEC 60812. However it is known that simplicity and popularity of the RPN has a price and that is that sometimes misleading conclusions can be drawn from the analysis. This has already been observed (Bowles 2003) and has now also led to cautionary advice in the standards. Immediately after Bowles's criticism a new approach to the construction of dependable RPN was proposed (Braband 2003).

This approach has also had its influence on standards, but the German DIN V VDE V 0831-100 is, according to the author's knowledge, the only standard dealing with concise procedures for handling PSDs, at least in the railway domain. Its scope is the functional safety of railway automation systems, the same scope as that of EN 50219 which defines four different safety integrity levels (SILs) to measure the criticality of safety functions. DIN V VDE V 0831-100 has been issued as a national pre-standard, since imminent international standardization was then not expected to be successful. However, after gaining some experience, it will soon also be proposed as the basis of an international standard. Legally, however, there is no difference between a standard and a pre-standard; both count as acknowledged codes of practice.

2.1 Risk acceptance

The objective of PSD assessment is to assess a potentially changed safety situation and, if required, to take measures for ensuring that the system affected by the PSD offers at least the same level of safety as a reference system (which may, for example, be the approved system without a PSD).

For this purpose, first of all basic considerations for proving the same level of safety by comparison with a reference system are required. In future, this approach will become more important because, in the case of significant changes, it is one of the three approaches towards risk acceptance which have been specified by the European Railway Agency (ERA) in EU Regulation 352/2009.

The process defined by the ERA is based on the principle that safety considerations focus on hazard control, i.e., on the basis of a system definition, hazards are defined for which control safety requirements are derived and proved. According to the ERA, a reference system R specifies a system which is proved in operation to provide an acceptable safety level and which can be used as a reference system when a system under assessment is checked for the acceptability of its risks.

The principle used as a basis by the ERA is ALASA (At Least As Safe As) compared to a reference system. This is because, if a reference system meets the requirements indicated above, the following applies, according to the ERA, to the system under assessment: the risks connected with the hazards covered by the reference system are regarded as acceptable.

Several national laws contain similar criteria, e.g. Article 2 (General Requirements) of the German Railway Building and Operation Regulations (EBO, 'Eisenbahn-Bau- und Betriebsordnung') provides for a similar relative safety criterion referring not to a reference system but to the recognized code of practice, i.e. regulations and standards.

What matters first is who determines which system is to be used as a reference system. According to EU Regulation 352/2009, this will be the applicant, i.e. the stakeholder who wants to obtain an approval.

2.2 Interpretation

It is undisputed among experts that, for the results of quantitative risk analyses and their related safety cases, at best only the order of magnitude is correct because of the uncertainties of the data and estimated values.

This rationale has also been followed by the ERA (ERA 2009) by specifying the following in Item 2.5.6.1 [G1] (h) of its CSM Guide:

> 'where quantitative criteria are used, either the admissible accuracy of the total result is within an order of magnitude or all parameters used for the quantification are conservative.'

These findings are also used by semi-quantitative risk analysis procedures such as risk graph or risk priority numbers which work with class subdivisions of the bandwidth b ranging from approx. 3 to 10, i.e. an average inaccuracy with a factor of $\sqrt{3} = 1.7$ to $\sqrt{10} = 3.2$ is accepted here. Similar statistical uncertainties exist when comparing approved systems on the basis of empirical data.

If such tolerance ranges are not accepted for the application of ALASA, an economically unreasonable automatism of a continuous increase in safety requirements has to be tolerated. EU Regulation 352/2009 also takes account of this fact in another way by defining the broadly acceptable risk:

> 'Basically risks resulting from hazards can be classified as broadly acceptable if the risk is so low that it is not reasonable to introduce additional safety measures.'

In particular, this also applies to broadly acceptable risk increases in the above tolerance ranges.

This consequently leads to the following interpretation of the risk acceptance criterion ALASA:

1. If ALASA is used for systems already approved, tolerance ranges must be accepted in doubt for the questioned system S, i.e. the assumption that ALASA compared to the reference system R is valid as long as a significant deviation of the event frequency from the average value of the reference system cannot be demonstrated.
2. If ALASA is used for a system S which is not approved, these tolerance ranges must not be used, i.e. for the purpose of proving ALASA compared to the reference system R, the same or possibly slightly higher requirements must be demonstrated.

Figure 1 shows this interpretation for the statistical demonstration of ALASA. Figure 2 shows the interpretation for semi-quantitative procedures where the parameter values are subdivided into classes with specific bandwidths. Here, ALASA means that the evaluation results fall into the same class.

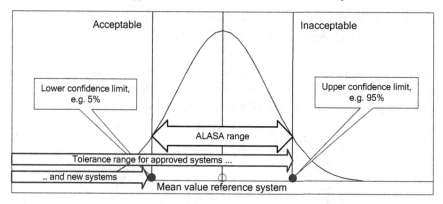

Fig. 1. Interpretation of ALASA for statistical demonstration

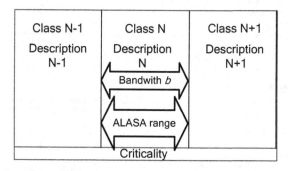

Fig. 2. Interpretation of ALASA for semi-quantitative demonstration

2.3 Assessment process

The standard DIN V VDE V 0831-100 (DIN 2009) explains in detail the individual process steps in the flow diagram in Figure 3. This describes only the basic steps; details must be regulated in the operator's or supplier's safety management system (SMS). Depending on the selected procedure, the process steps may include sub-steps which, for reasons of brevity, are not dealt with in detail here.

If, within the framework of the operator's SMS or the supplier's product supervision, it is assumed that specific safety-relevant events occur more frequently than expected or a PSD is detected, one of the parties comes to the conclusion that a changed safety situation may exist.

At the start of the process and possibly also during each process step, it must be checked whether the PSD meets the following requirements:

1. The PSD can occur in a system in operation.

214   Jens Braband

2. The PSD affects a safety-related function (SIL >0).
3. The PSD has a risk-increasing effect (compared to the explicit safety requirement).

If one of the conditions does not apply to an occurred PSD, the process should not be started. Alternatively, if it is discovered at a later date that a condition does not apply, the process should be aborted and terminated with documented evidence.

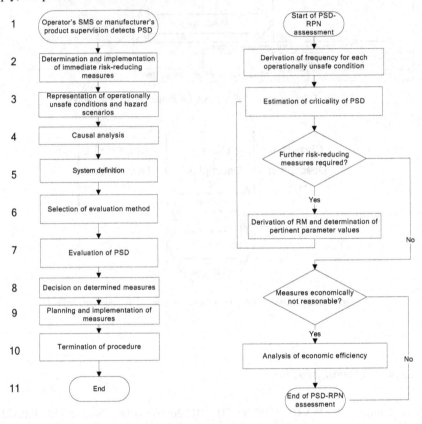

Fig. 3. Process flow diagram – general and detailed

2.4 Basic risk model

An operationally unsafe condition caused by a PSD exists if no other planned barrier which might prevent an in-service occurrence exists in the overall system. In such a case, only neutralizing factors exist as 'favorable' conditions which might prevent an accident (see Figure 4).

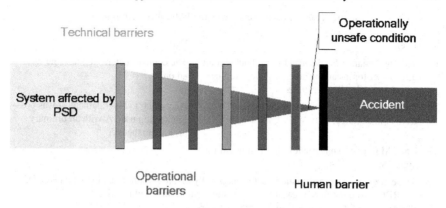

Fig. 4. Basic model

A path leading via the basic conditions, the operationally unsafe condition and failed hazard avoidance to the occurrence of damage is called the hazard scenario of a PSD.

It must be examined whether starting from a known operationally unsafe condition via the failure of any specific existing barriers, a hazard rather close to the cause can be identified. Starting from this hazard, further paths to other operationally unsafe conditions and thus also other hazard scenarios may exist. The identified hazard scenarios caused by the PSD must be described concisely.

To illustrate the concept we again take a look at the example from (UUS 2008), where the sequence of events depicted in Table 1 leads to the accident (with some minor simplifications and translations by the author).

It is evident that not all events can be regarded as barriers, but the following events could be identified as potential barriers, meaning that they could reduce the probability that the PSD triggers an accident:

- use of the emergency braking command for dispatching purposes (event 1)
- issue of emergency braking command exactly when the affected train is in transition to ETCS Level 2 (event 4)
- miscommunication between the signalman and the driver (event 5).

2.5 Assessment of PSD by RPN

In the case of semi-quantitative procedures, the parameters used for risk assessment are basically not quantified but classified by ranks. Usually, the same or similar parameters as for risk analyses are considered, i.e. severity and frequency of damage. These parameters are possibly also determined by assessing further subparameters, e.g. the possibility of hazard avoidance.

Table.1. Sequence of events from the Lötschberg derailment

No	Event	Explanation
1	The signalman (SM) decides to take back a route already set for a train by an emergency stop because of a delay in operations.	The control center (CC) does not give an order.
2	The SM decides not to contact the driver (D) of train A in advance.	According to his judgment, it was possible to stop train A with an ordinary braking maneuver.
3	The SM issues an emergency stop command for signal S.	
4	The emergency stop command is not processed by the RBC (radio block centre) and the movement authority (MA) for train A was not shortened accordingly.	Train A is in transition between ETCS Level 0 and Level 2.
5	The SM starts to reset the routes by the emergency command. As a result, the MA for train A is somewhat shortened, but not up to signal S.	The SM assumes that train A has already stopped.
6	D receives a message 'Emergency signal set by SM' on his cab display, stops and calls the SM via radio. The SM announces to D that train B will first pass through the tunnel. The SM issues a command to D to proceed until the EoA (end of authority).	SM assumes that the MA has been shortened up to signal S.
7	The SM manually sets a route for train B and checks it at his operator console.	
8	D proceeds with a speed of 100 km/h. He recognizes from a particular wayside signal that the points are not set correctly.	He immediately initiates emergency braking, but cannot prevent derailment at points no 34.
9	The traversal of points no 34 is automatically reported and the SM issues an emergency stop command for train B. The driver of train B recognizes the command and can stop his train in time.	

In DIN V VDE V 0831-100, procedures based on the FMECA of DIN EN 60812 are used. For each barrier, an evaluation table and a combination rule for the parameter values must be created for the purpose of determining criticality. Criticality, here expressed by the RPN, is a semi-quantitative metric of the risk. The risk acceptance criterion ALASA is interpreted here as 'at most the same criticality' or 'at most the same RPN'. With RPN evaluation, either a reference system or an explicit safety requirement (e.g. a SIL) must be defined (in either case called reference system R). In the latter case, it is also possible to determine the admissible removal period directly from the parameter values if the SIL is known.

In order to obtain reliable estimates, RPN procedures must have the following characteristics:

Rational scaling. The scaling of the evaluation tables must be at least approximately rational, i.e. the bandwidths b of the classes should be approximately equal.

Monotonicity. If the risk for scenario i is lower than the risk for scenario j, the RPN for scenario i must be smaller than or equal to the RPN for scenario j.

Accuracy. If the RPN for scenario i is equal to the RPN for scenario j, the risk for scenario i and the risk for scenario j should be approximately equal.

With the PSD, basically each safety deficiency identified must be eliminated (except in clearly defined exceptional cases), i.e. it must be determined within which period the defect must be eliminated and whether measures must possibly be taken simultaneously.

3 PSD-RPN procedure

The PSD-RPN procedure is used for performing a semi-quantitative criticality assessment with the objective that, after application of the procedure, the system with the PSD (system S) will not have a higher criticality than allowed by the explicit safety requirements. This means that, after application of the PSD-RPN procedure, the risk acceptance criterion ALASA is complied with.

The objective is to determine a justifiable period for removal of the PSD on the basis of its criticality with reference to the explicit safety requirements. The PSD-RPN procedure covers process step 7 from Figure 3 and meets the requirements defined in Section 2.

This procedure is only used if the cause is a fault of a safety-relevant function for which an explicit safety requirement in the form of a SIL is available or has been determined. The operationally unsafe conditions and the hazard scenarios are known from the superordinate process. The basic model for application of this procedure is shown in Figure 4. The essential process steps are represented in Figure 3 and described below.

3.1 Estimation of PSD frequency

In many hazard scenarios, the frequency of the occurrence of an operationally unsafe condition is the decisive factor when assessing the criticality of a PSD. Therefore, first the frequency of the potential operationally unsafe condition is estimated using Table 2. This table is approximately scaled (as are all other tables used in the PSD-RPN procedure) with the bandwidth $b = \sqrt{10}$. The parameter value H:

1. is determined for each function affected by the PSD and thus for each hazard scenario
2. refers to only one 'group of hardware and software elements' implementing the respective function

3. estimates for each function affected by the PSD the expected time until entry into the operationally unsafe state.

Table.2. Scales for the parameters frequency (H, abridged) and hazard avoidance (G)

Description for H	H	Description for G	G
Daily	17	Not possible	4
Twice a week	16	Knowledge-based action under unfavorable conditions	3
Weekly	15	Knowledge-based action under favorable conditions	2
Monthly	14	Rule-based action under unfavorable conditions	1
Quarterly	13	Rule-based action under favorable conditions	0
Yearly	12		
...	...		
Once in 300,000 years	1		
Once in 1,000,000 years	0		

For each hazard scenario, which circumstances must exist or must occur for the occurrence of the pertinent operationally unsafe condition are listed for that condition. These circumstances, here referred to as basic conditions, may be states or events.

If the values for the basic conditions cannot be taken from calculations or information documented elsewhere, an estimation session to be attended by experts shall be held. The named participants at this session shall unanimously agree on a value.

3.2 Estimation of PSD criticality

With the determined parameter H (and possibly the further parameter ΔRM if risk-reducing measures are required), each function affected by the deficiency is related to this function's SIL requirement using Table 3. In this table, the criticality of the PSD is set directly in relation to the criticality of the safety function (as expressed by its SIL) and the admissible PSD removal time is calculated according to ALASA.

This results in an admissible removal period for the respective function affected by the PSD. For pragmatic reasons, the upper limit has been set to 60 months though calculably even higher values would be admissible (in the cells in the upper left corner in Table 3).

If no risk-reducing measures are planned or have been taken, ΔRM is not considered.

Table 3. Determination of removal times

H-ΔRM	SIL 1 function	SIL 2 function	SIL 3 function	SIL 4 function
0				
1				60 months
2			60 months	36 months
3		60 months		12 months
4	60 months		36 months	4 months
5			12 months	1 month
6		36 months	4 months	
7		12 months	1 month	
8	36 months	4 months	Further risk-reducing measures are required.	
9	12 months	1 month		
10	4 months			
11	1 month			
>11				

3.3 Decision: are risk-reducing measures required?

The derivation of risk-reducing measures (RM) may be necessary because:

1. they are explicitly required according to Table 3 (highlighted section), or
2. removal of the PSD is not feasible within the determined period and the removal period shall be extended by the influence of the RM.

If no further RMs are required, the list of the derived measures ensures that, if the PSD is eliminated within the derived removal period, the criticality of the considered system will not be increased.

In the next process step, the expert committee shall first find and precisely define relevant additional measures which can be taken within the framework of the issue. Risk reduction corresponds to the difference in criticality with and without the considered additional measures.

Risk-reducing measures (RM) may have effects in each of the following ranges:

RMs with an effect on frequency. The planned measures either add a further barrier (basic condition) for one or several hazard scenarios or change the efficiency of an existing barrier. The planned measures can improve the efficiency of existing barriers (e.g. instructions to the operating personnel to react in a specific way in specific situations, shorter checking cycles) or create new barriers (e.g. operating personnel is provided for supervising specific processes).

RMs with an effect on the severity of the damage. The planned measures would reduce the severity of the damage of one or several hazard scenarios (e.g. reduction in speed, etc.).

RMs which have effects outside the system under consideration (additional hazard avoidance measures).

The evaluation of the parameter 'frequency (H)' is obtained as described above according to Table 2, but only with the basic conditions changed by the RM. In the case of train accidents (railway operating accidents with injury to persons and damage to property), determination of the parameter value 'extent of damage (S)' results from evaluation of the three sub-parameters:

1. type of accident (T)
2. number of affected persons (A)
3. applicable speed (V).

Tables are included in DIN V VDE V 0831-100. The results are added and lead to the parameter value $S = T + A + V$. In the case of passenger accidents (accidents exclusively with injury to persons), similar tables exist in order to estimate S.

Finally, the parameter 'hazard avoidance (G)' can be evaluated if RMs have been derived which have effects outside the system under consideration. Usually, hazard avoidance relates to additional human barriers. Therefore, for the affected function, the effect of hazard avoidance is determined by Table 2. This table is based on a conservative estimation of human factors in the railway domain.

Usually, the effect of RMs will be restricted to one field. Depending on the function for which the RMs have been derived, the parameter values HRM, GRM and SRM are obtained. These determined values are related to the values determined without RM: H, G and S. The input value ΔRM for Table 3 is derived by:

$$\Delta RM = (H - H_{RM}) + (G - G_{RM}) + (S - S_{RM})$$

3.4 Decision: are measures economically unreasonable?

The principle in the case of the PSD-RPN procedure is that all safety deficiencies must be eliminated. However, according to experience, cases exist which can be handled with the PSD-RPN procedure but where formal PSD handling is limited because the semi-quantitative method cannot adequately map all special cases (e.g. due to very low frequencies). Moreover, deficiencies are possible whose removal costs are highly disproportionate to the residual risk or deficiencies exist whose cause is not found within the removal period. The latter applies in particular to transient or individual phenomena which can be reproduced neither in the field nor in the laboratory.

In such cases, the unconditional removal of the deficiency would also be contradictory to, for example, the 'reasonable discretion' required in the EU Safety Directive and might also affect the railway's competitiveness. If the criticality of the PSD is low (deficiency removal time at least 60 months according to Table 3) and if, according to the expert's reasonable discretion, the case in question involves such a case, a detailed economic analysis can be started in the following process step. Details are described in DIN V VDE V 0831-100.

3.5 Example

In the example from (UUS 2008) the first step is to estimate H in conjunction with necessary RMs. The starting point is the use of an emergency braking command for dispatching means (event 1). We assume from the report that it is not explicitly forbidden but uncommon. Conservatively, we assume that this is practiced monthly (H=14).

In addition, the emergency braking command must be issued exactly when the affected train is in transition to ETCS Level 2 (event 4), which may last up to 10 seconds. We estimate this probability to be much less than 1:10, but we have no further data available.

Also, the miscommunication between the signalman and the driver has to be taken into account (event 5). In this case, both partners seem to have relied on the safety system, but there is a chance that, using more standardized communication, the error can be detected. Again we estimate a risk reduction of 1:10.

According to Table 2, we can derive H=10 as a result. In order to make an assessment according to Table 3, we have to take into account the SIL of the emergency braking command, which we assume to be SIL 4. Now, Table 3 shows as a first result that RMs are necessary as H=10 is not acceptable for SIL 4. The target would be a value for H-ΔRM of less than or equal to 5. An obvious measure would be to forbid the use of an emergency braking command for dispatching means, but this would not completely rule out the risk, as such orders can be misunderstood or not obeyed. Table 4 shows the tentative assessment of this and other possible measures. In the assessment, some uncertainty is indicated as not all circumstances necessary for the assessment could be found in (UUS 2008).

Table.4. Examples of RMs and their assessment

Event no	Description	ΔRM estimate
1	Forbidding the use of the emergency braking command for dispatching means	3
2,6	Communication to the driver before and after issue of the emergency braking command (including checking of effectiveness)	3-4
4	Checking that the affected train is already in ETCS Level 2	3-4
8	Speed restriction to 40 km/h	2-3

The result clearly shows that, while a single RM may not be sufficient, a reasonable combination of two RMs may lead to justification of the removal time for the PSD between 1 and 12 months.

Finally it is interesting to compare which RMs were taken in the real example (without PSD-RPN):

- Speed restriction to 80 km/h (manual input at the RBC).
- The affected train has to stop before the emergency command can be released again.
- The signalman has to make sure that the affected train is already in ETCS Level 2, before he is allowed to issue an emergency braking command.

Generally, it can be stated that the RMs seem appropriate for the case. By application of PSD-RPN, it could have been possible to reduce the number of RMs. Last but not least, it is to be noted that, in this example, the supplier removed the PSD within one month, while PSD-RPN would perhaps have permitted a slightly longer removal time. In summary, we observe that PSD-RPN seems to be quite suitable for practice in this example.

4 Justification of approach

Justification is based on ALASA as described in Section 2.2 supported by the EC CSM Regulation of the ERA (EC 2009). The goal is to provide, for a system affected by a PSD, an argument that ALASA is satisfied and that the system may stay in operation (perhaps with some restrictions imposed by RM) until removal of the PSD.

The basic approach is to compare the safety requirement for the affected function as expressed by its SIL with the safety performance of the function affected by the PSD. The SIL (CENELEC 2003) can be viewed as equivalent to a range of tolerable hazard rates (THR), which are meant as target failure measures for design of the function.

Thus, if the safety performance of the affected function taking into account the implemented RM is within the bandwidth of the associated THR of the safety function, ALASA is then satisfied. However, this basic approach does not take into account the removal time of the PSD and the fact that we want to apply the RM only temporarily.

So, we alternatively compare the probability that a failure of the function leads to a hazard within the lifetime of the component implementing the function. In the railways domain we may assume a lifetime of 30 years on average. If we now apply the ALASA criterion to this probability, we may take into account the removal time of the PSD and the effectiveness of the RM, and can construct Table 3 as a result.

We explain this in more detail using an example: consider a SIL 4 function for which the estimation of H-ΔRM has led to a value of 2, leading, by means of Table 3, to a removal time of 36 months. The probability that a failure of the function leads to a hazard within the lifetime of the component implementing the function, is required by EN 50129 to be in the range of between 10^{-8}/h and 10^{-9}/h. Now, the value of H=2 approximately corresponds to 10^{-9}/h, assuming we consider a function that is running more or less continuously. Comparing the probabilities over 36 months (the PSD removal time) and 30 years (the average lifetime of the component) leads to a ratio of between 0.1 and 0.01. These figures would both justify the ALASA criterion according to Figure 2 as well as the concept of a broadly acceptable risk from the EC (2009) Regulation. Having justified this cell in Table 3, extrapolation to the other cells is straightforward, given the definition of SIL by EN 50129 and the construction of the parameter tables such as Table 2.

5 Conclusions

PSD-RPN is a procedure which ensures that, for similar PSDs, measures with a similar effectiveness are applied and that the ALASA principle is practically enforced. It contributes to a rational and transparent handling of PSDs. Thus, it makes a major contribution to both increasing the cost-effectiveness of railway operations and improving quality, in particular in the field of complaint management. PSD-RPN belongs to a family of semi-quantitative risk assessment methods that have been designed in accordance with sound engineering principles. It produces dependable decisions if used correctly. The construction principle (Braband 2008) has been awarded the Walter Masing Prize for innovative quality management.

References

Bowles J (2003) An assessment of RPN prioritization in a failure modes effects and criticality analysis. Proc RAMS2003, Tampa

Braband J (2003) Improving the risk priority number concept. J Syst Saf 3: 21-23

CENELEC (2003) Bahnanwendungen – Sicherheitsrelevante elektronische Systeme für Signaltechnik. EN 50129

DIN (2009) Risikoorientierte Beurteilung von potenziellen Sicherheitsmängeln und risikoreduzierenden Maßnahmen. DIN V VDE V 0831-100

EC (2009) Commission Regulation (EC) No. 352/2009 of 24 April 2009 on the adoption of a common safety method on risk evaluation and assessment as referred to in Article 6(3)(a) of Directive 2004/49/EC of the European Parliament and of the Council

ERA (2009) Guide for the application of the Commission Regulation on the adoption of a common safety method on risk evaluation and assessment as referred to in Article 6(3)(a) of the Railway Safety Directive, European Railway Agency, ERA/GUI/01-2008/SAF

Braband J (2008) Beschränktes Risiko. Qual und Zuverlässigk 53(2): 28-33

UUS (2008) Schlussbericht über die Entgleisung von Güterzug 43647 der BLS AG auf der Weiche 34 (Einfahrt Lötschberg-Basisstrecke), Unfalluntersuchungsstelle Bahnen und Schiffe UUS, Reg. Nr. 07101601

At the Sharp End: developing and validating Safety Critical Software

Fergus Duncan

BitWise Group

Dunfermline, UK

Abstract Whatever methods and tools are used to generate and maintain the safety case for a project, at some stage the software needs to be developed, verified and validated. With its associated documentation set, this can easily become a very expensive and time consuming exercise, which is largely repeated for each version. This paper examines some of the key issues that impact time and cost, shares previous lessons learnt and describes some key methods that can reduce time and cost. Metrics are provided where available to help quantify the associated benefits.

1 Introduction

Developing safety critical software is a costly exercise, which grows non-linearly with the Safety Integrity Level (SIL). It is a large part of a total project budget. Although there is limited scope to 'cut corners' with regulatory bodies, there is always pressure to deliver. There are many variable aspects of the development lifecycle that can affect budget and timeline.

BitWise has developed safety critical solutions for many years spanning a number of sectors including medical, energy, automotive and defence. Safety critical software does not apply purely to embedded devices; it also covers PCs, servers and networks. This paper shares key aspects of that experience, which may vary slightly from other developers' perspectives.

Safety engineering is an evolving space. New and updated standards are being issued regularly and there is clearly a substantial future road map. For example, IEC80001 (IEC 2010a) has issued part 1 with other parts to come. New tools are also appearing, some of which are referenced later in this paper, but there are still many gaps. So developing safety software is carried out in a far from ideal environment.

Processes and tools need reasonable stability. It is not practical to have frequent churn. So improvements need to be managed carefully. In practice, there is a major disconnect between state of the art techniques and established engineering practice. Change at the sharp end is slow. For example, although formal modelling and support tools have been around for at least two decades, adoption is still very limited (estimated at around 5% of the software development market).

There are many standards aimed at developing safety critical software, with considerable overlap. Some are generic (e.g. IEC61508 (IEC 2010b)) but many have a sector focus (e.g. medical: ISO13485 (ISO 2003), IEC62304 (IEC 2006) and IEC80001). Since this paper is addressing issues that apply to multiple sectors, most of the standards references are to IEC61508.

2 Project lifecycle

A typical lifecycle for safety critical development is shown in Figure 1. This 'V' model fits the hierarchical approach of IEC61508 and other safety standards. Given that this paper is concentrating on the bottom layers of the 'V' model, the safety layers are omitted. The software requirements are a distillation of the safety and functional planning process.

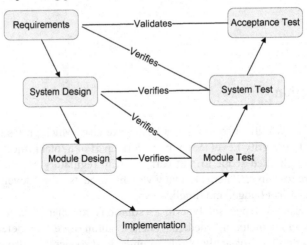

Fig. 1. Generic lifecycle model

Verification confirms that the software matches the design i.e. the 'how'. Validation confirms that the software matches the requirements, i.e. the 'what'. In practice, it is difficult to adhere strictly to the waterfall approach. Marketing departments often alter requirements and project understanding evolves as the development progresses, leading to a degree of churn. That is the real world but it puts pressure on the development processes.

Safety solutions can also iterate through a number of versions. These revisions can be driven by various factors such as component replacement, marketing input, rectification of faults or new regulatory requirements. Revisions typically change only modest parts of the system. Nevertheless, the rework costs can be substantial.

Managing this churn and avoiding cost and time escalation is a real challenge.

2.1 Requirements management and traceability

This is one area where tools support is far from ideal. For those with large budgets, a top end requirements management tool such as DOORS (IBM 2011) or Caliber (Borland 2011) will be used. However, the most frequently used requirements management tool remains Microsoft Word, with a wide variety of templates and styles. As long as there is a controlled process around its use, this is perfectly acceptable in safety critical development. However, it is not very efficient.

Safety critical development requires clear traceability from requirements to the other artefacts in the lifecycle model. Where formal methods are being used for requirements referencing, design, code generation and test case development, much of this process can be automated. However, this 'ideal' environment is often impractical.

Traceability serves several purposes. It enables checking that all requirements have been dealt with adequately at design, coding and testing stages. It also supports safety management where the impact of any change can be traced back to impacted requirements.

There is a range of generic artefact management tools on the market (e.g. CASE Spec (Goda 2011). These not only support requirements management but also other artefacts such as:

- hazards, mitigation techniques and other safety artefacts.
- design document sections, models, source code and test cases.

However, these tools are still fairly immature in that they do not integrate well with other tools. For example, importing requirements, particularly new revisions, can be painful.

DOORS has a complimentary product for test case management that integrates with its core requirements management. It is probably the most mature product of its type.

Many companies develop their own in-house tools to support this process, given the lack of commercially available solutions. For example, BitWise has a tool that builds a database to correlate test cases with requirements and auto-generate the traceability matrix document.

As tool support (hopefully) improves, the time consuming manual nature of traceability maintenance will be improved with associated reduction of total costs.

3 Formal methods

The use of formal or semi-formal methods is highly recommended for use in safety critical systems development. IEC61508 for example explicitly requires them for SIL-3 upwards. So what are formal and semi-formal methods and how are they used in practice?

Formal methods cover a range of notations and languages that captures software design in a precise, mathematical manner that then lends itself to formal proof. These languages are difficult to understand so are more likely to be transformed from a more user friendly modelling language such as UML (Unified Modelling Language). In turn, UML is typically generated using graphical editing tools.

Semi-formal methods use the graphical diagram formats and notations but without any formal generation of the underlying modelling or formal proof languages. They rely on manual review and testing.

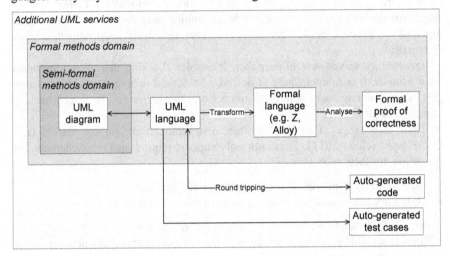

Fig. 2. Formal and semi-formal methods applied to UML

Modelling and UML have existed for many years, as have a variety of support tools. However, the formal proof elements of UML are relatively immature and there is not a complete equivalence between UML or any formal specification language. So the user has to resort to annotating the UML or avoiding certain types of construct. There are advanced tool sets for UML such as Rhapsody (IBM) and Enterprise Architect (Sparx Systems).

UML supports a range of model types that collectively support the description of complete solutions such as state machines, message sequences and classes. UML tools, such as those referenced above, address a number of lifecycle aspects:

- formal capture and definition of design
- traceability from requirements

- automatic code generation
- test case generation.

Over the years, many other languages and methodologies have been developed for formal methods. Most of these have never crossed the divide from academia to industry.

UML is the widest known modelling language. Enterprise tools such as Rhapsody or Enterprise Architect not only provide graphical methods of defining models but also support traceability, code generation and test case generation. They also provide some support for formal proof, but UML is generally regarded as not being sufficiently precise to be complete.

One recent tool of particular interest is ASD:Suite from Verum in Holland. ASD:Suite provides a solution for formal definition of interfaces between components in a multi-threaded system. Under the hood, it uses the formal language CSP (Communicating Sequential Processes) to enable formal proof of correctness and conformance to interfaces. This fits extremely well with a modular architecture, which is discussed later in this paper. Other features of ASD:Suite are separation of auto-generated and hand-written code, choice of execution models and policing of interfaces.

3.1 Automatic code generation

On the surface, the concept of automatic code generation is highly attractive. It avoids the need to hand generate code and should be much less error prone. However, it carries a number of pitfalls:

1. The execution model can be inflexible and incompatible with the target operating system.
2. Automatic code generation has not reached the 100% coverage level. Experienced users can achieve typically up to 70% but lower figures of between 30 and 50% are not uncommon. So this leaves the need to mix auto-generated code with hand-written code.
3. Following on, maintenance of the hand-written code can be challenging if it is mixed with auto-generated code.
4. Auto-generated code can be less efficient in memory usage and performance relative to hand crafted code.
5. Auto-generated code still needs to be thoroughly tested.
6. It can be very difficult for a software engineer, however well experienced, to become a proficient modeller. It requires a totally different mindset. The engineer needs to be able to work at a higher level of abstraction. There is an intellectual barrier to entry, which many engineers cannot aspire to. There is only a small subset of people with the right skills to use this approach effectively. Modelling tools in the hands of less able engineers generally leads to havoc.

7. As with any abstraction tool, in the right hands it can deliver major savings
    when applied to what it does well. However, a lot of time can be spent in fight-
    ing the corner cases where the envelope is being stretched.

Formal methods are therefore often only used for design and test case generation.
Code generation is performed manually. ASD:Suite addresses several of the issues
above and is being piloted by BitWise on several projects with auto-generated
code.

3.2 Reality of modelling and formal methods

The adoption of semi formal methods is commonplace. It is relatively easy to use
Visio or other drawing packages to produce state machine, sequence and class
diagrams. However, these rely on manual review for verification.

New projects try to embrace modelling tools, but a number regress back to
semi-formal methods, due to:

- difficulty in maintaining auto-generated code
- unsuitability of execution model
- unsuitability of test environment
- non-conformance with coding standards and defensive programming techniques.

There is considerably lower adoption of formal methods. Most projects work on
the basis that the auto-generation tool is not certified so the generated code still
needs to be fully covered by test cases.

The lack of certification also applies, at least currently, to ASD:Suite. However, it does address the first two (in the above bullet list) of the main causes of
fall-out from UML modelling.

Formal methods improve the quality of design verification. However, they do
not deliver any significant savings in development budget. The tools also typically
carry a high cost of ownership.

3.3 Manual code generation

Even with auto-generation of code from models, there is still a need for hand written software. A number of processes and standards need to be applied to this work
to minimise the risk of poor quality and resultant budget and timeline escalation.
While these may be obvious to some readers, BitWise is constantly amazed at how
often some or all of these are bypassed, even in safety critical development.

Coding standards, such as MISRA for C or in-house, avoid the use of danger-ous coding constructs. They also help enforce consistency of style and layout, making code easier to maintain.

Defensive programming techniques produce code that is much more robust. It also reduces the risk of defects being introduced at a later stage. For example, state variables should never be stored as a single value but abstracted though an access layer that duplicates and/or checksums the value.

4 Modularity and re-use

It is surprising how often a software based product or solution needs to be altered. It may have been sold to another customer but requires customisation. An existing customer may request additional or changed functionality. The associated churn in software traditionally leads to a process known as software erosion, where the code base becomes increasingly difficult to support. The cost of maintenance grows dramatically, given that each release needs to be shown to be fully verified and validated.

Many projects set out to establish a modular architecture. The software is di-vided into components, ideally with loose coupled and one-way interfaces. How-ever, new engineers join the team, experienced engineers leave, challenging new requirements come along, documentation is sometimes not kept up to date, and it becomes ever more difficult to maintain the original modular architecture.

Tools support for maintaining modular architectures is weak. BitWise has de-veloped an in-house tool that forms part of a project's build system. This manages dependencies between components and helps prevent abuse of interfaces. Even so, this is a difficult thing to maintain.

The advantages of re-use are potentially massive. A product revision may only require one or two components to change, offering a major reduction in re-testing. A new product may share many existing components, again offering major sav-ings. As an example, BitWise supplies software solutions for high-volume medical devices. These enjoy a large element of re-use.

Modularity fits very well with a layered safety architecture, e.g. LOPA (Layers Of Protection Analysis). Software systems can be very complex and difficult to understand. Unless these are broken down into understandable components with simple interfaces between them, it is extremely difficult to assess resultant safety levels. So modularity and its maintenance is a critical element of delivering safe software.

4.1 Software Product Lines

Software product lines (Clements and Northrop 2005) is a fairly recent concept that takes re-use to a new level. It formalises the processes and methods for maintaining components and even allowing them to migrate over time to support extended functionality, without breaking existing deliverables.

5 Testing

Testing is a major part of developing safety critical software. It can typically account for 40% or more of a project. Even with auto-generated code, it still needs to be tested.

Testing needs to be performed at a number of levels, corresponding to the various layers of the 'V' model. There is a modern phenomenon where some project teams put a great deal of effort into unit tests but a corresponding absence of effort into integration and system testing levels. While unit tests are valuable, they are no substitute for higher layers of testing.

For safety critical software, test cases need to be produced that:

- exercise all requirements
- exercise all (or most) code paths.

5.1 Automated testing

Automated testing is where tests can be executed without human intervention. This makes them repeatable across multiple test cycles and regression tests. It also makes them much more efficient and error-free to execute. Coupled with modular design and a software product lines approach, they can take a great deal of cost out of a product life cycle.

Automated testing works best when designed in at the start of a project. The architecture and high level design accommodate testing needs, being built in from the outset. This avoids the problems of separate test and production builds, which really needs to be avoided. It can be retrofitted to existing projects but can carry a significant refactoring exercise first.

There are pitfalls with automated testing. Maintenance can be very costly, which undermines much of the benefit. Managing test case maintenance requires a very clear approach to understanding allowable variant behaviour and avoiding brittle verification. A common approach is to compare results with golden data, which is particularly difficult to verify and maintain.

Another pitfall is around choice of test environment. There are a number of commercial and open source platforms on the market, particularly for unit tests. These often lack the flexibility to support multiple layers of testing.

User interfaces are also difficult to automate, given the need to manually inspect outputs. A good approach is to treat the user interface as a separate component and to minimise the functionality within it. This maximises what can be tested automatically.

Without doubt, automated testing, if handled effectively, is a key means of reducing costs in a safety critical development. However, it is dangerous to assume that all testing can be automated. As more test cases are added, the system becomes more immune to testing. Unstructured negative testing (angry monkey) must still form part of any test strategy.

5.2 SOUP validation

Recent standards have increased the emphasis in validating all the tools used in a project. It is no longer enough to test the deliverables. Every tool needs to be validated as well. Tools are generically known as SOUP (Software Of Unknown Provenance).

Tools are often very complex and in many cases, e.g. compilers, have an infinite set of potential inputs. So they cannot be proven in all cases. As with many aspects of software safety engineering, it comes down to a degree of confidence.

There are established processes for addressing SOUP validation. Some of these may draw on body of evidence e.g. Microsoft Word. Others will require an explicit test plan to validate the tool.

It makes sense to stick to a well proven tool set, avoiding the burden of SOUP validation on each project. This can act as a significant barrier to adopting new tools.

5.3 Reality

Despite the evolution of safety standards and accreditation authorities, the reality is that there is a spectrum of testing quality applied to safety critical projects. Market entry timing and funding pressures inevitably drive some businesses to cut corners where they can. These are not always filtered out by the accreditation authorities. This is quite disturbing and suggests that if a safety failure occurs, the ALARP judgment may not fall on the side of the supplier. The developer is taking a risk if full processes are not followed.

5.4 Code reviews and inspection

The cost of fixing any defect in software increases exponentially relative to which stage it is discovered at in the lifecycle. The earlier it can be found, the lower the cost impact. Reviewing code before it reaches the testing stage is therefore a good idea.

Effective manual code reviews require properly trained and qualified code inspectors. Specific areas include coding standards, architecture and domain knowledge. It also ties up a lot of senior staff time. However, this process can be augmented and simplified by use of automated tools.

In the embedded world, C and C++ are still dominant due to their modest memory footprints. Java and C# are much newer and have specified out some of the weaknesses of their predecessors. However, their run-time support code bases are large and hence not suitable for most embedded applications.

There are a number of classes of tool to assist with code inspection. These are categorised as different generations:

First generation. More robust compilers, with much stronger checks. The best known of these is PcLint.

Second generation. Code complexity analysis and standards compliance.

Third generation. Whole of code static analysers, such as Coverity, KlocWorks or Code Sonar.

Running these tools in conjunction with manual code inspection can make a major difference to code quality. It is also useful to have a checklist of things to look for during manual inspection that avoid overlap with automatic tools and act as an aide memoire.

6 Conclusions

Developing safety critical software involves a large number of potentially complex processes and tools. Entering into a project without a very clear plan and understanding of the product road map can easily lead to major creep in budget and delivery dates. More worryingly, some developers compromise on quality to address these issues.

There is no one process or tool that is a panacea. However, BitWise has learned from long and hard experience that combining a number of processes, trained staff and tools with clear product and quality plans can lead to substantial savings across a product's life. This paper has introduced the key aspects of this.

BitWise has found that the vast majority of safety critical projects experience some degree of evolution during their lifetime. Rarely is a project developed once and then cast in stone for its entire lifetime. So up-front investment in a modular and product-lines approach almost always delivers major benefits.

BitWise has also found that by following the approaches laid out in this paper, initial development estimates are more accurate. More importantly, the costs of product/system enhancements are reduced dramatically, rendering 50% or higher savings.

References

Clements P, Northrop L (2005) Software product lines, practices and patterns. Addison-Wesley

Borland (2011) Caliber requirements management tools. http://www.borland.com/us/products/caliber. Accessed 19 September 2011

Goda (2011) CASE Spec. Goda Software Inc. http://www.analysttool.com. Accessed 19 September 2011

IBM (2011) DOORS requirements management tools. http://www-01.ibm.com/software/awdtools/doors/productline. Accessed 19 September 2011

IEC (2006) Medical device software – Software lifecycle processes. IEC 62304. International Electrotechnical Commission

IEC (2010a) Application of risk management for IT networks incorporating medical devices – Part 1: Roles, responsibility and activities. IEC80001. International Electrotechnical Commission

IEC (2010b) Functional safety of electrical/electronic/programmable electronic safety related systems, Parts 1 to 7. ISO/IEC 61508. International Electrotechnical Commission

ISO (2003) Medical devices – Quality management systems – Requirements for regulatory purposes. ISO13485

Verum (2011) ASD:Suite. http://www.verum.com. Accessed 19 September 2011

The New Software Testing Standard

Stuart Reid

Testing Solutions Group

London, UK

Abstract In May 2007 ISO formed a working group to develop a new standard on software testing – a new area for ISO. This initiative is closely-supported by IEEE and BSI, both of which are providing existing standards as source documents to the project. The proposed standard, ISO/IEC 29119, comprises four parts. The first covers 'concepts and terminology', the second 'test process', the third 'test documentation', and the fourth 'test techniques'. An extension to the standard is already under development in the form of a test process assessment standard. This paper describes progress on the development of ISO/IEC 29119, which is now due for publication in 2012, and the challenges with creating a generic testing standard that is applicable to all organizations and all types of project.

1 Introduction

Software testing was an established and integral part of the software development process well before life cycle models were defined, with references to a separate software testing activity being made as early as 1954. Today estimates for the proportion of life cycle costs spent on testing vary from about 20% up to 80% for safety-critical systems (these estimates typically include testing costs across the full life cycle, and so comprise both static and dynamic testing). Despite its long history and high costs, testing has traditionally been poorly covered in standards; this corresponds with similar poor coverage in academic courses and research.

This paper covers a new international software testing standard, the development of which started in 2007 and which is now expected to be published in 2012. Some standards on different aspects of software testing have been published by bodies such as IEEE and BSI; these have either covered testing in individual life cycle phases (e.g. BS 7925-2 Software Component Testing (BSI 1998b)) or specific aspects, such as test documentation (e.g. IEEE 829 Test Documentation (IEEE 2008)). The new international standard (ISO/IEC 29119) is intended to be far more inclusive, covering testing processes at various levels, as well as test documentation, techniques for designing test cases, a testing vocabulary and the concepts on which the standard is based.

1.1 A software testing model

The underlying model used as the basis of the new standard is shown in Figure 1, and comprises four basic entities with the test processes forming the central core of the model. The test documentation is produced as a result of executing the test processes, thus the test documentation describes the outputs of the test processes. The requirement to use techniques to perform the testing (e.g. designing test cases) is defined as part of the processes, while the actual techniques are defined separately. The terminology used by the other parts of this model is defined in the vocabulary.

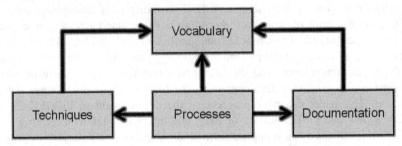

Fig.1. Underlying model of software testing

The processes covered by this model work at three different layers as shown in Figure 2. The organizational test process defines those activities required to manage the testing across a number of projects and would typically include the development and implementation of an organizational test policy and the organizational test strategy. Test management processes cover those activities that define and implement test plans; these could be at the overall project level or be concerned with the test management of individual test phases or test types (e.g. usability testing). The fundamental test processes define the actual testing activities (e.g. test design and test execution), but could include both static and dynamic testing.

1.2 Why testing standards?

Historically the demand for new standards has often been driven by serious failures and even major disasters (e.g. boiler standards and steamboat accidents, water standards and cholera epidemics). Although there are examples of inadequate software testing and associated serious failures (e.g. Ariane 5), the development of software testing standards appears to be more a balance between commercialism and an altruistic drive for increased professionalism in the industry.

Software testing standards provide a number of potential benefits to different stakeholders. For instance, use of such a standard could act as a form of guarantee to the consumer of a testing service that the testing is of a certain quality. From this perspective standards afford benefit to the consumer, their authors providing the expertise to a transaction that would otherwise be lacking.

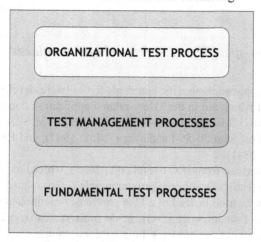

Fig. 2. Layers of software testing processes

Some expect standards to define best practice, but after a moment's reflection on the costs of implementing this, we would probably modify our view to expect a reasonable balance between best practice and cost (good practice).

The existence of a standard detailing good practice means testers do not have to start from scratch, but can build on the experience of the standard's authors. Thus standards can act as a means of technology transfer, distributing expert knowledge to readers in a cost-effective manner.

Unhappily, up until now there has been no *single* software testing standard. Consumers of software testing services cannot simply look for the 'kitemark' and testers have no single source of good practice. There are many standards that touch upon software testing, but many of these standards overlap and contain what appear to be contradictory requirements. Perhaps worse, there are large gaps in the coverage of software testing by standards, such as integration testing, where no useful standard exists at all.

1.3 Specific testing standards

Work on the first testing standard, IEEE 829 Software Test Documentation, began in 1979 and it was published 4 years later – the latest version was published in 2008 (IEEE 2008). Subsequently the IEEE published a unit test standard in 1987, which was revised in 2003 (IEEE 2003). BSI published two testing standards in 1998; part 1 is a testing vocabulary (BSI 1998a), while part 2 is a component testing standard that includes a test process for component (unit) testing, while the main contents are definitions (and examples) of test case design techniques (BSI 1998b).

1.4 Application-specific and safety-related standards

There are many application-specific standards for software development (and testing), nearly all of which are in the safety-related application domain. Examples of this type are DO-178B for avionics (RTCA 1992), MISRA for automotive (MISRA 1994), Def Stan 00-55 for defence (MoD 1997), and EN 50128 for railway (CENELEC 2001).

EN 50128 is derived from IEC 61508 (IEC 1998), which, according to its title, is 'applicable to electrical/electronic/programmable safety-related systems', and so could presumably be used instead of all the previously-mentioned standards.

IEC 61508 has four integrity levels, as do most standards using this concept, and is very comprehensive, covering both hardware and software (part 3 of this standard covers software requirements). It includes some rather strange software testing requirements (the relationship between the requirements for boundary value analysis and equivalence partitioning needs some work), and, as with all these standards, there is no rationale for the testing requirements. This is an area in need of research.

These standards require specific forms of software testing to be performed and specific test coverage levels to be achieved, but do not provide definitions of the corresponding processes, techniques and coverage measures. As different practitioners can have quite different perception of these, this can lead to a lack of consistency and misunderstandings. Hopefully, the availability of an international software testing standard should allay this type of problem.

2 ISO and IEC

The International Organization for Standardization (ISO) comprises a network of over 160 national standards bodies (one per member country) that had published well over 18,000 standards by the end of 2010. The ISO Strategic Plan (2011-2015) expresses a commitment to be '...the world's leading provider of high quality, globally relevant international standards'.

In the field of information and communication technologies ISO often collaborates with the IEC (International Electrotechnical Commission) to produce joint standards; in the region of 1,000 in the area of IT so far. As shown in Figure 4, ISO and IEC have set up a committee (SC7) on software and systems engineering under Joint Technical Committee 1 on information technology (JTC1), with terms of reference for the 'Standardization of processes, supporting tools and supporting technologies for the engineering of software products and systems'. In 2011 SC7 had 37 participating national standards bodies. Figure 3 shows the number of standards published and maintained by SC7 since its inception.

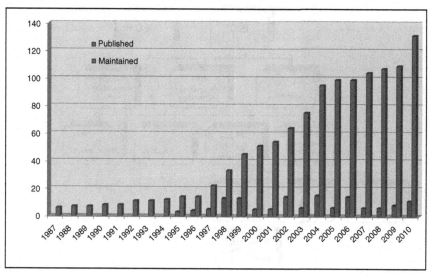

Fig. 3. SC7 software and systems standards

2.1 Standardization process

The development of a new standard begins with someone identifying a perceived requirement (e.g. being able to buy bullets from a wider range of suppliers based on a defined specification). A 'New Work Item Proposal' (NWIP) is produced describing the case for the new standard and the majority of participating SC7 members must support the NWIP for it to go ahead. Ideally, the proposers will have a draft version of the proposed standard already available at this stage, as there is a strict timetable for the production of a new standard and this is far easier to meet if a draft is already available.

Once approved, the NWIP is assigned to a Working Group (WG), who take responsibility for progressing the standard through a number of stages to publication. Figure 4 shows that WG26 (software testing) is one of approximately 15 WGs under SC7. Initially Working Drafts (WD) are produced and used to gain consensus between the experts on the WG, before a Committee Draft (CD) is sent out to the national bodies on SC7 for review and comment. Comments are received and incorporated (where appropriate) and, if necessary, a further CD is sent out. Once consensus on the CD within SC7 is reached it is sent out as a Draft International Standard (DIS) to all ISO members for further (technical and editorial) comments and finally as a Final Draft International Standard (FDIS) for approval to be published as an international standard. This progression is shown in Figure 13 for the new testing standard.

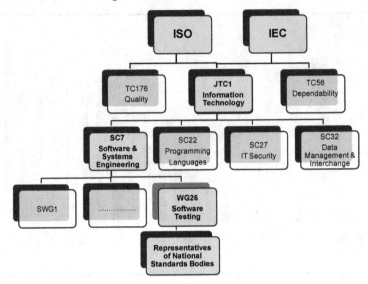

Fig. 4. ISO, IEC, JTC1, SC7 and WG26

Consensus in ISO is defined as:

'General agreement, characterized by the absence of sustained opposition to substantial issues by any important part of the concerned interests and by a process that involves seeking to take into account the views of all parties concerned and to reconcile any conflicting arguments. Consensus need not imply unanimity.'

To be accepted as an international standard, it must be approved by at least two-thirds of the national members that participated in its development, and not be disapproved by more than a quarter of all ISO members who voted on it.

The WG comprises a convener (chair), project editor (supported by editors), representatives of national standards bodies and technical experts. The representatives from national standards bodies should present their own technical expertise as well as the combined views of all stakeholders in their country. In some countries where there is widespread interest, views are collated by creating a mirror panel of the ISO WG. Interested organizations may also apply for representation on the WG, but they do not have voting rights like those held by the national standards bodies.

Individuals join WGs (and the mirror panel) for various reasons, but it can provide the obvious benefit of inside knowledge on future standards, and the ability to influence future standardization. Networking among WG members can also be beneficial.

SC7 holds two 'formal' meetings a year, each of which lasts a (working) week; the plenary meeting in late May and the interim meeting in October/November.

WGs may hold extra meetings between these, but these are more likely to be held as online meetings.

3 Background to ISO/IEC 29119

The NWIP for a new standard on software testing was approved by ISO in May 2007, to be based on existing IEEE and BSI standards (IEEE 829, IEEE 1008, BS 7925-1 and BS 7925-2). As no working group with software testing expertise existed within SC7 a new 'software testing' working group (WG26) was created. By 2011 over 20 different nations were represented on WG26.

The initial proposed four part structure of ISO/IEC 29119 showing how existing standards feed into the new parts is provided in Figure 5. Subsequently, 'part 5' on process assessment has been created as a result of a separate NWIP, although this part is being jointly developed by WG10 (Working Group on process assessment) and WG26, and is currently known as ISO/IEC 33063, but may be dual numbered as ISO/IEC 29119-5 in the future.

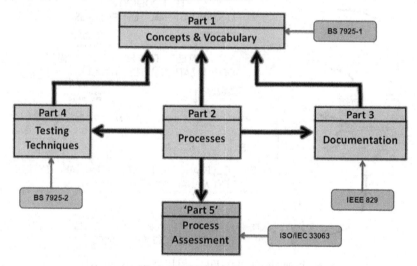

Fig.5. ISO/IEC 29119 structure

4 ISO/IEC 29119 part 2 – test processes

The processes in ISO/IEC 29119 part 2 are defined using a three layer model very similar to that in the software testing model described earlier and shown in Figure 1. Figure 6 provides an example of how these layers may be used in a relatively large and mature organization (mature enough to have an organizational test policy and large enough to make it worthwhile having an organizational test strategy). One slight difference in the ISO/IEC 29119 implementation of the earlier three layer model is that the lowest layer (the fundamental test processes) has been specifically defined as dynamic test processes, and so cannot include any static test processes. This is because it was not possible to gain consensus within WG26 (or SC7) on the inclusion of static testing in the standard.

Figure 6 shows the generic processes in part 2 of the standard being instantiated for use at different levels. The organizational test process is instantiated twice: once to develop and maintain the organizational test policy and once for the organizational test strategy. The test management processes are instantiated to develop and implement the project test plan, and also used for each subsequent phase or type of testing for which a separate test plan is created. Although test plans developed using ISO/IEC 29119 are expected to include consideration of both static and dynamic testing the lowest layer of processes in ISO/IEC 29119 is limited to dynamic testing. These dynamic test processes would be implemented whenever dynamic testing is required by a test plan (e.g. for unit testing, system testing, performance testing).

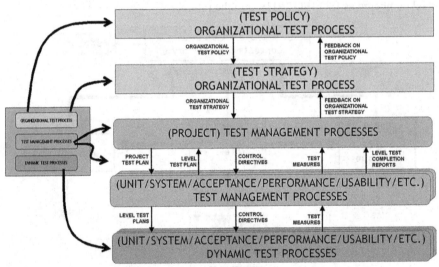

Fig.6. Example use of ISO/IEC 29119 three layer model

4.1 ISO/IEC 29119 organizational test process

There is just one organizational test process – this is shown in Figure 7. It is used for the development and maintenance of organizational level test specifications, the most common of which are the test policy and organizational test strategy. Organizational level test specifications typically apply across a number (if not all) projects in an organization, and so are not project-specific – they ensure that a consistent approach to testing is maintained across all projects. If the organization is large enough to run projects that are quite dissimilar (say in different programmes) there may be organizational test specifications that are specific to each programme.

A test policy defines the scope of testing, and describes the principles and high-level objectives expected of all testing within an organization. It is expected to be a high-level level document of only a couple of pages that is understandable by executives, and aligned with other executive level policies, such as the quality policy. The test policy provides guidance and constraints on the organizational test strategy and acts as a framework within which all the organization's testing should be performed. Example content of a test policy may be that all testing should comply with the ISO/IEC 29119 software testing standard.

In contrast to the test policy, the organizational test strategy is a technical document that defines the expected practice of testing on all projects in the organization – and, as such, may well comprise many pages. It must be aligned to the test policy (assuming there is one) and defines a set of reusable testing guidelines that can be used as the basis for specific test plans by test managers, thus reducing the decision-making required and ensuring consistency across projects. Example content of an organizational test strategy may be that an exit criterion for unit testing should be that 100% statement coverage is achieved.

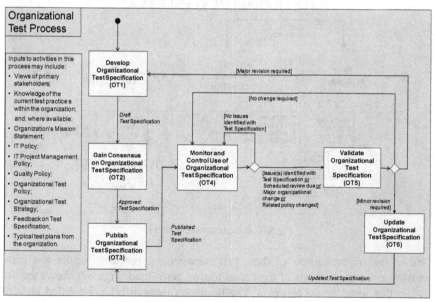

Fig.7. Organizational test process

4.2 ISO/IEC 29119 test management processes

There are three test management processes, as shown in Figure 8. These processes are used to manage lower level testing activities on a specific project, such as dynamic testing (as shown), static testing (not shown as currently not part of the standard) and lower level test management. When the test management processes are used at the project level and the project is large enough, then this project test plan may require test plans to be generated and implemented for individual test phases or specific test types.

While performing these test management processes, any constraints or guidelines provided by the test policy or the organizational test strategy should be complied with, unless there is a good reason not to, in which case any deviation should be agreed and documented.

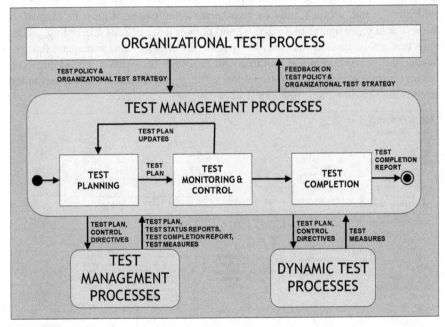

Fig.8. Test management processes

One of the major outputs of these test management processes is the test plan, which is used as the basis of the actual testing performed. Figure 9 shows the activities that generate the test plan. The figure is (necessarily) a simplified view of the process and although a simple linear flow is shown, in practice a considerable amount of iteration between activities would be expected to occur, especially as the test strategy is designed (in TP5), new risks are uncovered or old risks changed, and staffing and scheduling constraints discovered in TP6. As can be seen in activities TP4 and TP5, the standard mandates a risk-based approach to testing; it does not, however, specify the mechanism for performing the risk analysis. In a safety-critical application it could be appropriate to use integrity levels derived from perceived risks, while in a less critical application it would also be possible for the test manager to make subjective judgements based on simply asserted levels of risk.

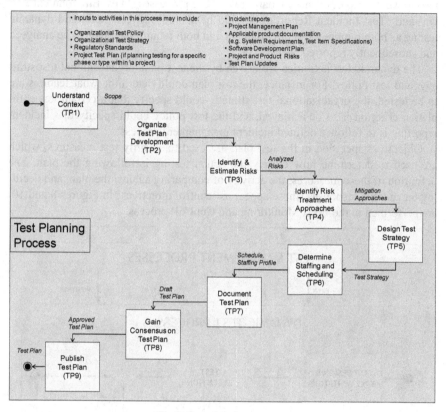

Fig.9. Test planning process

One of the most important test planning activities is TP5 'Design Test Strategy', where decisions such as which features are to be tested, which test phases, test techniques and test completion criteria are to be used are made. The 'test strategy' at this level is being derived as part of the test plan, and is quite different from the organizational test strategy. The organizational test strategy provides generic guidelines to how the testing should be performed on *all* projects, whereas the test strategy that forms part of the test plan defines specific testing to be performed on *this* project. Note, however, that the test strategy in the test plan should normally align with the guidelines and constraints provided in the organizational test strategy, and so there should necessarily be similarities.

4.3 ISO/IEC 29119 dynamic test processes

Figure 10 shows the four dynamic test processes. It should be noted that if static testing was also part of the standard, two of the processes ('Test Environment Set-Up' and 'Test Incident Reporting') could be shared between static and dynamic testing as both require a test environment and both require incidents to be analysed and subsequently reported, as necessary.

The dynamic test activities are driven by the test plan, organizational test strategy, and test policy. For instance, the test plan could determine what features are to be tested, the organizational test strategy could specify that a certain test completion criterion is to be achieved, and the test policy could specify that incident reporting is to follow a defined incident management process.

Objectives specified in the test plan are used to identify test measures, which are used to determine how closely the actual testing is following the plan. The definition of these measures, the activity of comparing against the plan, and deciding on suitable responses (these appear as 'control directives' in Figures 8 and 10) are performed in the 'Test Monitoring and Control' process.

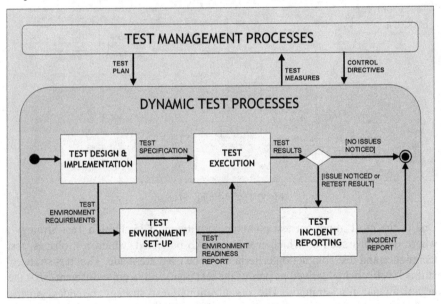

Fig.10. Dynamic test processes

The 'Test Design and Implementation' Process, shown in Figure 11, requires test cases to be derived to cover test coverage items, which are derived, in turn, from applying a test case design technique to the test conditions for those features that are to be tested. An example using the boundary value analysis technique would see boundaries identified as the test conditions and test coverage items could correspond to the value on the actual boundary and values an incremental 'distance' either side of it. For instance, in an exam grading program the boundary between pass and fail, say 50%, would be identified as one test condition (of several). Subsequently, assuming we are using integers, the values 49%, 50% and 51% would be derived as the test coverage items. Then test cases would be derived to ensure all three test coverage items were exercised by tests (and these would also include expected results).

Test cases may be grouped into test sets (perhaps based on whether they are to be executed using manual or automated test execution) and then the test cases in the test sets are typically ordered into test procedures based on dependencies between the test cases.

A requirement of the standard, also shown in Figure 11, is that the traceability through the process should be documented, so that it is possible to link the test procedures all the way back to the original test basis (requirement).

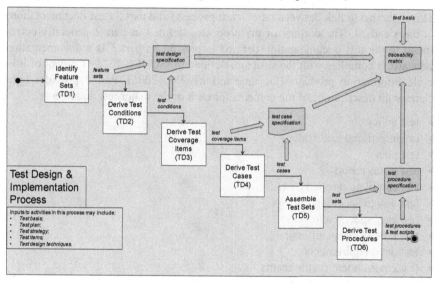

Fig.11. Test design and implementation process

4.4 ISO/IEC 29119 process descriptions

Each of the processes included in part 2 of the standard is described using the format for process descriptions defined in ISO/IEC TR 24774 Guidelines for process description (ISO 2010). This technical report provides guidelines that a process should be described in terms of:

- title
- purpose
- outcomes

- activities
- tasks
- information items.

It is noteworthy that this structure includes no description of who performs the activities and no process inputs (the 'information items' correspond to the process outputs). These ISO guidelines changed while the test processes were being defined and all process inputs, roles and responsibilities had to be stripped out in the next version to ensure compliance with the guidelines.

5 ISO/IEC 29119 part 3 – test documentation

There is a strong link between part 2 (test process) and part 3 (test documentation) of the standard. The outputs of the processes defined in part 2 generally correspond to the test documentation defined in part 3. As part 3 is a documentation standard, it complies with the structure defined in ISO/IEC 15289 Content of lifecycle information products (Documentation) (ISO 2006). Part 3 provides templates with descriptions of the contents for each of the major test documents:

- test policy
- organizational test strategy
- test plan
- test status report
- test completion report
- test design specification
- test case specification
- test procedure specification
- test data requirements
- test environment requirements
- test data readiness report
- test environment readiness report
- test execution log
- incident report.

Probably of more use to test practitioners are the examples of each of the test documents that are also provided in the annexes of part 3.

6 ISO/IEC 29119 part 4 – test techniques

Those following part 2 of the standard are required to produce test plans that include requirements for test case design techniques to be specified (and used) and test completion criteria to be achieved. Test case design techniques and corresponding coverage measures are defined in part 4 of the standard. Each test case design technique is formally defined (in the normative part of the standard), but corresponding examples showing how the techniques could be applied are provided in the annexes.

The current list of test case design techniques included in part 4 is:

- specification-based testing techniques

    - boundary value analysis
    - cause-effect graphing
    - classification tree method
    - combinatorial test techniques
    - decision table testing
    - equivalence partitioning
    - error guessing
    - random testing
    - scenario testing
    - state transition testing
    - syntax testing

- structure-based testing techniques

    - branch / decision testing
    - branch condition testing
    - branch condition combination testing
    - data flow testing
    - Modified Condition Decision Coverage (MCDC) testing
    - statement testing.

7 Verification, validation and testing

The development of a software testing standard within ISO has raised a number of questions. Probably one of the most emotive has been the relationship between verification and validation (V&V) and testing. Many members of SC7, especially those with a defence background, hold a 'traditional' view of testing as being one of the four forms of V&V (the other three being inspection, simulation and demonstration). This view that inspection was separate from testing was reinforced by defence standards, but most members of WG26 (and especially those without a defence background) held a view that inspection was a type of static testing, and hence a form of testing. This view was reinforced by numerous texts, published over a number of years, from as early as Myers's seminal 'Art of Software Testing' from 1979, and the common practice of test plans including requirements for static testing.

These two opposing perspectives inevitably introduced the potential for disagreement and a study group was set up within SC7 to consider the position of

V&V within ISO standards. Even though many members of this working group come from the defence community (who may have to change the way they do testing if the new standard is adopted for defence contracts), the taxonomy shown in Figure 12 was agreed (although it is quite possible it will change in the future).

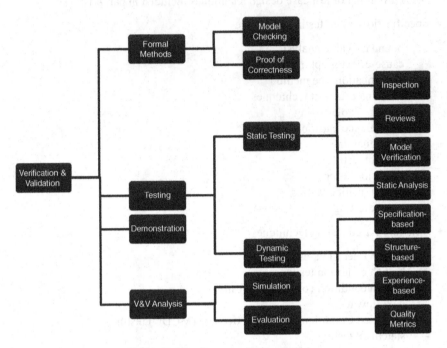

Fig.12. Verification and validation taxonomy

Despite this agreement, it has not yet been possible to gain consensus on the inclusion of static testing processes in the new standard (at least for the initial publication).

8 ISO/IEC 29119 and risk-based testing

Most of those working on the development of the new standard do not believe that it includes any 'leading edge' technology that should act as a barrier to its adoption by professional testers. It should be noted, however, that the standard mandates the use of a risk-based approach to the testing.

Risk-based testing (RBT) has been around in various forms for over 20 years, and accepted as a mainstream approach for over half that time, now being an integral part of popular certification schemes, such as ISTQB (with more than 150,000 ISTQB-qualified testers worldwide). Despite this, and the fact that RBT is not a complex approach in theory, it is still rare to see RBT being applied as successfully as it could be and many practitioners appear to be still 'blissfully' ignorant of it, although happily this does not apply to the safety-related community.

When using RBT, risk analysis is used to identify and score risks, so that the perceived risks in the delivered system (and to the development of this system) can be prioritized and categorized. The prioritization is used to determine the order of testing (higher priority risks are addressed earlier), while the category of risk is used to decide the most appropriate forms of testing to perform (e.g. which test phases, test techniques, and test completion criteria to use). A valuable side-effect of using this approach is that at any point the risk of delivery can be simply communicated as the outstanding (untested) risks. The results of performing testing against perceived risks and also the evolving business situation will naturally change the risk landscape over time thus requiring RBT to be considered as an ongoing activity. As wide a range of stakeholders as possible should be involved in these activities to ensure that as many risks as possible are considered and their respective treatments (or not – we may decide to not address some risks) are agreed.

The application of RBT is not, however, applied in an effective manner on many of the projects that do use it. This is often due to the scope of RBT as applied being too narrow, by it not encompassing the higher levels of testing, such as in the organizational test strategy, and by it not being used as the basis for test planning that covers the whole life cycle. RBT can also fail to fulfil expectations when it is not integrated into the wider risk management practices within an organization, or when RBT is only used to address risks in the deliverable software rather than also considering the risks to the testing itself. These challenges can largely be addressed by the industry changing its perspective on RBT and widening its view. The new standard, however, cannot, in itself, solve this problem as although it mandates RBT, it does not specify how RBT should be applied.

The new standard can, however, raise awareness of RBT within the testing community. Probably the biggest challenge to the effective use of RBT is the lack of maturity of test practitioners, and if the new standard forces recognition and the take-up of RBT by test practitioners it will strongly 'encourage' maturation in this respect.

9 Plans for 29119

Progress on the publication of the standard has been slower than expected – mainly from the perspective of SC7 as a whole, rather than from WG26 itself.

As was mentioned earlier, an 'ideal' NWIP is accompanied by a draft standard, thus making its progress through the development process quicker. The NWIP for ISO/IEC 29119 was based on pre-existing IEEE and British Standards (see Figure 5) and over the years it has become apparent that the majority of SC7 (outside of WG26) understood this to mean that the development of ISO/IEC 29119 would largely be a re-badging exercise. This was despite WG26 regularly reporting that this was not the case. In fact, the 'donated' standards only provide (conflicting) processes for unit testing, and no processes at any other level (so no organiza-tional-level or management processes), thus necessitating most of the work on the test processes (which form the 'core' of the set of standards) to be started from practically a 'blank sheet'.

The WG decided that the creation of new test processes should involve as wide a review community as possible and many testers from around the world have been involved in this process, resulting in thousands of comments over two infor-mal rounds of reviews and subsequent updates. This extensive review process (see Figure 13) has, however, necessarily extended the development time for the stan-dard, and a formal extension of the rigid delivery schedules applied by ISO was granted in May 2009.

As can be seen in Figure 13, it was decided that the standard would be devel-oped in two 'tranches'. This was partly due to the lack of available editors to start working on all four parts at the same time, and that part 1 can only be completed after the others as it contains the definitions for the other three parts.

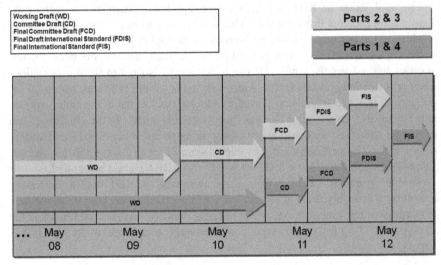

Fig.13. Timelines for ISO/IEC 29119

10 Conclusions

Given the high cost of testing and the maturity of the discipline it is somewhat surprising that a comprehensive testing standard is still unavailable. Apart from demand from the consumers of test services and test practitioners looking for a guide on good practice, there is also now a stated demand for a standard to act as a body of knowledge for test certification schemes. For many years safety-critical and/or application-specific software development standards have required forms of testing to be performed and various test completion criteria to be achieved, but there has been no definitive standard describing how this testing should be done, nor how test coverage should be measured. The new ISO/IEC 29119 software testing standard should help to fill this gap.

The new standard defines good practice for testing at the organizational level (across multiple projects), at the management level (planning, monitoring and control, test completion), and for the processes for designing and performing dynamic testing. As well as the test processes (which mandate a risk-based approach to the testing), test documentation, test case design techniques and a testing vocabulary are all covered by the new standard. An extension to the standard is already under development in the form of a test process assessment standard.

This standard is being developed under the auspices of ISO/IEC by a group of experts from over 20 countries, and, if current plans are followed, should be published in 2012. The testing standards provided as source documents to the new standards from IEEE and BSI will be 'retired' some time after its launch.

References

BSI (1998a) BS 7925-1-1998, Software testing – vocabulary. BSI

BSI (1998b) BS 7925-2-1998 Software component testing. BSI

CENELEC (2001) EN 50128-2001 Railway applications – Software for railway control and protection systems. CENELEC

IEC (1998) IEC 61508:1998 Functional safety of electrical/electronic/programmable electronic safety-related systems. IEC

IEEE (2003) IEEE 1008-1987(R2003) Standard for software unit testing. IEEE

IEEE (2008) IEEE 829-2008 Standard for software test documentation. IEEE

ISO (2006) ISO/IEC 15289:2006 Content of life-cycle information products (Documentation). ISO

ISO (2010) ISO/IEC TR 24774 Guidelines for process description. ISO

MISRA (1994) Development guidelines for vehicle based software. MISRA

MoD (1997) Def Stan 00-55 Requirements for safety-related software in defence equipment. Issue 2. Ministry of Defence

RTCA (1992) DO-178B Software considerations in airborne systems and equipment certification. RTCA Inc.

Goal-Based Safety Standards: Promises and Pitfalls

John McDermid and Andrew Rae

Department of Computer Science, University of York

York, UK

Abstract This paper contrasts goal-based and prescriptive safety standards and regulation based on their respective 'worldviews' – the assumptions and expectations that lead to a preference for one form of regulation over another. It considers whether these worldviews are entirely subjective, or whether there may be an empirical basis for favouring one worldview over another. Our analysis does not draw definitive conclusions on this matter, but indicates how evidence might be identified. It also indicates benefits of goal-based regulation – which would arise if that worldview 'holds', and the pitfalls if it doesn't. It is hoped that this way of looking at these contrasting approaches to safety standards and regulation will provide some insight for those charged with developing standards.

1 Introduction

There is a growing number of system safety engineering standards which are goal-based, i.e. they state required end-states or outcomes rather than prescribing methods and processes. Coglianese (Coglianese et al. 2002) provides a summary of the arguments for goal-based regulation, as well as identifying some counter-arguments and potential limitations. One of the authors has previously written arguments in favour of goal-based standards based on a safety-case approach (Kelly et al. 2005), and both authors believe that there is a strong logical argument for goal-based safety regulation.

The purpose of this paper is not to repeat the arguments for goal-based regulation; instead we discuss whether and how questions of regulation can be answered using experience and evidence rather than argument. The types of questions we are interested in range from the simple:

'Are goal-based standards better than prescriptive standards?'

to more nuanced issues such as:

'Under what circumstances are goal-based standards or prescriptive standards advantageous?'

and:

'How can we minimise the weaknesses and capitalize on the strengths of prescriptive and goal-based standards?'

It is not practicable to answer the above questions directly in this paper – indeed it may not ultimately be practical to answer them objectively – however there *is* benefit in considering how we might go about answering them. By doing this it might be possible to produce more objective evidence of the promises and pitfalls of goal-based standards, and thus guide the development of standards. This is inevitably a long-term agenda, but if we are to make progress in reducing the 'Library of Babel' (Borges 2000) of system safety engineering standards (it is hard to count, but there are probably several hundred such standards) then it is necessary to bring a fresh and analytical perspective to their development and evolution.

The paper starts by reviewing the purpose of standards in system safety engineering, focusing on those issues that we do not believe to be contentious, e.g. producing safer products than would otherwise be the case. A premise of this paper is that the goal-based versus prescriptive standards debate reflects different 'worldviews' about what makes standards effective. One of the keys to improving the debate is to articulate those 'worldviews' and to identify how data from development or operation could identify which (if either) of those views is most representative of the 'real world' of safety-critical systems engineering. The core of the paper focuses on analysing these 'worldviews' to identify ways in which we can shed light on the above questions. This also enables us to address the 'promises and pitfalls' of the title in what is hopefully a more objective manner than we have presented previously.

The above may seem rather philosophical – and at times the paper does take a rather philosophical standpoint – but the intent is also to be practical. Spending money on activities that do not contribute to safety (although they are meant to) is not very desirable; not carrying out activities that are essential to achieve safety may have dire consequences. Thus, the latter part of the paper seeks to identify some pragmatic steps that can be taken, in the context of existing projects and standards developments, to use the insights gained from trying to address the above questions.

2 Standards: what are they for?

There are different types of standard, e.g. those that relate to technical aspects of products, such as data buses, those that relate to whole products, e.g. aircraft, and those that relate to processes. Some product standards are relevant to safety – indeed in some areas, e.g. civil aviation, there are extensive sets of standards and other documents which specify in considerable detail the safety-related technical characteristics of aircraft. However our focus here is on process standards, i.e. those that relate to the conduct of the system safety engineering activities, as that is where the goal-based/prescriptive debate is most pertinent.

In system safety engineering there are formal standards, e.g. MIL-STD 882D (DoD 2002), and other types of document, some of which are referred to as guidelines, e.g. DO-178B (RTCA 1992). We will use the term 'standard' generically for any document intended to help achieve at least a minimum level of quality in system safety engineering activities (and thus desirable qualities of the end product).

In principle, we might want to say that standards are intended to make systems objectively safer – and this might be the basis for comparison between goal-based and prescriptive approaches. In practice, measuring the relative success of the approaches in achieving this goal is impracticable, due to the longevity of systems, the very low unsafe failure rates which need to be achieved, the plethora of factors which impact safety, the fact that we won't produce two versions of a system under different standards, and so on. Thus, whilst we need to keep the laudable aim of making systems safer in mind, we need to be realistic about what we can empirically determine about the influence of standards.

Further, before we can ask: 'What are standards for?' we need to consider their context of use. Systems can be developed in a regulatory framework, where there is a formal acceptance process, or for unregulated markets. In the regulated domain standards can be used to govern the relationship between a supplier and a customer, between a supplier and a regulator, or between companies in a supply chain. We will focus on the supplier-regulator interface because this appears to give sharper 'questions' but we will also make comments on the other relationships where appropriate.

The primary purpose of a system safety engineering standard can therefore be said to be:

Purpose 1. Require a minimum standard of safety to be achieved and demonstrated.

We say: 'require' rather than 'ensure' because a document cannot ensure – but a regulator may be able to do so. This is something of a regulator perspective – but it is also pertinent to the supplier, as it gives a 'floor' to their activities. This leads to two further important, if not primary, purposes:

Purpose 2. Where further safety can be achieved above a minimum, require safety improvement to be balanced with the cost of safety improvement.

Purpose 3. Minimise the cost required to achieve and demonstrate safety.

Purpose 3 is clearly more the interest of the supplier (although a regulator should not wish to impose unreasonable costs) and Purpose 2 is rather more balanced – both regulators and suppliers should wish to see safety improved, but not at any cost. It is hoped that Purpose 1 is not contentious, although Purpose 2 and Purpose 3 might be – for example some might think that economics should not be considered at all; that leads us to the notion of 'worldviews'.

3 Safety worldviews

By a 'worldview' we simply mean the way that some group of people look at an issue. We believe that the differences in opinion between those that favour goal-based standards and those that advocate prescriptive standards reflect different worldviews – particularly regarding the behaviour of regulators and suppliers. We give broad descriptions of the different views then identify some assumptions and predictions which we believe characterize those views.

To amplify on the idea of worldviews we note that Kant, in his Critique of Pure Reason [6], includes the *Antinomies*: a set of contradictory theses. The first pair is:

- The world has a beginning in time, and is also limited as regards space.
- The world has no beginning, and no limits in space; it is infinite as regards both time and space.

Kant proceeds to provide strong arguments in favour of each point of view – on careful reading it becomes clear that each argument is coherent and quite compelling, and the differences lie in terms of the underlying assumptions in each (the different worldviews). Kant was (indirectly) making the point that there is a limit to what we can know about the world from within the world, and that we cannot always resolve such disagreements from empirical observations.

In our discussion here we do not aspire to the philosophical heights of Kant. Further, it seems more helpful to articulate questions which might shed some light on the merits of the different views. We can do this as we have the luxury of something which Kant didn't have – some evidence, even if it is less extensive than we might wish!

Our pragmatism introduces some imperfections into the philosophical framework. The first is that the standards themselves shape reality – believing in a worldview can make it more true. The second imperfection is that to some extent our description of each worldview is relative to the other worldview. This reduces objectivity but aids comparison.

We use the terms 'PrescriptionStan' and 'GoalTopia' as rhetorical labels for the differing worldviews, although we endeavour to make the analysis as objective as possible. Rather than setting out assumptions and predictions explicitly, we instead identify what we call 'features' of the worldviews – characteristics which we would expect to hold.

3.1 PrescriptionStan

In PrescriptionStan standards are used by regulators to both tell suppliers *what* to achieve, and *how* to go about it. Examples of such standards are EN50126, EN50128 and EN50129 (CENELEC 1999, 2001a, 2001b) in the railway-signalling domain. These standards, for example, identify safety integrity levels

(SILs), and define development processes in terms of techniques that are highly recommended (HR), or recommended (R); in some cases, techniques can be mandatory (M) or not recommended (NR).

The underlying worldview is competitive (or perhaps sceptical): suppliers will do as little as possible and prescription is essential to get them to do what is necessary (to meet Purpose 1).

Balance between Purpose 2 and Purpose 3 is achieved through a contest between the regulator (championing improved safety) and the supplier (championing reduced costs). This contest may occur once (during the standard-writing process) or on a case-by-case basis where flexibility of action or interpretation is included in the standard (as it is in most).

To some degree one can argue that in PrescriptionStan Purpose 1 is prioritized over Purpose 2 and Purpose 3. A clear minimum standard is preferred to giving suppliers and regulators flexibility which may lead to abuse or uncertainty.

We can now articulate features of this worldview, which, whilst not directly testable themselves may give rise to testable predictions.

PrescriptionStan Feature 1 (PF1). Suppliers usually will not voluntarily undertake sufficiently thorough safety activities.

This feature is at the heart of an adversarial worldview. Suppliers must be taught or made to do (enough of) the right thing. This feature could be observed by measuring:

- whether there is a low incidence of suppliers undertaking activities not required by the standards
- whether the amount and quality of safety activity undertaken by suppliers varies in proportion to the activity level of the standards enforcer (regulator).

PrescriptionStan Feature 2 (PF2). There is a direct relationship between clarity and precision of requirements and successful compliance with those requirements.

This feature drives the limitation of supplier choice seen in prescriptive standards. Provide too many options, and the supplier becomes confused or finds loopholes. This feature could be observed by measuring:

- whether there is an inverse relationship between the level of prescriptive detail in a standard and the rate of submissions being rejected as non-compliant
- whether there is a direct relationship between the level of prescriptive detail in a standard and the ability of a regulator to enforce the requirements of the standards
- whether there is an inverse relationship between the level of prescriptive detail in a standard and the incidence of systems which gain regulatory approval but prove to be unsafe.

This latter gets close to the fundamental questions about making systems safer.

PrescriptionStan Feature 3 (PF3). There will be minimal variation in the approaches used to conform to the standards.

This feature speaks to the practicality of prescriptive standards.

The feature can be observed by measuring:

- whether there is similarity in documentation produced for regulatory approval for similar systems developed by different organisations in different countries.

PrescriptionStan Feature 4 (PF4). Techniques can be selected independently of the systems being analysed.

This feature is also a pre-requisite for prescriptive standards to be effective. If the feature does not hold in the real world, prescriptive standards cannot work effectively. The feature can be observed by measuring:

- whether there is a relatively low incidence of suppliers needing to use techniques that are not in the standard(s)
- whether there is a relatively low incidence of techniques being used purely for standards compliance (as opposed to achieving some safety benefit).

PF4 is closely related to standards evolution. It implies that the standards are updated at a rate matching the change in knowledge about effective techniques.

3.2 GoalTopia

In GoalTopia standards set objectives saying what has to be achieved, but not saying how (although guidance may be given). Recent examples of such standards are DS 00-56 Issue 4 (MoD 2007), ISO 17894 (ISO 2005) and ISO 26262 (ISO 2011). Goal-based standards are often thought of as a new concept but both MIL-STD-882 and DO-178B are goal-based. The core of MIL-STD-882 articulates some very simple objectives (at issue D (DoD 2002), the mandatory part that defines objectives is less than two pages), although this is perhaps masked by the fact that there has been extensive documentation on how to do things, e.g. the tasks in MIL-STD-882C (DoD 1996). DO178B (RTCA 1992) has 66 objectives for the most stringent assurance level (development assurance level (DAL) A); it is often perceived as a process standard, perhaps because there are so many objectives, but only two of them stray into prescription.

The underlying worldview is collaborative, or one of partnership: suppliers and regulators will agree an effective and cost-effective way to (achieve and) demonstrate safety. This perhaps reflects a greater balance between Purpose 1, Purpose 2 and Purpose 3. From the PrescriptionStan border partnership and flexibility threaten Purpose 1, but in GoalTopia they are attractive means to achieve and demonstrate safety. Stating requirements as objectives gives flexibility – e.g. to use new technology where it is cost-effective – but still requires meeting the objectives).

GoalTopia Feature 1 (GF1). Suppliers will use the flexibility granted by goals rather than prescriptive processes to choose cost-effective solutions to achieving and demonstrating safety.

This feature is the main rationale for goal-based standards. The feature could be observed by measuring:

- whether there is significant variation in the means chosen to achieve and demonstrate safety between projects and organisations
- whether there is an inverse relationship between the level of prescription and the incidence of techniques being used purely for standards compliance (as opposed to gaining some safety benefit).

GoalTopia Feature 2 (GF2). It is practicable for regulators to distinguish between projects that meet the goals and projects which fall short of the goals.

This feature speaks to the workability of goal-based regulation (and the concerns of the PrescriptionStan worldview). Flexibility is only workable if it is possible to observe whether the goals have been met. The feature can probably not be directly measured 'in the wild', but could be observed by qualitative studies of the objections raised by regulators to proposals (both initial safety plans and system acceptance), and by quantitative studies of the ability of regulators to discriminate between projects that meet and do not meet the goals.

GoalTopia Feature 3 (GF3). Selection of techniques and methods should be based primarily on the class of system.

For example for an application which is essentially one of logic, perhaps a railway interlocking system, formal techniques, e.g. model-checking, could be used for a significant part of the safety demonstration. In contrast, model-checking will be relatively ineffective for safety-critical control systems, where it is necessary to assess control stability, jitter, timing, etc. of discrete approximations to continuous control problems. From another perspective, analysis of even quite critical avionics systems shows significant variation in architecture and approach to redundancy based on system type and criticality (Reinhardt and McDermid 2010).

The feature could be observed by measuring:

- whether there is significant variation in the means chosen to achieve and demonstrate safety between systems in the same projects and organisations.

GoalTopia Feature 4 (GF4). Standards will need updating only in response to changes in goals, not changes in technology or knowledge of techniques.

This feature is a necessary implication of the GoalTopia worldview. If the feature isn't real, then the worldview itself is challenged. This feature can be observed by monitoring changes in goal-based standards. Forces other than changes in technology and knowledge may drive change, but we should be able to analyse individual changes for their causes, hence assess this feature.

This selection of features is intended to facilitate comparison.

3.3 Questions for comparison

The description of the worldviews, especially the features, gives us a basis for asking questions that might provide evidence in support of one or other of the worldviews. The proponents of each worldview might disagree with the statements made above; by making them explicit, however, we have made it possible to discuss the assumptions underlying the worldviews. As self-acknowledged natives of GoalTopia we welcome correction from across the border, and from fellow citizens, recognising that we may even find that GoalTopia is not one nation!

Whilst the features of the worldviews don't align directly, they do address some common topics from which we can draw questions linked to the worldviews.

These topics, to be addressed in more detail below, are:

1. the selection of techniques and methods by suppliers
2. the interaction between regulators and suppliers regarding system acceptance
3. the evolution of standards and guidance.

On the selection of techniques and methods, PrescriptionStan and GoalTopia make diverging assumptions. PrescriptionStan suggests that within a given industry, techniques will be mainly uniform regardless of the technology or organisations involved in each project. GoalTopia suggests that there will be variety driven by the needs of the technology. We can investigate this topic as direct questions:

Q1. Within a given industry, to what extent do methods and techniques vary?

Q2. What are the factors that drive method and technique variation?

On the interaction between regulators and suppliers, PrescriptionStan and Goal-Topia make different but not directly incompatible assumptions. PrescriptionStan predicts that more prescription will empower the regulator and facilitate agreement between supplier and regulator. GoalTopia predicts that more prescription will increase the rate of conduct of prescribed but unhelpful safety activity and omission of valuable but not prescribed safety activity.

Q3. Is the type of standard a factor in the power and effectiveness of a regulator?

Q4. Is the type of standard a factor in the time and effort required to come to an agreement between regulator and supplier?

On the evolution of standards, PrescriptionStan and GoalTopia make assumptions unimportant to the other worldview. PrescriptionStan predicts that prescriptive safety process standards can keep pace with technological change. GoalTopia predicts that goal-based standards won't need to keep pace with technological change and so will remain relatively stable.

Q5. Do prescriptive standards evolve as rapidly as technology and knowledge about effective methods?

Q6. Are goal-based standards relatively stable compared to prescriptive standards?

3.4 Evidence problems

There are numerous confounding factors which increase the difficulty of addressing the above questions. We provide a brief list here of issues other than the veracity of the worldviews which might affect the answers to the questions. In our view this does not undermine the approach being advocated – but it does mean that care is needed in analysing evidence (see evidence below).

Standards Processes. It may be that organisational and market forces have a greater influence than the worldview on the evolution of standards. For example, it might be that goal-based standards are more stable in principle (GF4) but in practice change faster as they are simpler, or require simpler consensual processes. It may be that standards with a prescriptive worldview incorporate flexibility as a side-effect of consensus-building instead of as part of the regulator philosophy.

Industry Norms and Events. The questions can only be addressed within a coherent regulatory framework, and lack external validity beyond this. Standards evolution and regulator power may be driven by the history of an industry sector, particularly with respect to heavily publicised accidents.

National Context. The legal frameworks in some countries make adherence to standards a defence in a court of law; this is likely to place greater emphasis on the merits of prescriptive standards. Further, it may be that variations in culture and practices across nations means that longer is spent negotiating acceptable processes (so the answers to Q3, Q4 and Q5 could vary with country, not just standard type).

Variation across the Supply Chain. It may be that the flexibility of goal-based approaches is valuable higher up the chain, but is a net disadvantage lower down. Looked at another way, a prime may gain from negotiating processes with a regulator, but may face significant difficulties if tier 1, tier 2, etc. suppliers are able, themselves, to negotiate wide variations in process. This might suggest that goal-based standards at the prime level could be supported by prescriptive standards, set by the prime, at lower tiers. However, this shouldn't remove the ability to be flexible; e.g. on an aircraft it might be that quite different methods are appropriate for cockpit displays than for a flight control system (see GF3).

3.5 Evidence possibilities

The most natural context for evaluating the questions is the relationship (interaction) between suppliers and regulators. To do this requires the questions to be addressed within a coherent regulatory framework, e.g. railway signalling, civil aviation, to provide fair comparisons. As there are well-defined regulators, e.g. the Federal Aviation Administration (FAA) and European Aviation Safety Authority

(EASA) in civil aerospace, several (perhaps all) of these questions could helpfully be addressed in collaboration with the regulators. Variation across nations and markets could be evaluated by, or in conjunction with, major industrial primes who work across multiple industrial sectors.

To evaluate the above questions systematically would require one, or several, coordinated 'campaigns' to obtain evidence. The authors have not done this, and the aim here is only to show that it is plausible to collect and evaluate such evidence – more by way of trying to show that the approach is practicable, than to try to draw any firm conclusions. We consider a small number of cases (where a case is one source of evidence) for each question:

Q1. Within a given industry, to what extent do methods and techniques vary?

Q2. What are the factors that drive method and technique variation?

In the case of military aviation, there is evidence that 'standard practices' arise for system and software design which go beyond the requirements of standards (Reinhardt and McDermid 2010); in particular, evidence shows that good practice has been evolved which means that more critical systems are developed with greater defence-in-depth; this tends to support the value of the use of goal-based standards (as was used, in the main, although these are military aircraft systems).

The procurement and assessment of civil nuclear power plant seems to lead to significant homogeneity of processes, whereas there are military systems with significant variation in standards used (even in the same company for the same client!). This suggests that this is an area where the complicating factors are significant.

Q3. Is the type of standard a factor in the power and effectiveness of a regulator?

Q4. Is the type of standard a factor in the time and effort required to come to an agreement between regulator and supplier?

Whilst the authors are aware of no direct evidence in the public domain, there is some indicative evidence. There was considerable industry 'push back' on DS 00-56 Issue 4, and some companies refused to work to it (partly because of the way in which ALARP responsibilities were allocated, not just the goal-based nature of the standard). This is not supportive of the features identified for goal-based standards, although note the caveat about the industry norms and events.

Further, UK MoD's procurement of the C130J involved a substantial amount of additional work, to a significant degree applying static code analysis to code produced according to DO178B. This significantly extended the acceptance time, but also led to an improvement in the integrity of the product (software flaws were found and then removed). Whilst there is, of course, no evidence it is interesting to speculate whether or not the same thing would have happened if using the current version of DS 00-56, rather than the earlier prescriptive standard and the associated (now obsolete) DS 00-55 (MoD 1997). Of course, there also remains the question of the impact on safety of the remedial work.

Q5. Do prescriptive standards evolve as rapidly as technology and knowledge about effective methods?

Q6. Are goal-based standards relatively stable compared to prescriptive standards?

DO-178B has been very stable and even the introduction of DO-178C which is likely to be 20 years after the publication of DO-178B will not really modify the core part of the standard (there is additional material to deal with new technologies). The core of MIL-STD-882 has stayed fairly stable, although there has been rewording, and a significant change in the volume of informative material (the task definitions). By contrast IEC 61508 has changed quite substantially between Issue 1 (IEC 1998) and Issue 2 (IEC 2009).

These examples tend to support the worldview of goal-based standards, but the iteration of DS 00-56, though Issues 3 and 4, and the recent commencement of work on Issue 5, only seven years after the publication of Issue 3, provides some countervailing evidence (although the main driver arises from non-technical issues including the Haddon-Cave enquiry (Haddon-Cave 2009).

Unsurprisingly, there is no clear, unequivocal, evidence to support either the goal-based or prescriptive worldviews. What we hope we have shown, however, is that it is not impossible to shed light on these questions and the two worldviews. We consider the utility of the approach, and the ability to 'do better' in answering the questions below.

4 Assessment

It is clearly infeasible to conduct controlled experiments to contrast safety regulation, and we do not suggest that this should be attempted. Further, it is hard to separate cause and effect, so even if there was unequivocal evidence in support of a feature, it does not imply success of the related worldview.

For example, evidence for PF4 – 'Techniques can be selected independently of the systems being analysed' – such as consistent use of a process across a range of disparate systems may arise from engineers and management 'making things work despite the standards' rather than confirming the PrescriptionStan worldview.

In the absence of suitable controls, is our approach scientific? We would argue that it is, for two primary reasons.

Firstly, a scientific approach does not seek to confirm but to reject hypotheses. Whilst any confirmation of a worldview feature will be doubtful, it may certainly be possible to robustly disprove the existence of a feature.

Consider GF1 – 'Suppliers will use the flexibility granted by goals rather than prescriptive processes to choose cost-effective solutions to achieving and demonstrating safety'. If, for example, in the defence context the same civil standard was always used to meet the requirements of DS 00-56 then this would be evidence to reject the hypothesis. Armed with such information we can make progress in refining standards towards achieving their desired intent.

Second, it is very hard to write standards such that they are clear to readers who were not involved in their development (there is substantial evidence for this, albeit not scientifically documented). If standards developers describe their world-view explicitly, it should help them to articulate clearly their intent, and also to do 'thought experiments' to see whether or not the expected features are likely to be manifest. It may also indicate where standards are confused, or have problems.

For example applying the GoalTopia worldview to ISO 17894 would suggest that prediction GF3 – 'Selection of techniques and methods should be based primarily on the class of system' – would not be met. The standard is so flexible that it is hard to see why any two projects would follow the same course. This might suggest to the standards developers they need to be more specific; it certainly should suggest to users that they should develop and promulgate their own interpretation of the standard[1]. The same 'test' might also prove useful in the revision of DS 00-56 Issue 4 to produce Issue 5, leading to the standard being more specific for different classes of system, or including a more detailed set of objectives, as is seen in DO-178B, for example. Put another way, the approach of identifying how one might evaluate standards might prove to be a useful tool for standards developers.

5 Promises and pitfalls

The evaluation criteria and questions also help to identify promises and pitfalls. There are several promises; the summary here paraphrases some of the features, and extends them to some degree:

- Developments can be undertaken cost-effectively, using techniques appropriate to a system type, and hence addressing Purpose 3 – GF1, GF2.
- It will be possible to chose appropriate processes for different types of system, but to reuse experience on related classes of system – GF1, GF2, GF3.
- Processes will not be disrupted by changes in standards – GF4.
- Processes will be cost-effective, as it is possible to identify the most appropriate methods and tools, and there will be no need to undertake activities which do not 'add value' – GF1 plus!
- Development of safety-critical systems and software will become more evidence-based, as there is value in collecting evidence on the utility of methods in order to optimize processes.

The latter two promises are clearly long-term benefits, if they are to be realisable. In contrast the questions identify some pitfalls; again we have paraphrased:

- Methods used will not vary significantly, and the cost of agreeing processes will outweigh the benefits of the flexibility offered – Q1, Q3, Q4.

---

[1] Some of the classification societies have done this.

- Standards change anyway, as it is not possible to write them clearly enough, or sufficiently independent of technology, to achieve stability – Q2.
- Standards will remain flexible across the supply chain, giving primes (system integrators) significant difficulties in integrating systems and demonstrating safety – Q5.

These pitfalls indicate risks to projects, and potentially to the safety of the end product of the development.

6 Conclusions

Developing standards is difficult; doing so in the context of safety-critical systems is particularly difficult. In essence, such standards are hypotheses – 'doing things this way will make systems safer and/or reduce costs of achieving an appropriate level of safety'. These hypotheses cannot be evaluated during the production of the standard, nor even during system development, and it is quite unlikely that they can be evaluated during the operation of systems developed using the standards. Even if they can, it is likely that the knowledge so gained will be of little utility, as technology will have changed enormously in the intervening time (as required failure rates are so low). To be more explicit, the authors are aware of systems developed in the 1970s which have now amassed enough operational hours to show that safety targets have been met – but the systems employ standards and technology which is now obsolete, so the findings have no predictive value.

The above suggests that trying to evaluate standards is nugatory – we accept it is challenging, but believe that merit can be gained from the endeavour. The approach outlined can help to disprove hypotheses (about the merit of particular approaches) even if it cannot prove them. Avoiding unhelpful approaches to standardisation would be highly beneficial. Further, the discipline of articulating a worldview for a standard may help in the development and presentation of the ideas, and thus increase the effectiveness of the standard.

We have shown that it is possible to shed some light on questions which would show the comparative merit of goal-based and prescriptive standards, using only 'naturally occurring' evidence. This suggests that a greater and more coordinated attempt in the community to collect evidence and seek to validate standards and other engineering methods should yield benefit. This paper will have succeeded in its purpose if it stimulates more widespread and principled evaluation of standards for developing and assessing safety-critical and safety-related systems.

References

Borges JL (2000) Labyrinths: selected stories and other writings. Penguin Classics
CENELEC (1999) EN 50126 Railway applications – the specification and demonstration of reliability, availability, maintainability and safety (RAMS). CENELEC

CENELEC (2001a) EN 50128 Railway applications – software for railway control and protection systems. CENELEC

CENELEC (2001b) EN 50129 Railway applications – communication, signalling and processing systems. CENELEC

Coglianese C, Nash J, Olmstead T (2002) Performance-based regulation: prospects and limitations in health, safety and environmental protection. KSG Working Paper Series No RWP02-050. http://ssrn.com/abstract=392400. Accessed 15 September 2011

DoD (1996) MIL-STD-882C Standard practice for system safety, Change Notice 1. US Department of Defense

DoD (2002) MIL-STD-882D Standard practice for system safety. US Department of Defense

Haddon-Cave C (2009) The Nimrod review: an independent review into the broader issues surrounding the loss of the RAF Nimrod MR2 aircraft XV230 in Afghanistan in 2006. HC1025. Her Majesty's Stationery Office, London

IEC (1998) Functional safety of electrical/electronic/programmable electronic safety related systems. IEC 61508. International Electrotechnical Commission

IEC (2009) Functional safety of electrical/electronic/programmable electronic safety related systems. IEC 61508, Issue 2. International Electrotechnical Commission

ISO (2005) Ships and marine technology – computer applications – general principles for the development and use of programmable electronic systems in marine applications. ISO 17894. International Standardisation Organization

ISO (2011) Road vehicles – functional safety. ISO FDIS 26262. International Standardisation Organization

Kant I (1907) Critique of pure reason. The Macmillan Company

Kelly TP, McDermid JA, Weaver RA (2005) Goal-based safety standards: opportunities and challenges. In Proc 23rd Int Syst Saf Eng Conf, System Safety Society, San Diego

MoD (1997) Requirements for safety related software in defence applications. DS 00-55 Issue 2. UK Ministry of Defence,

MoD (2007) Safety management requirements for defence systems. DS 00-56 Issue 4. UK Ministry of Defence

Reinhardt DW, McDermid JA (2010) Assuring against systematic faults using architecture and fault tolerance in aviation systems. In: Improving systems and software engineering. Engineers Australia

RTCA (1992) DO178B Software considerations in airborne systems and equipment certification. Radio Technical Commission for Aeronautics

Safety Levels in a Commercial Context

Mike Parsons

Logica UK

London, UK

Abstract Within Logica UK, a new risk assessment framework has been introduced for safety-related bids, projects and services. This framework incorporates both safety (harm) assessment and commercial risk aspects and utilizes a simple questionnaire which can be used by project and bid staff. The output is a risk score and a safety level in the range 1 to 4. The risk level then determines the assurance regime to be applied to the supply, during bidding, development or service provision. The scheme has proved successful and has been rolled out across the UK.

1 Introduction

1.1 About Logica

Logica is a business and technology service company, employing 41,000 people. It provides business consulting, systems integration and outsourcing to clients around the world, including many of Europe's largest businesses. Logica creates value for clients by successfully integrating people, business and technology. It is committed to long term collaboration, applying insight to create innovative answers to clients' business needs (Logica 2011).

1.1 Safety-related projects

There are about 40 safety-related development projects running in Logica UK today including work in the space, defence, health, utilities and government sectors. These development projects span a variety of safety risk levels, to formal external standards, e.g. DEF STAN 00-56 (MoD 2007) and DO-178B (RTCA 1992). The highest Safety Integrity Levels (SILs) are currently to DO-178B Level B and SIL 2 of IEC 61508 (IEC 2010). Many involve bespoke code development and high levels of verification and assurance activity.

1.2 Safety-related services

There are about 100 safety-related service projects currently running, including work in the following areas: aviation and airports, healthcare, government, policing, rail, and offshore oil and gas. Although these services are based around IT systems, there is generally little *development* activity within the contract. Instead the focus is on delivering the service to a contracted level, usually involving maintenance, support, helpdesk and enhancements. As of today, none of the software in these services is developed to a formal safety integrity level: all mitigations required to reduce the safety risks to acceptable levels are placed in the overall processes and procedures in the service, or are otherwise handled by the client or operations staff.

1.3 Safety-related bids

At any given point in time there are about 20 safety-related bids and significant changes to existing contracts under consideration. Bidding follows a process which ensures that appropriate steps are taken to mitigate safety risks. The process is also intended to ensure that relevant internal stakeholders (including safety experts) are engaged early enough in the process. All safety projects require a mandatory safety gate review, supported by guidance materials and checklists to help with hazard identification.

1.4 Origins of work

Historically Logica utilised a simple safety flag (Yes/No) for each bid, project or service. When the flag was set it triggered a standard set of process-based safety risk mitigations to be applied. This situation existed for some years and worked well for high risk programmes, but tended to create issues around low risk projects: should they be considered safety-related (with the process overhead creating additional cost and effort), or not safety-related (thereby possibly creating low-level risks)? There was also some ambiguity in situations where the client had not identified any safety requirements before producing the Invitation To Tender. Finally the existing process did not encompass any of the wider commercial risk aspects related to safety (e.g. brand damage). Eventually this scheme was decided to be too coarse and something more sophisticated was needed.

A set of safety levels was clearly required; various schemes were proposed, initially starting with three levels, finally extending to four. It was clear from the outset that commercial risks related to the safety aspects were required to be considered in an integrated way with the accidental harm aspects. As a commercial company it is important that the legal, regulatory and brand risks of accidents are fully considered.

1.6 Existing materials

Established system safety standards such as IEC 61508 tend to focus on pure safety (harm) risks, with no mention of wider commercial aspects. This means that there is little formal established guidance available to help develop mitigations for these other areas. The main sources of material therefore had to include both existing safety standards and internal commercial guides. The existing internal Logica guide LCG-032 (Logica 2010) was found to be useful to supplement other material, but was concerned largely with safety-critical development projects.

2 The assessment framework

The key concept of a Logica Safety Level (LSL) was developed to categorize the inherent risk within a supply and to establish an appropriate assurance regime to manage the risks.

There are four LSLs, plus a zero non-safety level for completeness. A summary of the LSLs is given in Table 1.

2.1 Deriving an LSL

The LSL is initially derived using a straightforward questionnaire. This is designed to be simple enough for technical and managerial staff to complete in most cases.

Firstly if there is no credible safety risk at all then LSL 0 is assigned and the process is stopped. If there is any possible safety risk, or any doubts that there may be risk, then the five 'word picture' questions below are considered.

The single answer that most closely matches the expected or actual situation is chosen. The scores for the selected answers are added up and used with a lookup table to assign an LSL. The single most likely or best matching answer is chosen (no intermediate values are allowed).

In many cases, bid, project or service staff are able to choose an initial answer themselves, but help is available from experienced safety engineers as required. The LSL is always subject to regular review by safety managers regardless of initial assessment.

The questions are shown in Tables 2 to 6. The score for each question is shown in the final column.

Table 1. Overview of Logica Safety Levels (LSLs)

LSL	Risk to Logica	Summary overview	Safety assurance regime	Typical external view
0	No current risk (and there never will be)	No credible safety risk and working in a sector/industry where safety is not an issue	Nothing	No safety
1	No current risk (but there could be)	No significant safety risk now, but working in a sector or industry where safety is an issue, so that a contract change or change of usage could introduce risk	Occasional monitoring	No safety
2	Low risk	Our responsibility is small, the impact is low and there is plenty of time to check for errors.	Light-weight safety management	Safety-related
3	Medium risk	We have significant responsibility, where accidents can be serious, but where there is some time to detect and correct errors. There may be client or sector standards specified.	Formal safety management	Safety-related
4	High risk	There is an element of control and little time to detect or correct errors, or errors are likely undetectable. We have a key role or are priming. Usually working to a safety standard and may have real-time aspects. Accidents may be severe.	Formal safety management plus independent oversight	Safety-critical

Question 1 (shown in Table 2) is the real key to the assessment, considering severity (impact) of possible accidents and how close our supply is to them.

Table 2. LSL questionnaire 1

	Score
1. **Severity and Proximity.** How severe could an accident be that is related to our supply? Could it be caused directly by our system/service?	Score
a) All possible routes to an accident from our supply are considered incredible.	1
b) Our supply could cause operational inconvenience only. It has no real influence on any eventual accident, except via lengthy and indirect routes.	2
c) Our supply could lead to slight or temporary injuries affecting one or two people. Several other people/systems are involved in checking/making decisions. Minor environmental impact possible.	4
d) Our supply could lead to serious injuries affecting a small number of people. At least one human or independent check is involved for all results/outputs/controls. Significant environmental impact possible.	7
e) Our supply could easily lead to death or permanent disablement for several people. The accident could be caused by our system/service with little chance of anything else catching our errors. The accident could affect the general public or have wide and long lasting environmental impact.	12

Question 2 in Table 3 considers the possible impact of accidents on corporate Logica.

Table 3. LSL questionnaire 2

2. **Corporate Impact.** How would a serious accident in this sector be tolerated by the industry sector or general public? How much would it affect Logica? Would a claim be likely? Would it generate press interest?	Score
a) Little interest, accidents happen all the time in this sector. Negligible chance of claims or investigations. No adverse publicity likely.	1
b) Some concern from the client, but accidents happen occasionally. Small chance of claim against us. Local or specialist press interest. Minor investigation or audit.	2
c) Public would be concerned, accidents are rare in this sector. Significant chance of claim against us. Regional press interest. Client inquiry or investigation likely.	5
d) Public would be alarmed and consider the accident a result of poor practice. Claims very likely. National press or TV coverage a possibility. Legal or independent inquiry may follow.	8
e) Public would be outraged and consider such an accident unacceptable. Multiple claims/fines from regulators or courts are likely. Headline news on TV. Official and/or public enquiry possible.	12

Question 3 in Table 4 looks at our contractual and commercial responsibility.

Table 4. LSL questionnaire 3

3. **Responsibility.** How much responsibility do we have for safety aspects within the project/service? What specific liabilities for consequential losses/3rd party claims do we have via the contract or other means?	Score
a) We are not responsible for any safety aspects. No liabilities for accident claims with us. Client or other party has accepted full safety responsibility. We are fully indemnified by client or 3rd party.	1
b) We are a small part of a large consortium. We have minimal liability for safety via the contract. We are partly covered by explicit client or 3rd party protections. All safety work is performed by subcontractors, we only review and monitor.	2
c) We are a significant part of the consortium or team. We have some share of the safety responsibility. Specific safety liabilities to the client via the contract are mentioned. There are no indemnities in our favour. All key safety obligations have been explicitly flowed down to subcontractors.	4
d) We are prime for a small programme or have the bulk of the safety responsibility within a team. Specific accident-related liabilities in the contract are significant. We provide some indemnities to others via the contract. Some significant safety obligations have not been flowed down to subcontractors.	7
e) We are priming a major programme or we have whole safety responsibility. Specific accident-related liabilities in the contract are large (or unlimited). We provide explicit indemnities in favour of client/3rd party for accidents related to our supply. Safety obligations have not been discussed or flowed down to subcontractors.	10

Question 4 (Table 5) relates to the nature of the implementation of the system or service

Table 5. LSL questionnaire 4

4. **Size, Complexity and Novelty.** What is the scale and sophistication of the system/service? How much new technology is used?	Score
a) Tried and tested design. One main, well established technology. Clear and simple interface. No timeliness aspects. Less than 20,000 LOC (Lines Of Code) or simple one-COTS (Commercial Off The Shelf) package design. One safety-related application supported. Simple and conventional hosting/hardware.	1
b) Standard design but some configuration or tailoring. A few key interfaces. Some non-critical timing aspects. Little new technology used. 20,000 - 100,000 LOC or design based on few COTS packages. Up to 5 safety-related applications supported. Standard network, few servers and PCs, or typical hosting.	3
c) Typical design but significantly modified or enhanced. Several critical interfaces. Some timing aspects. One or two new technologies used. 100,000 - 500,000 LOC or design based on several COTS packages. Up to 10 supported safety-related applications. Significant infrastructure including network management, many servers and PCs, non-standard hosting or remote/multi-site elements.	5
d) Mostly bespoke design with some COTS. Many key interfaces. Some real-time aspects. Several new technologies used. 500,000 - 1,000,000 LOC or design based on many COTS packages. Up to 50 safety applications supported. Distributed multi-site infrastructure including data links, remote or handheld devices, network management, multiple servers/PCs/Cloud aspects, single control centre.	7
e) Bespoke design. Hard real-time functions. Multiple new technologies. Numerous key interfaces. More than 1,000,000 LOC or design based on large number of COTS packages. More than 50 supported safety applications. Highly complex and widespread infrastructure including specialist or bespoke devices, multiple data links, remote or handheld devices, network management, servers/PCs/extensive use of Cloud, multiple control centres.	10

Question 5 in Table 6 is concerned with usage of the system or service.

Table 6. LSL questionnaire 5

5. **Usage Exposure.** How much usage and what type of users are there likely to be of the delivered system/service?	Score
a) Unlikely ever to be deployed.	1
b) A small number of operational users. Small scale operation. One site in the UK. No general web access. No public access.	2
c) A number of operational users. Medium scale operations. Several deployed sites. Some web access. Specialist user or limited public access.	5
d) A large number of users. Wide scale operations. Multiple sites including one or two abroad. General web access. Public access to certain aspects.	8
e) International usage. Several sites round the world. General public or mainstream usage.	12

2.2 LSL lookup table

The total score from the questionnaires is used to look up the LSL in Table 7.

Table 7. LSL lookup table

Total Score	Logica Safety Level
≤9	LSL 1
10-25	LSL 2
26-34	LSL 3
≥35	LSL 4

2.3 Worked example

As an example of using the questionnaire, consider a maintenance tasking system for a regional utility based on a client-chosen COTS package and a handheld pad device (Figure 1).

Fig. 1. Utilities handheld pad device

Consider we are part of a consortium and doing tailoring and configuration of the COTS software but little or no bespoke work. Another supplier is providing the specifically designed hardware and training the staff. The client has not quoted any standards, safety levels or given us any specific systems safety requirements. The contract has no mention of limits of accident claims or indemnities in our favour.

The system is understood to have risks if the data is corrupted or lost, as a maintenance engineer could be sent to a site to service potentially hazardous equipment for which Health and Safety warnings are missing, or maintenance information (e.g. replacement part types) are incorrect.

Although there are possible dangers to the maintenance operator, it is considered unlikely that the public could be directly affected as the work takes place on secure, mainly remote, sites.

The design is based on a similar solution we have produced for another utility already, however because it is COTS based, errors are expected to happen occasionally.

1. **Severity and Proximity.** How severe could an accident be that is related to our supply? Could it be caused directly by our system/service?
   c)   Our supply could lead to slight or temporary injuries affecting one or two people. Several other people/systems are involved in checking/making decisions. Minor environmental impact possible. (4)

2. **Corporate Impact.** How would a serious accident in this sector be tolerated by the industry sector or general public? How much would it affect Logica? Would a claim be likely? Would it generate press interest?
   b)   Some concern from the client, but accidents happen occasionally. Small chance of claim against us. Local or specialist press interest. Minor investigation or audit. (2)

3. **Responsibility.** How much responsibility do we have for safety aspects within the project/service? What specific liabilities for consequential losses / 3rd party claims do we have via the contract or other means?
   c)   We are a significant part of the consortium or team. We have some share of the safety responsibility. Specific safety liabilities to the client via the contract are mentioned. There are no indemnities in our favour. All key safety obligations have been explicitly flowed down to subcontractors. (4)

4. **Size, Complexity and Novelty.** What is the scale and sophistication of the system/service? How much new technology is used?
   b)   Standard design but some configuration or tailoring. A few key interfaces. Some non-critical timing aspects. Little new technology used. 20,000 - 100,000 LOC or design based on few COTS packages. Up to 5 safety-related applications supported. Standard network, few servers and PCs, or typical hosting. (3)

5. **Usage Exposure.** How much usage and what type of users are there likely to be of the delivered system/service?
   c)   A number of operational users. Medium scale operations. Several deployed sites. Some web access. Specialist user or limited public access. (5)

In this case the sum of the scores is 4 + 2 + 4 + 3 + 5 = 18, giving LSL 2.

3 Discussion of the assigned LSL

The LSL here is different to the standard Criticality, SIL (Wikipedia 2011a), Design Assurance Level (DAL, Wikipedia 2011b) or Software Level used in many safety standards, because it includes the notion of corporate risk which can change the assessment significantly. Some examples:

1. We have developed a large police database system, just entering service, which has no specific safety requirements, no safety standard or SIL specified and yet is assessed as LSL 3. This is due to the sensitivity of data it contains, the possible uses to which the data may be put, and the potentially large public impact and press interest should it produce incorrect results leading to an accident.
2. Work we are doing for a rail company is considered LSL 3 as it could potentially put trackside workers at risk, even though the customer has not specified a SIL or safety standard for the work.
3. Some work we are performing in the health sector is assessed at LSL 2 (one level lower than might be expected) as the supplier of the main COTS product in use has provided us with an extensive legal indemnity, covering possible claims against us related to the product.

Some important points to note:

- The LSL doesn't replace any client imposed SIL or DAL, the LSL stands separately as our internal assessment of the inherent corporate risk in the work.
- The LSL is useful as a communication vehicle to discuss safety with the client. If our assessment is very different to theirs then the gap needs discussion.
- The LSL is subject to change if there is a significant change to any part of the supply. This could be due to a contract change, or may due to a change in the way the client is using the system/service (e.g. by deploying at additional sites).
- The LSL is always reviewed every 12 months regardless of any other change.
- The LSL is reviewed during internal safety audits.

4 LSL and requirements

Once the LSL is assigned it is used to select the applicable requirements from the Logica internal Safety Management System (SMS) via a series of tables. Some examples are given below. (It is important to note that these Logica internal requirements are used in addition to any client, legal, regulatory or standards obligations imposed.) Excerpts from the tables are shown from:

- General Requirements (Table 8)
- Staffing Requirements (Table 9)
- Document Requirements (Table 10)
- Release and Configuration Requirements (Table 11).

Note that the full set of tables (not shown here) covers the entire Logica safety management system – from requirements through design to verification.

Table 8. Excerpt from General Requirements

Type	Requirement	LSL 1	2	3	4	Notes
	General Requirements ● – Required, ○ – To be considered, ✗ – Not acceptable, - – Not required					
Legal	The applicable legal system and jurisdiction for the supply shall be established.	○	●	●	●	
	If the contract has an international dimension, the worst case claim origin shall be considered.	-	○	●	●	
	If the applicable legal system is significantly different to the UK, local advice regarding safety obligations shall be sought	-	○	●	●	
Regulatory	The regulatory environment for the sector shall be established.	-	○	●	●	Including applicable standards and practice guides
Subcontractor or Supplier	Subcontracts shall consider flowdown of: • safety standards and regulatory obligations • functional or operational requirements regarding safety • support or service aspects of safety • indemnities in our favour • liabilities we hold in favour of client or third parties.	-	○	●	●	
Contract Risks	Risks and liabilities extending beyond the lifetime of the contract shall be considered.	-	○	●	●	Risks may not materialize for some years after delivery. Liabilities may include obligations to inform the client of faults found in similar systems.
	Adequate warnings and caveats on the use of the supply shall be considered: in documentation and within the supply itself.	-	●	●	●	E.g. consider warnings/caveats on startup screens or report templates.
Insurance	The Group insurance policy shall be checked to establish that it covers this type of work.	-	●	●	●	Review to be done by a competent person e.g. Commercial Manager.

Table 9. Excerpt from Staffing Requirements

Safety Staffing

● – Required, ○ – To be considered, ✗ – Not acceptable, - - Not required

Area	Level	LSL				Notes
		1	2	3	4	
Safety Staffing	Part-time Project Safety Engineer (PSE) role covered by project staff (Supervised Practitioner Level)	-	●	✗	✗	PSE (Practitioner) supervision needed
	Part-time by PSE (Practitioner Level)	-	○	●	✗	PSE may work on more than one project.
	PSE (at Practitioner or Expert Level) fully embedded in project	-	-	○	●	The PSE may undertake other tasks but primary role is on one project.
Safety Competency	Some informal knowledge and awareness of safety within key project staff	●	✗	✗	✗	
	Bid Manager, Project Manager, Quality Manager and Design Authority staff have safety knowledge and have attended safety courses.	-	○	●	●	
	PSE is Supervised Practitioner.	-	●	✗	✗	
	PSE is Practitioner.	-	○	●	●	
	PSE is Expert.	-	-	○	●	
	External Safety Board/Safety Committee	-	-	○	●	

5 LSL results

The LSL assessment scheme has now been rolled out to all bids, projects and services running in Logica UK. The pie chart in Figure 2 shows the distribution across LSLs. As expected, this shows that the vast majority of the Logica work is at the lower risk levels (LSL 1 and LSL 2), however a significant number are at higher risk level 3. Only 1 percent of all work is at the highest (LSL 4) level.

6 Conclusions

A new, *composite* safety risk assessment framework has been introduced and this has been shown to be effective in assessing the combination of corporate and safety risks. All UK projects and services have now been assessed, and all new bids go through the same process. The use of a straightforward questionnaire has simplified the assessment process and has been used extensively over the last year.

Table 10. Excerpt from Document Requirements

Safety Documents

● – Required, ○ – To be considered, × – Not acceptable, - – Not required

Type	Document	LSL				Notes
		1	2	3	4	
Contractual	Contract or Change containing explicit safety requirements, liability protections and mitigations	-	○	●	●	E.g. safety requirements section and indemnities in our favour
	Supplier or subcontractor contracts containing explicit flow-down of requirements and liabilities	-	○	●	●	Also removal of restrictive clauses
Planning	Shortform Safety Management Plan (SSMP)	○	●	×	×	Only one of these required
	Safety Management Plan (SMP)	-	○	●	●	
	Accident Management Plan	-	○	●	●	
Safety Justification Report	Safety Story	○	●	×	×	Only one of these required
	Safety Overview Report	-	●	×	×	
	Safety Summary Report	-	-	●	●	
	Safety Case Report	-	-	●	●	
Client-level Agreements	SLA which explicitly addresses safety issues	-	○	●	●	If a service
Internal Agreements	OLA which explicitly addresses safety issues	-	○	●	●	If a service

For the first time commercial and safety risks have been considered together in an integrated and consistent way, and used to drive the safety risk mitigation regime across the company. Overall this has been very well received: safety staff benefit from a simple assessment framework which can be discussed easily with project and service staff, and service and project managers have also welcomed the clarity that the tables of clear requirements provide. This has resulted in better engagement all round.

The key benefit is commercial – Logica now does the appropriate amount of risk mitigation for the level of safety and corporate risk. This has cost and schedule benefits as many low-risk bids, projects and services benefit from less process overhead.

Table 11. Excerpt from Release and Configuration Requirements

Release and Configuration Management

● – Required, ○ – To be considered, ✗ – Not acceptable, - – Not required

Area	Level	LSL 1	2	3	4	Notes
Release Board	Informal	-	●	✗	✗	
	Formal with PSE	-	○	●	✗	
	Formal with PSE (minuted)	-	-	○	●	
Configuration Management	Informal	-	●	✗	✗	
	Procedures defined and documented	-	○	●	✗	
	Fully and formally managed	-	-	○	●	
Release Reporting	Mention of any safety issues in release notes	-	●	✗	✗	
	Formal list of Limitations/Restrictions/External Mitigations in release notes and Safety Justification	-	-	●	●	
Problem Management	Informal check of problem reports/ORs for safety aspects	-	●	✗	✗	
	PSE review of problem reports/ORs for safety aspects	-	○	●	●	

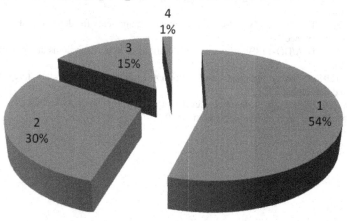

Fig. 2. Distribution of Logica UK supplies across LSLs

7 Future work

This work could easily be extended to cover requirements in other process areas, creating a wider and more consistent SMS. It could also be extended to integrate with other areas such as the quality and security process frameworks already in place to encompass related risks and requirements. Other Logica geographies which conduct safety-related work would also benefit (particularly the Netherlands, Malaysia and Australia).

7.1 Use of database/web application

Currently the LSL assessment is recorded using a Word form. This works well for individual assessments but doesn't enable easy analysis of assessments done, tracking of version changes, or allow easy sharing across the company. Currently the survey functionality available within the Microsoft Sharepoint framework is being investigated as a better implementation of the form. The ultimate aim is to create a web-accessible database of all the LSL assessments.

References

IEC (2010) IEC 61508 Functional safety of electrical/electronic/programmable electronic safety-related systems. Edition 2.0. International Electrotechnical Commission
Logica (2010) Mandatory procedures: systems safety management. LCG032, Logica
Logica (2011) About Logica. http://www.logica.co.uk/we-are-logica/about-logica. Accessed August 2011
MoD (2007) DEF STAN 00-56 Safety management requirements for defence systems. Issue 4. Ministry of Defence
RTCA (1992) RTCA/DO-178B Software considerations in airborne systems and equipment certification
Wikipedia (2011a) Safety Integrity Level. http://en.wikipedia.org/wiki/Safety_Integrity_Level. Accessed September 2011
Wikipedia (2011b) Design Assurance Level. http://en.wikipedia.org/wiki/Design_Assurance_Level#Software_level. Accessed September 2011

A Devil's Advocate on SIL 4

Odd Nordland

SINTEF ICT

Trondheim, Norway

Abstract The concept of safety integrity levels is well established and for many safety critical systems SIL 4 is demanded by default. The problem with SIL 4 is that it is impossible to prove and the demand is often not justified. A devil's advocate view is adopted and a number of questions related to demanding SIL 4 are asked and the problems to be addressed when answering them are discussed.

1 Introduction

The concept of safety integrity levels was introduced in the UK Defence Standard DS 00-55 as early as 1991 and was adopted by IEC 61508 (IEC 1998) and later by the CENELEC railway application standards, e.g. EN 50129 (CENELEC 2003), that have subsequently become adopted as IEC standards. The idea is in itself fairly simple: a safety integrity level is a measure of the reliability of a safety function. A failure of a safety function can lead to a hazardous situation, so the higher a safety function's failure rate is, the higher the hazard rate will be. Now a failure of a safety function may not necessarily lead to a hazardous situation, so theoretically a safety function could have a failure rate that is higher than the hazard rate. However, safety experts always assume worst case scenarios in order to be on the safe side, so it is usually assumed that every failure of a safety function will lead to a hazard.

Hazards can have varying degrees of severity, and some will be considered to be tolerable, so ranges of tolerable hazard rates are defined and associated with safety integrity levels. For SIL 4, the corresponding hazard rate is between 10^{-8} and 10^{-9} hazards per hour. This means the maximum failure rate for a SIL 4 function will be 10^{-8} failures per hour; now of course we don't consider fractions of failures, so it would be more sensible to talk about 1 failure per 10^8 hours, which is equivalent.

The standards require detailed hazard analyses to determine the hazards associated with a given safety function, their severity and probability and thus the maximum tolerable hazard rate that leads to the SIL classification. This, however, is often not done: it is much more convenient to simply demand the highest safety

integrity level, i.e. SIL 4, in order to avoid lengthy discussions and having to justify accepting a lower SIL. Particularly in the railway sector, many operators and
infrastructure owners demand SIL 4 in their contracts 'because the authorities
won't accept anything less'.

In the following, some questions related to demanding SIL 4 are asked and the
problems to be addressed when answering them are discussed.

2 What does SIL 4 really mean?

A SIL 4 safety function can have a failure rate of 1 failure per 10^8 operational
hours. Wrong! All the calculations used for determining reliabilities are statistical
calculations giving average values based on large numbers of samples. The failures won't occur at regular intervals once every hundred million hours, so in order
to have statistically relevant figures, we should operate with around 100 failures in
10^{10} operational hours. Then at least we can talk about an average of 1 failure per
10^8 operational hours.

The figure 100 is also an order of magnitude, and variations of plus or minus
5% are still within the limits, so in reality we're talking about between 95 and 105
failures in ten billion operational hours. That gives us an average between 0.95
and 1.05 failures per 10^8 operational hours, and here the first problem becomes
visible: 1.05 failures per 10^8 operational hours is more than 1, so it wouldn't be
accepted even though it is in fact within the limits of the calculations!

So SIL 4 does not even mean an average of at most 1 failure per 10^8 operational hours. The average failure rate can in fact be slightly higher without automatically disqualifying for SIL 4.

It should be noted that most statisticians would probably prefer to replace the
figure 100 by 1000, but then we would be talking about around a 1000 failures in
a hundred billion operational hours. Now while this would give us good statistics
with a high accuracy of the results it would be even more prohibitive to prove.

The important fact is that SIL 4 does not mean that nothing will go wrong for
the first 99,999,999 operational hours and then an accident occurs. We can equally
well have five accidents in the first ten operational hours and then 500,000,000
operational hours where nothing goes wrong. The average is then less than 1 hazard per 10^8 operational hours.

3 How can you prove SIL 4?

Basically there are two possibilities: by measurement or by calculation.

3.1 Measurement

Measurement is impossible. The numbers of hours are accumulated hours of operation, so if we want to measure between 95 and 105 failures in ten billion operational hours, we need a lot of equipment operating continuously for a very long time. A year is 8,760 hours, for simplicity let's say 10,000. That means we need a million units operating for a year, or a hundred thousand operating for ten years, in order to achieve the necessary amount of operational experience. If we assume a life span of 40 years (which is a very long time for safety critical equipment), we still need 25,000 units operating continuously for their entire life cycle. Even if we weaken the requirement of between 95 and 105 failures in ten billion operational hours to 1 in a hundred million, we're still talking about 250 identical units operating continuously and without modification for forty years. Which still doesn't prove anything, because they will not all have been subject to identical operational and environmental conditions during the entire forty year period. So direct measurement is impossible.

3.2 Calculation

Let's try calculations. The most widespread form of reliability calculation is the fault tree analysis which enables us to calculate the probable failure rate of a function based on the failure rates of its components and their interactions. The accuracy of such calculations is heavily dependent on the accuracy of the underlying data, and that accuracy is usually pretty poor.

The manufacturers of components sometimes – but far from always – provide reliability data for their equipment, but how do they determine them? They don't get every unit that ever fails returned to them with detailed information on how long it had been in operation until it failed, let alone any information about the environmental conditions. If the hard disk of your computer crashes, do you send it back to the manufacturer and tell him how often you switched your computer on and for how long it was on? Do you even know how often you switch your computer on and how long it takes before you switch it off again? Or do you return your mobile phone to the manufacturer when it breaks down, or do you just buy a new one?

So the manufacturers have to use some form of simulation. They take more or less random samples from their production and subject them to simulated operation. Sometimes the simulation will involve extreme conditions from which one can deduce how long the sample would have survived under normal conditions. In other cases, the simulation will involve continuous operation under the predefined 'normal' conditions. But what are 'normal' conditions?

A weakness of simulations is that they cannot correctly reflect the conditions that occur in real life. A climate chamber can simulate high or low temperatures, and high or low humidity, but not vibrations, pressure variations or other physical influences at the same time. An arctic storm in the North Sea with gale force winds, enormous waves, temperatures below freezing and salt water and ice flying through the air is not what a simulator can produce, but it's the normal operating environment on many an oil platform.

Whatever kind of simulation the manufacturer has used, it will not cover all the operational scenarios that will occur in real life, so his figures will be inaccurate. How inaccurate they are, nobody can tell because that would require a detailed analysis of real life operational scenarios and a comparison with the simulated scenarios. Even then, there is no guarantee that the equipment will always be operated as it should be and under the correct environmental boundary conditions. Indeed, safety systems are often conceived in order to cope with erroneous handling or abnormal, extreme conditions.

The above-mentioned measurements can be performed for fairly simple components, but become effectively impossible for more complex subsystems. For example, if a safety function depends on data being handled by a server, the failure rate of the server will contribute to the failure rate of the safety function. The failure rate of a server cannot be measured by simulation and will itself depend on a vast number of factors. In such cases, databases with reliability data are sometimes used. Failures of complex systems are reported to the database so that a rough estimate of the complex systems' reliabilities can be made. But they are very rough estimates, because there is no guarantee that all the failures are reported, that they are reported correctly and that the additional information about operational environment and profile is included. And since complex systems will be less common than simple components, the number of systems being evaluated will usually be too small to give statistically reliable figures.

Not all manufacturers provide any reliability figures for their products at all. They simply don't know how reliable their products are. Often they produce components which are not solely intended for safety critical applications and their customers will accept that the component lasts at least as long as the final product is intended to operate. Modern electronic devices become antiquated so quickly that there is little interest in making them durable, so the manufacturers of the components are not required to demonstrate how long their components will survive. So very many can only provide at best approximate orders of magnitude with little or no evidence.

Another solution is to use 'expert judgement'. This is an even more inaccurate figure, because it is effectively a qualified guess based on the expert's personal experience. Experts also don't always agree, so a different expert will very likely give a different estimate.

There will also be basic events that are virtually impossible to quantify. For calculating the reliability of a ventilation system in a tunnel, it was necessary to estimate the probability of a fire near the tunnel entry causing smoke to be blown into the tunnel. How often do fires break out, how often do they produce large amounts of smoke, how often does the wind blow in the direction of the tunnel instead of away from it? These figures could only be very coarse estimates.

So the basic data used in the reliability calculations is always inaccurate. How inaccurate the data is will vary, but when the basic data that is used in the calculations is inaccurate, the inaccuracies will perpetrate and accumulate through the calculation and give a final result that is hardly more accurate than the most inaccurate basic figure. So it is at best an order of magnitude, but certainly not a reliable number.

All this also assumes that the underlying model for the calculations has been correct. A fault tree is based on an analysis of how components can fail and how that will affect the system. If any failure modes or other influencing factors are overlooked, the entire calculation becomes even more questionable.

Now the nasty part of the calculations is that the numbers get bigger and bigger as the calculations proceed. In order to have a final result in the order of magnitude 10^{-8} failures per operational hour, the input data must have reliabilities down to 10^{-12} failures per operational hour or even less! If we can't prove 10^{-8} failures per operational hour by direct measurement, we certainly can't demonstrate 10^{-12}. So the whole calculation is based on improbable data that cannot be confirmed.

Finally, there will always be factors that are explicitly out of scope for the calculations. Human error or the effects of administrative procedures are difficult to quantify, and often systematic failures are explicitly excluded from the calculations. So whatever the result of the calculation is, the truth will be a considerably higher figure.

4 Why do you demand SIL 4?

As mentioned earlier, one of the reasons is just being on the safe side: if you demand the highest safety integrity level, nobody can accuse you of not having been strict enough with respect to safety. In particular, nobody can sue you if something goes wrong! This is a regrettable trend that we have in our society: if something goes wrong, we have to find a scapegoat. It must be somebody's fault and that unfortunate person can then be made responsible for all the consequences, including the financial ones.

This does not contribute to safety in any way. Making somebody liable for damages that he could not reasonably have prevented is not going to prevent those damages from occurring. And when the damages go into the millions, the scapegoat will not be able to pay them anyway. When an engineer is accused of being responsible for a dozen people being killed, his defence lawyer's biggest concern is preventing the man from committing suicide before the court case begins.

But there are other reasons for demanding SIL 4 than simply fear of being sued. Safety integrity levels are – as mentioned earlier – associated with tolerable hazard rates, and the standards define which tolerable hazard rates correspond to which SIL. What they don't say is how to determine when a hazard rate is tolerable. For this we have hazard (or risk) acceptability principles.

The perhaps most widespread principle is the ALARP principle (As Low As Reasonably Practicable) which divides risk into three regions: an unacceptable region, a tolerable region and a negligible region. Where the boundaries lie is not explicitly stated, and the common assumption is that the current level for a given system is already tolerable. It demands that risks shall be reduced as far as practicable to a level within the tolerable region. This necessitates a cost-benefit analysis for any risk reduction measure, which unfortunately is often restricted to a pecuniary point of view. There are even definitions of the price of a human life in order to facilitate such calculations.

The French GAMAB principle (Globalement Au Moins Aussi Bon, sometimes known by its English acronym GALE, Globally At Least Equivalent) is similar in that it starts with a risk level that is presumed to be tolerable and requires that any alteration shall result in a total risk that is at the same level or lower. This means that a worsening in one part of a system can be acceptable if it is more than compensated by an improvement elsewhere. This is a qualitative case of the ALARP principle, where the cost of the alteration is the worsening of a portion of the system, whilst the benefit is the improvement elsewhere. But here again we are assuming that the currently achieved hazard rate is acceptable.

The problem is that the level that is regarded as tolerable is not objectively defined. It's based on assumptions on what the general public will accept, and that is a very fuzzy figure. The fact is that the figures that are used in the standards are not definitions of what a tolerable hazard rate should be; they are simply a scale for measuring safety integrity levels based on possible tolerable hazard rates. The standards require that for each individual hazard the tolerable rate should be determined, but they don't say how. They contain tables classifying risks according to frequency and severity; these tables are explicitly stated to be examples, but they are more often than not simply adopted in a given, real case. But they still don't identify tolerable hazard rates. They identify combinations of severity and frequency that can be defined as tolerable, and the associated hazard frequencies are then taken to be the tolerable hazard rates. But there is no empirical data that the tolerability criteria are actually correct.

In most European countries the number of people annually killed in road accidents is in the order of magnitude of some hundreds, with about ten times as many being injured. That's roughly one person killed and ten injured every day or two (per country!) which corresponds to a hazard rate of around one hazard per five hours. Hardly anybody demands all motor traffic to be banned, so a hazard rate of two hazards every ten hours is evidently acceptable. That's a long way from SIL 4.

The figures given in the standards are also generic. A tolerable hazard rate depends on the hazard and in particular on its severity, so the assumption that the hazard frequencies that are used in the tables are equivalent to tolerable hazard rates is evidently not justified.

5 What could be an alternative?

The second problem with ALARP is the definition of what is reasonably practicable. Instead of demanding SIL 4 by default based on fictitious – or at least questionable – tolerable hazard rates, a more pragmatic approach could be used. Hazards are binary events: there's no such thing as half an accident. So if the probability of a hazardous event can be reduced to less than half an event in a system's lifetime, we can reasonably assume that the event will not occur before the system is decommissioned. And there is no need to consider a longer period of time.

Let us assume again that a safety critical system will have a lifetime of forty years. This is not completely unrealistic, although many systems are designed for only thirty or less. Forty years are about 350,000 hours, so let's add about 50% and say 500,000 hours. That means we're considering up to sixty years for a system that is only planned to run for forty, so the lifetime can even be substantially prolonged without endangering the result. Half a hazardous event in 500,000 hours is one in a million hours. That corresponds to SIL 2!

6 Conclusion

From the foregoing we can see that it is impossible to prove that a safety function actually achieves SIL 4. It cannot be demonstrated by actual measurements, and the calculations that are used are of questionable credibility, based on even less credible input data. Nevertheless, safety authorities are willing to accept such calculations as 'proof'. This is probably because they are not aware of what the figures really mean. The probabilities are at best relative numbers; SIL 4 is 'safer' than SIL 3, but that doesn't mean it has to be demanded. And SIL 4 cannot be proved.

The tolerable hazard rates on which safety integrity levels are based are arbitrary. There is no empirical evidence that society actually demands those hazard rates, on the contrary, society is evidently willing to accept considerably higher risks than the standards postulate. A comparison with road traffic reveals that a horrendous hazard rate is willingly accepted by the vast majority of our society. A realistic estimate of what is reasonably practicable leads us to SIL 2 rather than SIL 4.

Now this does not mean that we should never demand more than SIL 2. But when we demand SIL 4, we must be able to justify why we demand something that is impossible to prove and then accept evidence that is questionable and certainly not a proof.

There's nothing wrong with SIL 4 if you can justify and prove it.

References

CENELEC (2003) Railway applications – Communication, signalling and processing systems – Safety related electronic systems for signalling. EN 50129. CENELEC, Brussels, Belgium

IEC (1998) Functional safety of electrical/electronic/programmable electronic safety-related systems. IEC 61508. International Electrotechnical Commission, Geneva, Switzerland

AUTHOR INDEX

Keith Armstrong 97
Allan Bain 11
George Bearfield 75
Jens Braband 209
Graham Braithwaite 177
Audrey Canning 25
Sirma Celik 43
Fergus Duncan 225
Derek Fowler 115
Paul Hampton 137
Chris Hobbs 159
Reiji Ishima 55

Chris Johnson 85
Peter Ladkin 189
Martin Lloyd 159
John McDermid 257
Minoru Mori 55
Odd Nordland 285
Mike Parsons 271
Ronald Pierce 115
Andrew Rae 257
Stuart Reid 237
Roger Rivett 35
Martyn Thomas 1